T0338907

THE CONQUERED

Extravagantes is a series conceived to attract exceptional books that enhance the distinctive profile of Dumbarton Oaks in the humanities. These volumes explore topics at the intersections and boundaries of one or more of our programs of study or call for formats that take them beyond the scope of already established series.

THE CONQUERED

Byzantium and America on the Cusp of Modernity

ELENI KEFALA

DUMBARTON OAKS RESEARCH LIBRARY AND COLLECTION
WASHINGTON, DC

Printed in the United States of America by Sheridan Books, Inc.

Texts and translations of "Huexotzincayotl" and "Tlaxcaltecayotl" are taken from J. Bierhorst, ed. and trans., *Cantares mexicanos: Songs of the Aztecs* (Stanford, CA, 1985). © 1985 by the Board of Trustees of the Leland Stanford Jr. University. All rights reserved. Used with the permission of Stanford University Press, www.sup.org.

ISBN: 978-0-88402-476-7

Library of Congress Cataloging-in-Publication Data

NAMES: Kefala, Eleni, author.
TITLE: The conquered : Byzantium and America on the cusp of modernity / Eleni Kefala.
OTHER TITLES: Extravagantes (Dumbarton Oaks)
DESCRIPTION: Washington, DC : Dumbarton Oaks Research Library and Collection, [2020] | Series: Extravagantes | Includes bibliographical references and index. | Summary: "In the middle of the fifteenth century, ominous portents like columns of fire and dense fog were seen above the skies of Constantinople as the Byzantine capital fell under siege by the Ottomans. Allegedly, similar signs appeared a few decades later and seven thousand miles away, forecasting the fall of the Mexica capital of Tenochtitlan-Tlatelolco to the Spanish and their indigenous allies. After both cities had fallen, some Greeks and Mexica turned to poetry and song to express their anguish at the birth of what has come to be called the "modern" era. This study probes issues of collective memory and cultural trauma in three sorrowful poems, the "Lament for Constantinople," the "Huexotzinca Piece," and the "Tlaxcala Piece." Composed by anonymous authors soon after the conquest of the two cities, these texts describe the fall of an empire as a fissure in the social fabric and an open wound on the body politic. They are the workings of creators who draw on tradition and historical particulars to articulate, in a familiar language, the trauma of the conquered"—Provided by publisher.
IDENTIFIERS: LCCN 2020028901 | ISBN 9780884024767 (hardcover)
SUBJECTS: LCSH: Collective memory and literature—Turkey—Istanbul. | Collective memory and literature—Mexico—Mexico City. | Civilization, Modern. | Psychic trauma in literature. | Conquerors in literature. | Istanbul (Turkey)—History—Siege, 1453. | Mexico City (Mexico)—History—To 1519. | Istanbul (Turkey)—Social conditions. | Mexico City (Mexico)—Social conditions—16th century.
CLASSIFICATION: LCC PN56.C618 K44 2020 | DDC 808.8/03582—dc23
LC RECORD AVAILABLE AT HTTPS://lccn.loc.gov/2020028901

Book design and text composition by Melissa Tandysh.

To the Blisses,
for bringing the Byzantines and the Mexica
under the same roof.

CONTENTS

Preface

ix

ONE

Serendipities

1

TWO

Byzantium, America, and the "Modern"

11

THREE

Tradition and Theory

15

FOUR

Imparting Trauma

27

FIVE

Texts and Their Afterlife

117

References

137

Index

149

PREFACE

What we call chance is our ignorance
of the complex mechanism of causality.

JORGE LUIS BORGES, *Seven Nights*

N 1920 MILDRED BARNES BLISS AND ROBERT WOODS BLISS PURCHASED THE
Georgetown estate that they named Dumbarton Oaks. By the time the
couple donated the property to Harvard two decades later, they had turned
what they described as "an old-fashioned house standing in rather neglected
grounds" into a "home of the Humanities," boasting an outstanding art collection and library.[1] The Blisses had set the stage for a world-class research
center. Former Dumbarton Oaks director Jan Ziolkowski would tell you that
Dumbarton Oaks is proud of its unique community that is as conducive to
intellectual inquiry as it is to lifelong friendships and partnerships. The center's
matchmaking potential was, in fact, anticipated by a most unexpected academic
pairing, the product of the Blisses' "avocations in Byzantine and Pre-Columbian
art."[2] To my knowledge, Dumbarton Oaks is the only international research

---

[1] J. N. Carder, "Mildred and Robert Woods Bliss: A Brief Biography," in *A Home of the
Humanities: The Collecting and Patronage of Mildred and Robert Woods Bliss*, ed. J. N. Carder
(Washington, DC, 2010), 1–25, at 1, and idem, "The Architectural History of Dumbarton
Oaks and the Contribution of Armand Albert Rateau," in Carder, *Home of the Humanities*,
93–115, at 93.

[2] J. M. Ziolkowski, "Foreword," in Carder, *Home of the Humanities*, xiii–xiv, at xiii.

institution dedicated both to Byzantine and Pre-Columbian studies.[3] Thanks to the Blisses, for decades Byzantinists and Pre-Columbianists have been gathering together, week after week, to attend each other's research reports and public lectures in what for many remains an improbable marriage. What is there in common between Byzantium and preconquest America[4] beyond their fortuitous encounter at Dumbarton Oaks, the result of the personal interests of two visionary art collectors inspired by early twentieth-century antiquarianism? What follows should be read as a partial answer to this question and as a decided attempt to turn the improbable marriage into a meaningful partnership, one that, in my opinion, is highly relevant today.

This study probes issues of collective memory and cultural trauma in the *threnos*, or poetic lament, "Anakalema tes Konstantinopoles" ("Lament for Constantinople") and the *icnocuicatl*, or songs of sorrow, "Huexotzincayotl" ("Huexotzinca Piece") and "Tlaxcaltecayotl" ("Tlaxcala Piece"). Composed by anonymous authors relatively soon after the conquest of the Byzantine and Mexica Empires in the mid-fifteenth and early sixteenth centuries, these texts convey the tragedy of the fall of Constantinople and Tenochtitlan as they stood at the threshold of modernity. The focus on Mexico among other indigenous cultures is guided as much by necessity—that is, matters of length and balance—as by choice. Not only do "Huexotzincayotl" and "Tlaxcaltecayotl" reenact the trauma of the siege and fall of one of the most important cities of pre-Columbian America, they do so within the context of the *Cantares mexicanos* (*Mexica Songs*), a unique corpus of ninety-one songs rooted in pre-Hispanic cultural practices.

Legend has it that the Mexica, who had migrated from a place called Aztlan to the Valley of Mexico, were guided by their supreme god Huitzilopochtli to settle down in an area where an eagle perched on a cactus eating a snake. There they founded Tenochtitlan (*tenochtli* is a variety of nopal cactus) around 1325.[5] While it remains unclear whether Aztlan ever existed, it is unlikely that the Mexica who received Hernán Cortés in 1519 referred to themselves as Aztecs or *Aztecah* (plural of *Aztecatl*, a person from Aztlan), a name widely employed since the nineteenth century. The word "Nahua" is now commonly used for the Nahuatl-speaking peoples of Central Mexico, but "Aztec" is still often reserved

---

3   A third research program at Dumbarton Oaks focuses on garden and landscape studies.

4   A range of terms is used to refer to pre-Hispanic America, including preconquest, precontact, pre-Columbian and pre-Cortesian.

5   D. Caplow, *Leopoldo Méndez: Revolutionary Art and the Mexican Print* (Austin, TX, 2007), 186. Not all sources reference the snake in the founding story of Tenochtitlan.

for the Mexica Empire.[6] Likewise, the Byzantines called themselves *Romaioi* (Romans), their empire *Romania* or *Romaïs* (Eastern Roman Empire), and their capital city Constantinople, after Emperor Constantine the Great, who founded it on the site of the ancient city of Byzantion in 324. The term "Byzantine" was not current, save in relation to the residents of Constantinople, before 1557, when the German scholar Hieronymus Wolf applied it to the Eastern Roman Empire. "What emperors had considered Roman, and Westerners . . . had called Greek," notes Robert Nelson, "thereby became Byzantine to distinguish it from ancient Greece. The name stuck."[7] Although mutually unknown and traditionally unconnected, we shall see that these historically misnamed peoples meet in more than one way.

Although this book was written during a nine-month fellowship at Dumbarton Oaks in 2016 and 2017, its seeds can be found in my decade-long project on cultural modernity in twentieth-century Argentina. In the final stages of that project, I ended up researching modernity's conceptual others— those "premoderns" and "nonmoderns" against which modernity would eventually define itself—partly in an attempt to understand the complex and elusive phenomenon that we call modernity, partly out of intellectual curiosity. It was an exciting journey of rediscovery going all the way back to my first academic steps as an undergraduate student in Byzantine and modern Greek studies at the University of Cyprus in the 1990s, when I was introduced to the fascinating world of Byzantium by Panagiotis Agapitos. After fifteen years in a Spanish department in Scotland where I have cultivated a passionate interest in postcolonial thought, writing on Byzantium and pre-Columbian America felt like a much-anticipated intellectual homecoming.

6   J. Bierhorst, ed. and trans., *Cantares mexicanos: Songs of the Aztecs* (Stanford, CA, 1985), 51; L. M. Burkhart, *The Slippery Earth: Nahua-Christian Moral Dialogue in Sixteenth-Century Mexico* (Tucson, AZ, 1989), 4; M. Z. Christensen, *Translated Christianities: Nahuatl and Maya Religious Texts* (University Park, PA, 2014), 5.

7   R. S. Nelson, "Byzantium and the Rebirth of Art and Learning in Italy and France," in *Byzantium: Faith and Power, 1261–1557*, ed. H. C. Evans (New York, 2004), 515–23, at 523; A. Kaldellis, *Hellenism in Byzantium: The Transformations of Greek Identity and the Reception of the Classical Tradition* (Cambridge, 2007), 42; F. Haarer, "Writing Histories of Byzantium: The Historiography of Byzantine History," in *A Companion to Byzantium*, ed. L. James (Oxford, 2010), 9–21, at 18. Constantinople took its name in 330 (C. Mango, "Constantinople," in *The Oxford Dictionary of Byzantium*, ed. A. P. Kazhdan et al., 3 vols. [New York, 1991], 1:508–12, at 508). On the term "Byzantinism," see D. G. Angelov, "Byzantinism: The Imaginary and Real Heritage of Byzantium in Southeastern Europe," in *New Approaches to Balkan Studies*, ed. D. Keridis, E. Elias-Bursać, and N. Yatromanolakis (Dulles, VA, 2003), 3–23, at 9.

Since its inception, my project has enjoyed a loving extended family of bright and generous scholars who welcomed, supported, and helped it grow in too many ways to mention here. My friend Anthi Andronikou was the one to point to Dumbarton Oaks as the most suitable place for this project. I often remember that long night in late October 2015 that I spent in the library at St Andrews finalizing the fellowship application, while Anthi tirelessly brought me every single book I asked for like a spoiled child. I must thank her for her endurance that night, but also for the many productive discussions we have had about Byzantium since and for kindly preparing the drawings and maps included here. None of this, of course, would have happened had that application not been supported by my three referees, Roderick Beaton, Will Fowler, and Geoffrey Kantaris, and the senior fellows in Byzantine studies at Dumbarton Oaks: Dimiter Angelov, John Duffy, Ioli Kalavrezou, Derek Krueger, the late Ruth Macrides, and Robert Ousterhout. I wholeheartedly thank them all, as well as Michael Maas, then director of Byzantine studies.

Writing a book on two seemingly unrelated fields required a good deal of energy and perseverance, much of which I owe to my Dumbarton Oaks friend Michalis Kappas, with whom I had inspiring conversations about Byzantine art and culture over long walks in Georgetown and across the Potomac River, and to the wonderful team of fellows in Byzantine and Pre-Columbian Studies: Marco Aimone, Brian Bauer, Nicolas Beaudry, Ari Caramanica, Ximena Chávez Balderas, Ryan Clasby, Andrea Cuomo, Hendrik Dey, Lori Boornazian Diel, Eric Dyrdahl, Adam Goldwyn, Sergey Ivanov, Polina Ivanova, Anna Leone, Jessica MacLellan, Mihail Mitrea, James Morton, Agnieszka Szymanska, and John Zaleski. Special thanks to Ximena and Lori in particular for sharing with me their knowledge of the Mexica, as well as to the directors of Byzantine and Pre-Columbian Studies, Elena Boeck and the late Colin McEwan, who made a comparatist like myself feel at home in both disciplines.

My stay at Dumbarton Oaks would have been entirely different, and so would the fortune of this book, had my fellowship not by chance coincided with that of Tom Cummins. As my favorite author once said, "what we call chance is our ignorance of the complex mechanism of causality." I still remember our meeting in the director's residence when I first mentioned the project to Tom. I must admit that he is one of the very few people I have ever talked to who did not need any explanation for the unusual comparison of the Byzantines and the Mexica. In a different lifetime, I am convinced that he would have written this book, no doubt with far better results; in this one, I will be forever grateful for his unwavering support and for his inherent passion and ability to motivate.

David Holton, whom I first met during my graduate studies at Cambridge in 1997, has been incredibly generous with his knowledge, making the English rendition of "Anakalema tes Konstantinopoles" flow much more smoothly, while ensuring accuracy and preserving the tone of the original. I thank him for taking the time to carefully read the poem and make nuanced and perceptive suggestions that have improved the translation greatly.

The book could not have had more competent and caring editors than Joel Kalvesmaki, Colin Whiting, and Lisa Shea. To them and to the anonymous readers, whose insightful comments have benefited the manuscript immensely, I owe a great debt of gratitude. Director of Publications, Kathy Sparkes, has been a model of patience and graciousness, going out of her way to ensure a timely publication of the book. Working with her has been a special privilege and a pleasure.

Jan Ziolkowski not only enthusiastically embraced the project but also saw in it the opportunity to launch this new series, *Extravagantes*. His role in the production of the book was critical, and so were his unflagging efforts to support, in his capacity as director of Dumbarton Oaks, the Blisses' vision of the center as a sanctuary for the humanities. I am hugely indebted to him and his wife, Elizabeth Ziolkowski, for making my time there enjoyable as well as productive.

I cannot think of any other library besides the one at Dumbarton Oaks that is so well endowed in Byzantine and Pre-Columbian studies, such that literature is readily available on even the most obscure texts. Nowhere else can one so easily meet and talk to scholars from both areas. This book would have never been written had the Blisses not transformed that old-fashioned house into Dumbarton Oaks. It is to them that this work is dedicated.

ONE

SERENDIPITIES

IN THE YEAR 1394 A POWERFUL EMPEROR SOUGHT A PREDICTION. WOULD "the end of the world" and "the conquest of the city" occur as anticipated or would "the time . . . be prolonged?"[1] According to calculations based on the Scriptures, doomsday would come in the year 1492. Some estimates were apparently bolder, detailing the exact day and time of the events: "On a Sunday, in the seventh hour of the night."[2] The anxious emperor seeking out prophecies was not Acamapichtli (r. 1376–1395), the first *tlatoani* (ruler) of the Mexica, but Manuel II Palaiologos (r. 1391–1425), the *basileus* (king) of the Eastern Roman Empire, later dubbed "Byzantium." Many Romaioi, or Byzantines, including the patriarch Gennadios Scholarios, expected the end of the world in 1492, which in the Orthodox Christian calendar corresponded to the seven-thousandth year since Creation.[3] As the time approached, they waited with nervous anticipation,

---

1   M.-H. Congourdeau, "Byzance et la fin du monde," in *Les traditions apocalyptiques au tournant de la chute de Constantinople*, ed. B. Lellouch and S. Yerasimos (Paris, 1999), 55–97, at 62–63.

2   I. Bryennios, Ἰωσὴφ μοναχοῦ τοῦ Βρυεννίου τὰ εὑρεθέντα, ed. E. Voulgaris, 2 vols. (Leipzig, 1768), 2:371.

3   P. Magdalino, "The Year 1000 in Byzantium," in *Byzantium in the Year 1000*, ed. P. Magdalino (Leiden, 2003), 233–70, at 237–38. See also C. Mango, "Byzantinism and Romantic Hellenism," *Journal of the Warburg and Courtauld Institutes* 28 (1965): 29–43, at 34. On Byzantine eschatology, consult M.-H. Congourdeau, "Les Byzantins face aux catastrophes naturelles sous les Paléologues," *Revue des études byzantines* 67.1 (2009): 151–63; Congourdeau, "Byzance"; and P. Guran, "Eschatology and Political Theology in the Last Centuries of Byzantium," *Revue des études sud-est européennes* 45 (2007): 73–85.

Fig. 1. The personification of the Earth riding a lion (middle) and an angel (upper right) playing his trumpet to raise the dead from the sarcophagus (bottom right). The inscription reads, "The Angel of the Lord trumpeting over the Earth" (ΑΓΓΕΛΟΣ Κ[ΥΡΙΟ]Υ ϹΑΛΠΙΖΩΝ ΤΗΝ ΓΗ). Fresco, 1391, Roustika, Crete, Church of Panagia. Photograph by Michalis Kappas.

bracing themselves for the predicted apocalyptic events of "the end of the world," or *synteleia* (fig. 1).

Writing at the turn of the twentieth century, the American historian Alexander del Mar posited that "while the Greek church were looking for this catastrophe, the Latin church, which enjoyed the advantage of a different Anno Mundi, employed its energies in persecuting the Moslems and Jews," a venture that culminated in the fall of Granada in 1492. Meanwhile, in the same year,

Fig. 2. King Ferdinand and Queen Isabella of Spain bidding farewell to Columbus at his departure for the Indies in 1492. Theodor de Bry, *Americae*, book 4, engraving 8 (Berlin, 1596), Kunstbibliothek, Staatliche Museen zu Berlin. Courtesy of bpk / Kunstbibliothek, SMB / Knud Petersen.

Columbus "found a New World, the plunder of which enabled the almost extinguished torch of European progress to be lit afresh" (fig. 2).[4] In an eerie stroke of irony, the Byzantines were right in their fears. Their predictions may have been slightly off in the timing of the capture of Constantinople, which took place on the morning of Tuesday, 29 May 1453, when the army of the Ottoman sultan Mehmed II entered the city through the western walls, but they had nevertheless foretold with uncanny precision the end of the world as they knew it. From a retrospective and secular point of view, eschatological narratives did not announce the *synteleia* and resurrection of the dead "from one end of heaven to the other," but bore the news of the fall of two empires and the birth

---

4   A. del Mar, *The Worship of Augustus Caesar* (New York, 1900), 221. For the narrative accompanying Theodor de Bry's illustration, see G. Sievernich, ed., *America de Bry, 1590–1634*, trans. A. Kovacsics (Madrid, 2003), 163.

of two others, from one end of the world to the newly "discovered" other.[5] "In less than a wink of Cronos's eye," notes Tom Cummins, "the ancient world of the Americas became a New World," while the values of the two worlds were set "in open competition."[6]

On 13 August 1521, also a Tuesday, Tenochtitlan, the imperial city of the Mexica, and its twin city Tlatelolco on the island of Mexico in Lake Texcoco would fall into the hands of an alliance formed by Cortés and several indigenous city-states. Perhaps nowhere is the uneasy encounter between the two worlds more eloquently articulated than in the *General History of the Things of New Spain (Historia general de las cosas de Nueva España)*, known as the *Florentine Codex*—a monumental ethnographic work compiled with the help of Nahua scholars under the supervision of Franciscan friar Bernardino de Sahagún, who taught at the Real Colegio de Santa Cruz de Tlatelolco in the sixteenth century. Written in both Spanish and Nahuatl using the Roman alphabet, "the texts are arranged in parallel columns of mutually unintelligible words—languages with no common linguistic origin."[7] The long process of epistemic adaptation, subversion, and cross-fertilization that was set off by the conquest is also reflected in Spanish chronicles of the time, many of which stress the inability to describe in a familiar idiom what the conquistadors saw. Bernal Díaz del Castillo, who joined Cortés, relates that "some of [their] men, who had been at Constantinople and Rome, and travelled through the whole of Italy, said that they had never seen a market-place of such large dimensions, or which was so well regulated, or so crowded with people as this one at Mexico."[8] Speaking of the marketplace in Tlatelolco, Cortés similarly observes that it was twice the size of the one in Salamanca, displaying "every kind of merchandise produced in these lands." The Spaniard enumerates some of those goods before he concedes

---

5   The full passage from Matthew reads: "And he shall send his angels with a great sound of the trumpet, and they shall gather together his elect from the four winds, from one end of heaven to the other" (Matt. 24:31).

6   T. Cummins, "Competing and Commensurate Values in Colonial Conditions: How They Are Expressed and Registered in the Sixteenth-Century Andes," in *The Construction of Value in the Ancient World*, ed. J. K. Papadopoulos and G. Urton (Los Angeles, CA, 2012), 358–75, at 359.

7   Ibid.

8   B. Díaz del Castillo, *The Memoirs of the Conquistador Bernal Díaz del Castillo*, trans. J. I. Lockhart, 2 vols. (London, 1844), 1:238. The original title of Díaz del Castillo's account is *Historia verdadera de la conquista de la Nueva España (True History of the Conquest of New Spain)*, written between the 1550s and 1584 but not published until 1632. On the dating of the work, see R. Adorno, *Polemics of Possession in Spanish American Narrative* (New Haven, CT, 2007), 348.

Fig. 3. A towering flame over Hagia Sophia, 21 May 1453. Drawing by Anthi Andronikou, after Nestor-Iskander's account.

that "because of their great number and because I cannot remember many of them nor do I know what they are called I shall not mention them."[9]

On the cusp of modernity, we shall see that the Byzantines and the Mexica faced historical changes reportedly forecast by ominous signs on both sides. "On the twenty-first day of May," details Nestor-Iskander, an eyewitness of the siege of Constantinople, there was "a frightful sign in the city. As a consequence, on the eve of Friday, the entire city was illuminated. . . . Many people gathered and saw on the Church of the Wisdom of God [Hagia Sophia], at the top of the window, a large flame of fire issuing forth," which "encircled the entire neck of the church for a long time" (fig. 3). Before the flame "took to the sky," it "gathered into one" and "there was an indescribable light." "Those who had seen it," the author tells us, "were benumbed; they began to wail and cried out in Greek: 'Lord have mercy!' The light itself has gone up to heaven; the gates of heaven were opened;

9   H. Cortés, *Letters from Mexico*, ed. and trans. A. Pagden (New Haven, CT, 1986), 103–4.

the light was received; and again they were closed."[10] The towering flame over Hagia Sophia alarmed nobles and laymen alike, who asked for advice from the patriarch. "God's grace and generosity have gone from us," the latter admonished them, "God wishes to hand over our city to the enemy."[11] Michael Kritoboulos, one of the four Greek historians of the fall and Mehmed II's biographer, narrates that for a whole day the imperial city was in dark and that "on the next day, in the morning, a dense fog covered the whole city, lasting from early morning till evening." This sign, he writes, "evidently indicated the departure of the Divine Presence, and its leaving the City in total abandonment and desertion."[12]

A handful of decades later and seven thousand miles away, a similar sign appeared in the sky: "It was like a tongue of fire, like flame, as if showering the light of the dawn."[13] According to the *Florentine Codex*, which provides the most important indigenous account of the events of the conquest in Nahuatl, the omen occurred approximately ten years before the Spaniards' arrival in Mexico: "It looked as if it were piercing the heavens. [It] was wide at the base and pointed [at the head]. To the very midst of the sky, to the very heart of the heavens it extended. . . . When it arose and thus came forth, when it appeared at midnight, it looked as if day had dawned."[14] For an entire year the sign "came forth" and "when it appeared, there was shouting; all cried out striking the palm of the hand against the mouth. All were frightened and waited with dread."[15] The *Florentine Codex* reports a second omen involving the house of Huitzilopochtli, the principal god of Tenochtitlan: "Quite of its own accord fire broke out in the house of the demon Uitzilopochtli [sic], and flared greatly. No one had set fire to it; only of itself it burst into flames." When the "tongues of fire" consumed the house, "there was an outcry" and the priests said: "'O Mexicans, hasten here to put out [the fire! Bring] your earthen water jars!' And when they cast water

---

10   Nestor-Iskander, *The Tale of Constantinople (of Its Origin and Capture by the Turks in the Year 1453)*, trans. W. K. Hanak and M. Philippides (New Rochelle, NY, 1998), 63.

11   Ibid. Marios Philippides and Walter Hanak link this event to St. Elmo's fire (M. Philippides and W. K. Hanak, *The Siege of Constantinople in 1453: Historiography, Topography, and Military Studies* [Farnham, 2011], 223).

12   M. Kritoboulos, *History of Mehmed the Conqueror by Kritovoulos*, trans. C. T. Riggs (Princeton, NJ, 1954), 59.185.

13   B. de Sahagún, *Florentine Codex: General History of the Things of New Spain*, ed. and trans. A. J. O. Anderson and C. E. Dibble, 12 vols. in 13 (Santa Fe, NM, 1950–1982), book 12, ch. 1, 1.

14   Ibid. The *Florentine Codex* dedicates chapter 1 of book 12 to omens about the conquest of Mexico.

15   Ibid.

Fig. 4. The burning of the Temple of Huitzilopochtli, in *Florentine Codex*, 1577, Florence, Biblioteca Medicea Laurenziana, MS Med. Palat. 220, fol. 409r. Courtesy of the Ministero per i beni e le attività culturali e per il turismo.

upon it, when they sought to smother it, all the more did it flare" (fig. 4).[16] The burning of the house of Huitzilopochtli was of great significance as the god was associated with the founding myth of Tenochtitlan and the empire.

Like the rise and fall of Huitzilopochtli's house, the life of Hagia Sophia was a synecdoche for the city. Built on the orders of Emperor Justinian I from 532 to 537, Hagia Sophia was, in the Byzantine imagination, a symbol for Constantinople, and by extension the empire. The resemblance between the omens in the so-called Old and New Worlds is not accidental. The latter were a colonial device, constructed after the fact and informed by the former. For the Nahuas, notes Louise Burkhart, such prophetic texts were a "key strategy for coping with change." They invented them to make sense of the conquest as part of a "counternarrative of continuity," which, as will become clear, presented the colonial era not as a rupture with the past, but as its continuation.[17]

Nestor-Iskander adds another twist to the narrative. In his account of the foundation of Constantinople by Constantine the Great, he tells of a fight between an eagle and a snake. The emperor, he recounts, "gathered great lords,

---

16 Ibid., book 12, ch. 1, 2.

17 L. M. Burkhart, *Holy Wednesday: A Nahua Drama from Early Colonial Mexico* (Philadelphia, PA, 1996), 92–93. See also M. Restall, *When Montezuma Met Cortés: The True Story of the Meeting That Changed History* (New York, 2018), 204–5. For the notion "counternarrative of continuity," see J. Klor de Alva, "Nahua Colonial Discourse and the Appropriation of the (European) Other," *Archives de sciences sociales des religions* 77 (1992): 15–35.

Fig. 5. An eagle and a snake, mosaic, ca. 527–565, Istanbul, Great Palace Mosaic Museum. Courtesy of the Erich Lessing Kunst- und Kulturarchiv GmbH.

dignitaries and masters, and began to consider the layout of the city's walls, towers, and gates" when "this snake suddenly came out of a hole and raced over the place; at the same moment an eagle, having escaped from aloft, descended, snatched the snake, and flew on high." But the snake "began to gather its strength around the eagle" until the two of them fell "on that place" where the city would be erected. Constantine was "in great dread," seeking the advice of his wise men. "This place," they told him, "will be called Seven Hills and will be glorified and exalted above other cities throughout the world." The wise men, however, warned the emperor that "the eagle is a sign of Christianity while the snake is a sign of the non-Orthodox. Since the snake overpowered the eagle, it reveals how Mohammedanism will overwhelm Christianity."[18]

A recurring trope across different cultures, the struggle between eagle and snake was portrayed in a famous mosaic in the Great Palace in Constantinople (fig. 5), probably commissioned by Emperor Justinian I, as well as in numerous

18   Nestor-Iskander, *Tale of Constantinople*, 25–26.

Fig. 6. Huitzilopochtli's sign to the Mexica, in *Codex Durán*, ca. 1581, Madrid, Biblioteca Nacional de España, VITR/26/11, fol. 14v. Courtesy of the Biblioteca Nacional de España.

Mexican manuscripts.[19] The eagle motif was, in fact, very important to the peoples of Central and South America and, as noted before, played a pivotal role in Nahua lore and the foundation myth of Tenochtitlan (fig. 6).[20] Meanwhile the theme's prominence among the Mexica is still echoed today in its appearance on the modern Mexican flag.

But what is there in common between Byzantium and America apart from what seem to be some shared semiotics and bemusing serendipities, drawn together by my fancy? Where do these geographically remote and culturally distinct civilizations meet, if we agree they do, save for the fortuitous settings of libraries, museums, and palaces under whose roofs a great deal of the intellectual and material culture of Byzantium and preconquest America has found refuge? What is there to compare between the imperial cities of Constantinople and Tenochtitlan beyond the fact that, on the grand scale of history, they were conquered nearly simultaneously? In my view, the answer partly lies in Del Mar's earlier comments about the year 1492.

19   Even though this particular mosaic was probably not visible around 1453, similar depictions elsewhere may have been a source of inspiration for Nestor-Iskander (Philippides and Hanak, *Siege of Constantinople*, 221). For more examples of relevant scenes in Byzantium, see R. Wittkower, "Eagle and Serpent: A Study in the Migration of Symbols," *Journal of the Warburg Institute* 2.4 (1939): 293–325, at 318.

20   Wittkower, "Eagle," 304.

TWO

BYZANTIUM, AMERICA,
AND THE "MODERN"

THE MIDDLE AGES, DEL MAR TELLS US, "ALMOST EXTINGUISHED [THE] TORCH of European progress." This was "lit afresh" in the New World, where Europe's utopian imaginings could be forged anew. In short, the doomsday of the Romaioi turned out to instead concern the peoples of the Anahuac (Valley of Mexico) and Tawantinsuyu (Inca Empire), among others. The conquest inaugurated Europe's "American" dream, the dream of modernity.

Meaning both "new" and "just now," the word "modern" is constantly displaced by itself, the "just newer." Its first appearance in Latin as *modernus* dates to the late fifth century, when Pope Gelasius used it to distinguish between contemporary events (*admonitiones modernas*) and the early Christian years (*antiquis regulis*).[1] The notion subsequently underwent several resignifications before it was associated in the eighteenth century with linear, future-oriented progress. Free from the burden of the Greco-Roman past, which until then was thought of as superior to the present and therefore as a standard that should be emulated, the Enlightenment heaved anchor and sailed headlong into its modern future. In this way Europe set itself up as scientifically, technologically, and culturally superior to the past and to other parts of the world.

The term "modernity" may have been traditionally employed in connection with the eighteenth-century Enlightenment, but a number of scholars have

---

1   H. R. Jauss, "Modernity and Literary Tradition," trans. C. Thorne, *Critical Inquiry* 31.2 (2005): 329–64, at 333.

identified the colonization of America in the late fifteenth and sixteenth centuries as "first" or "early modernity," reserving the phrase "second modernity" for the Enlightenment, the French and Industrial Revolutions, and the second wave of European colonialism in the nineteenth and twentieth centuries.[2] In both cases, modernity's assumed superiority, what Enrique Dussel describes as "the irrational myth of modernity,"[3] was paired with the alleged inferiority of exogenous and endogenous histories. These "modern" Europeans regarded what was external in space (non-European cultures) and time (the Middle Ages) as dark and regressive.

The first process—exogenous inferiorization, that is, the defining of non-European peoples and cultures as inferior—is clearly reflected in the attitudes of Columbus and European colonizers. According to the Genoese admiral, the native people "should be good servants" and could "easily be made Christians" because "they appeare[d] to [him] to have no religion,"[4] while conquistadors like Cortés saw them as "innocent or savage, childlike or barbarous."[5] These negative stereotypes lived on into the Enlightenment. Voltaire thought of indigenous people like the Caribs and Iroquois as "plunged into barbaric stupidity for the most part," lacking "reasoned knowledge," and Buffon, with the exception of Mexico and Peru, spoke of savages (*sauvages*) at the mercy of the forces of nature.[6] At the same time, the debate about whether the indigenous "were peoples in the infancy of mankind or degenerated populations" continued into the eighteenth century between "the partisans of progress and human perfectibility" and "the proponents of the senescence of the world and

2   A. Escobar, "'Mundos y conocimientos de otro modo': El programa de investigación de modernidad/ colonialidad latinoamericano," *Tabula rasa* 1 (2003): 51–86, at 60. See E. Dussel, *The Invention of the Americas: Eclipse of "the Other" and the Myth of Modernity*, trans. M. D. Barber (New York, 1995); idem, *The Underside of Modernity: Apel, Ricœur, Rorty, Taylor, and the Philosophy of Liberation*, trans. E. Mendieta (New York, 1996); A. Quijano, "Colonialidad del poder, eurocentrismo y América Latina," in *La colonialidad del saber: Eurocentrismo y ciencias sociales. Perspectivas latinoamericanas*, ed. E. Lander (Caracas, 2000), 201–45; idem, "Colonialidad del poder y clasificación social," *Journal of World-System Research* 6.2 (2000): 342–86; and W. D. Mignolo, *The Idea of Latin America* (Oxford, 2005).

3   Dussel, *Underside*, 52.

4   C. Columbus, *The Four Voyages*, ed. and trans. J. M. Cohen (London, 1969), 56.

5   M. Restall, *Seven Myths of the Spanish Conquest* (New York, 2003), 107.

6   Voltaire, *Les œuvres complètes*, vol. 26A, *Essai sur les mœurs et l'esprit des nations*, ed. B. Bernard et al. (Oxford, 2013), 212–13; and G.-L. Leclerc, Comte de Buffon, *Histoire naturelle générale et particulière, avec la description du Cabinet du Roy*, Suppl. 5 (Paris, 1778), 247–48.

degeneracy of America."[7] Together with these negative portrayals, we encounter the image of the noble savage (*bon sauvage*), which originated in the works of Rabelais, Ronsard, and Montaigne and persisted in the writings of Rousseau, Lafitau, and others.[8]

The second process—endogenous inferiorization, that is, the defining of Europe's own past as inferior—is exemplified by Filippo Villani, who in the early 1380s denounced the past (later dubbed the Middle Ages) as the abyss or depth of darkness (*abyssus tenebrarum*). In its humanist fervor, incipient modernity saw the medieval period as the way of negation (*via negationis*).[9] But while the Western Middle Ages were gradually rehabilitated—to some extent, at least, by the historical revisionism of the Enlightenment that culminated in romanticism's idealization of medieval culture—outside and sometimes within the circles of Byzantinists, the history of the eleven-century-long Eastern Roman Empire is typically regarded as a rehash of antiquity or contemporary Islamic, Latin, and Hebrew material. According to this narrative, Byzantium, hobbled by dogma and despotism, was unable to produce anything new; its contribution to the world is restricted to preserving ancient knowledge. In due course this knowledge was passed on to the West, which used it for the advancement of humanity. This disparagement of Byzantium, first emerging in the Enlightenment, still holds sway over our collective consciousness. Gibbon labels the Byzantines a "degenerate people," Voltaire sees their history as "a worthless collection" of "declamations and miracles" and "a disgrace to the human mind," while Montesquieu describes it as "a tissue of revolts, seditions and perfidies."[10] The philosophes' reading of Byzantium fed into modernity's narrative of superiority, and its endurance can be verified in contemporary pejorative uses of the epithet "Byzantine" in English, French, German, Italian, and Spanish. With the modern rhetorical construction of indigenous America

---

7   C. J. Jaenen, "'Les Sauvages Ameriquains': Persistence into the 18th Century of Traditional French Concepts and Constructs for Comprehending Amerindians," *Ethnohistory* 29.1 (1982): 43–56, at 44–49.

8   P. P. Boucher, *Cannibal Encounters: Europeans and Island Caribs, 1492–1763* (Baltimore, MD, 1992), 118–23.

9   In Jauss, "Modernity," 340.

10 E. Gibbon, *The History of the Decline and Fall of the Roman Empire*, 13 vols. (London, 1997), 5:515. For Voltaire, see A. A. Vasiliev, *History of the Byzantine Empire, 324–1453* (Madison, WI, 1952), 6. For the original French, see Voltaire, *Les œuvres complètes*, vol. 67, *Œuvres de 1768*, ed. S. Davies, J. Renwick, B. Guy, and C. Todd (Oxford, 2007), 296. C.-L. de Secondat, Baron de Montesquieu, *Considerations of the Causes of the Grandeur and Decadence of the Romans*, trans. J. Baker (New York, 1882), 437.

strongly contested, the Islamic contribution to the birth of modernity duly recognized, the role of classical antiquity long acknowledged, and that of the Western Middle Ages slowly restored, today Villani's trope of the abyss of darkness is kept largely for Byzantium.

America illustrates what I refer to as "the irrational myth of modernity abroad," that is, modernity's rhetoric of superiority over non-European cultures. Byzantium, on the other hand, epitomizes what we could call "the irrational myth of modernity at home." The discursive construction of the indigenous people as savages and the Middle Ages as dark and retrograde are two tributaries of the same river. They are conceptual siblings, the progenies of a single historical process that forced the Eastern Roman Empire and indigenous America into an unlikely relationship that was as much unthinkable as it was inexorable. As modernity became increasingly self-conscious, it saw itself as a distinct and inevitable historical period whose putative supremacy over the rest of history was plain. With the Enlightenment idea of linear development in particular, "modern" Europeans were heading full speed toward a future of infinite progress. Outside modernity's exceptionalism, the premodern and nonmodern were relegated to the sphere of the underdeveloped, regressive, belated, or simply inferior. Byzantium and America are examples of endogenous and exogenous inferiorization. They are complementary strands in the mirror of a narcissistic modernity, and both represent its "underside"—coloniality. They are, of course, also both constitutive of modernity.[11] In addition to playing a crucial part in modernity's self-imagining, they made its actualization epistemically and materially possible. America and Byzantium were instrumental in the rise and consolidation of the modern.

This theoretical digression historicizes the comparative approach of the conquests of Constantinople and Tenochtitlan on the threshold of modernity before looking at how the Romaioi and the Mexica saw and conveyed the fall of their empires. Drawing on theories of cultural trauma and collective memory, I will investigate affective, cognitive, and aesthetic crossovers and variances in learned poetry and song to explore how their authors understood the events in question and their aftermath. I focus on a close, selective reading of three relevant texts to reach some meaningful conclusions about the discursive production of collective memory and cultural trauma at the time.

---

11   Dussel, *Underside.*

THREE

TRADITION AND THEORY

OUR THREE TEXTS ARE "ANAKALEMA TES KONSTANTINOPOLES" ("LAMENT FOR Constantinople"), "Huexotzincayotl" ("Huexotzinca Piece"), and "Tlaxcaltecayotl" ("Tlaxcala Piece"), all created by anonymous authors fairly soon after each conquest and recorded in sixteenth-century manuscripts. One of the most famous poems dedicated to the fall of Constantinople, "Anakalema" belongs to the tradition of *threnoi*, learned laments for cities that evolved in parallel and often in dialogue with folk songs on the same theme. "There has been an unbroken tradition of such historical laments in Greek, both learned and vernacular," argues Margaret Alexiou.[1] Like folk songs and a sizeable body of threnoi, "Anakalema" is drafted in political verse (*politikos stichos*), an iambic, fifteen-syllable verse without rhyme and with a caesura after the eighth syllable.[2] The "national" or "native" meter of modern Greece, political verse has dominated vernacular poetry since the fourteenth and fifteenth centuries.[3] Unlike

---

1   M. Alexiou, *The Ritual Lament in Greek Tradition*, rev. D. Yatromanolakis and P. Roilos (Lanham, MD, 2002), 83. For folk laments in particular, see R. Beaton, *Folk Poetry of Modern Greece* (Cambridge, 1980), 95–102.

2   Like folk songs, "Anakalema" avoids enjambment, making use of it only rarely. See, for example, lines 12–13, 67–68, 109–10 (E. Kriaras, "Εισαγωγή," in *Ανακάλημα της Κωνσταντινόπολης*, ed. E. Kriaras [Thessaloniki, 2012], 9–17, at 14).

3   It is still puzzling why Byzantine authors called it political verse. "One thing certain," writes Roderick Beaton, "is that it never had anything to do with politics. The adjective πολιτικός in the twelfth century seems to have meant 'down-to-earth,' 'day-to-day.' . . . The word seems

folk poetry, which was sung and passed on orally, threnoi like "Anakalema" were written by learned men, occasionally priests or monks, although the lack of certainty regarding authorship and date "suggests a degree of anonymity and perhaps a period of oral transmission." This hypothesis is backed by the common pool of motifs and stylistic elements present in a range of threnoi.[4] The poet who wrote "Anakalema" was well informed about the events of the conquest, had a deep knowledge of Greek folk verse, and was most likely a member of the upper class.[5] He borrowed tropes and formulas from established traditions, among them threnoi, monodies (prose laments) and *moirologia* (folk laments) for cities and for the dead, and various legends and founding myths to express what seemed inexpressible: the fall of the Queen City or *Basileuousa*.

For all that the "Anakalema" author employs the standard Greek of the time—the Byzantine *koine*, which in theory would allow him to get through to different communities across the Greek world—his text displays some idiomatic traces that, as Emmanuel Kriaras has shown, point to Cyprus, Crete, and the Dodecanese (fig. 7). While all the linguistic clues identified by Kriaras appear on Cyprus, not all of them are found in the other places.[6] The residual dialectal diction of the poem seems to be Cypriot, including the titular noun *anakalema* (lament), which, Kriaras tells us, is only reported on Cyprus.[7] In fact, while the verb *anakaliemai* or *anakalioumai*, meaning to mourn, weep, or lament, appears in other parts of the Greek world, such as the islands of Naxos, Syros, and Crete, the noun *anakaleman* (also *anakaleton, anakalion, nekalion, nekaleman*), meaning weeping or mourning, seems present only on Cyprus.[8] Kriaras's conclusion is seconded by Jean Darrouzès, who explains that paleographic evidence, especially orthography, indicates that the manuscript, or at

---

to have referred to the private life of the citizen (πολίτης), if not actually to the dweller in Constantinople, commonly known as 'the City' (Η Πόλις)" (R. Beaton, *The Medieval Greek Romance* [London, 1996], 98).

4   Alexiou, *Ritual Lament*, 88. For a range of formulas shared by relevant learned and folk laments, see ibid., 83–101.

5   G. Kehayoglou, "Επίμετρο," in Kriaras, *Ανακάλημα της Κωνσταντινόπολης*, 35–100, at 70.

6   Kriaras, "Εισαγωγή," 11–13.

7   For more examples of idiomatic elements in the poem, see Kriaras, *Ανακάλημα της Κωνσταντινόπολης*, 6–8.

8   Ibid., 6; idem, *Λεξικό της μεσαιωνικής ελληνικής δημώδους γραμματείας, 1100–1669*, 21 vols. (Thessaloniki, 1968–), 2:78–79; Academy of Athens, *Ιστορικόν λεξικόν της νέας ελληνικής*, 4 vols. (Athens, 1933–53), 2:50–51; K. Yangoullis, *Θησαυρός κυπριακής διαλέκτου* (Nicosia, 2009), 54. On Cyprus, the verb *nekalioumai* is also used (ibid., 54, 305).

Fig. 7. The eastern Mediterranean in the fifteenth century. Map by Anthi Andronikou, after J. Harris, *The End of Byzantium* (New Haven, CT, 2010), map 2.

least the folios containing the poem, must have been produced in Cyprus.[9] However, not all scholars agree that the poem is from Cyprus, with some suggesting Crete or the Dodecanese. For the sake of this discussion I follow Kriaras's theory, but it should be clear that whether Cypriot, Dodecanesian, or Cretan, the exact provenance of the song has little impact on the actual analysis of the text, its author's claim of trauma, and its afterlife.[10]

9   J. Darrouzès, "Bulletin critique," *Revue des études byzantines* 25 (1967): 259–60.

10 The reference to Cretans in "Anakalema" (31, 38–39) had led a number of earlier scholars, including Karl Krumbacher, Athanasios Papadopoulos Kerameus, Agathangelos Xirouchakis, Dirk Christiaan Hesseling, and Stephanos Xanthoudidis, as well as some of Kriaras's contemporaries, among them Stylianos Alexiou and Gareth Morgan, to assume that the poem was of Cretan origin (Kriaras, *Το Ανακάλημα*, 3–5). On the Cypriot authorship of the poem, see ibid., 5–11; idem, "Εισαγωγή," 10–14; G. Kehayoglou, "Το γραμματειακό 'πολυσύστημα' του ύστερου Μεσαίωνα και η ποικιλία της ελληνόγλωσσης λόγιας, ημιλόγιας, δημώδους και ιδιωματικής λογοτεχνίας ως το τέλος της φραγκοκρατίας (12ος αι.–1489)," in *Ιστορία της νεότερης κυπριακής λογοτεχνίας*, ed. G. Kehayoglou and L. Papaleontiou (Nicosia, 2010), 19–90, at 84–86; idem, "Επίμετρο," 54–55, 94; and A. Karanika, "Messengers, Angels, and Laments for the Fall of Constantinople," in *The Fall of Cities in the Mediterranean: Commemoration in Literature, Folk-Song, and Liturgy*, ed. M. R. Bachvarova, D. Dutsch, and A. Suter (New York, 2016), 226–51, at 235.

The limited presence of dialect in "Anakalema" must not come as a surprise, argues Kriaras, because the use of *koine* with certain idiomatic vestiges was not uncommon. He provides as an example the poem "Lament for Cyprus" ("Threnos tes Kuprou"), attributed to the Cypriot author Solomon Rodinos (1515–1585/1586).[11] Referring to the Ottoman conquest of the island in 1571, Rodinos's poem, notes Kriaras, is drafted in a mixed language that combines idiomatic elements with archaisms.[12] Such a linguistic blend could point to authorial intentions similar to those of "Anakalema." Giorgos Kehayoglou says that by the fourteenth century the Byzantine *koine* was mostly used in Constantinople and the few regions still under its political control (for example, part of the Peloponnese known as the Morea, Thrace, and Macedonia), while in other areas of the Greek world, "the Greek *koine* seems to dissolve again into dialects or idioms, as in antiquity."[13] In contemporary Cyprus in particular, where the earliest use of idiomatic language is observed in the writings of Saint Neophytos Enkleistos (the Recluse) in the twelfth century, we find texts almost entirely in the local dialect. Among them are the legal corpus *Assizes* (fourteenth century) and the chronicles of Leontios Machairas and Georgios Boustronios (both fifteenth century).[14] Given that by the sixteenth century Cypriot texts written in Greek favor the dialect over the standard Greek of the time,[15] and assuming a Cypriot origin for the poem, we may read the application of *koine* in "Anakalema" as a conscious choice of the author to disseminate his trauma claim as widely as possible.[16]

Concrete information on the performance of Byzantine threnoi is scarce, save for religious threnoi. Performed on Good Friday to this day, for instance,

11   See T. Papadopoullos, ed., "Ὁ θρήνος τῆς Κύπρου," *Κυπριακαί σπουδαί* 44 (1980): 1–78. Among the scholars who have attributed the "Lament for Cyprus" to Rodinos are Simos Menardos, Theodoros Papadopoullos, and David Holton (G. Grivaud, "Ὁ πνευματικός βίος και η γραμματολογία κατά την περίοδο της Φραγκοκρατίας," in *Ιστορία της Κύπρου*, ed. T. Papadopoullos, vol. 5, *Μεσαιωνικόν βασίλειον: Ενετοκρατία*, part 2, *Πνευματικός βίος, παιδεία, γραμματολογία, βυζαντινή τέχνη, γοτθική τέχνη, νομισματοκοπία, βιβλιογραφία* [Nicosia, 1996]: 863–1207, at 1181–82).

12   Kriaras, "Εισαγωγή," 13. Interestingly, while Rodinos's threnos (composed after 1571) employs a mixed language, the lyric poems contained in the anonymous Cypriot *Canzoniere* (ca. 1546–1570) are written in the local dialect.

13   G. Kehayoglou, *Από τον ύστερο Μεσαίωνα ως τον 18° αιώνα: Εισαγωγή στα παλαιότερα κείμενα της νεοελληνικής λογοτεχνίας* (Thessaloniki, 2009), 31.

14   Kehayoglou, "Το γραμματειακό 'πολυσύστημα,'" 56, 88; and idem, "Επίμετρο," 72.

15   Grivaud, "Ὁ πνευματικός βίος," 1123, 1206.

16   For the use of dialect in the literature of Renaissance Crete, see D. Holton, "The Cretan Renaissance," in *Literature and Society in Renaissance Crete*, ed. D. Holton (New York, 1991), 1–16, at 13–15.

"Epitaphios Threnos" ("The Lamentation at the Tomb") is a service of lamentations for the burial of Christ.[17] Speaking of rhetoric in twelfth-century Byzantium, Margaret Mullett mentions threnoi as part of a larger body of performative works, such as funeral orations (whose primary function was to praise), consolations (to console), and monodies (to mourn).[18] Defining the "social setting" of any of these death genres, writes Mullett, is often difficult. Some may have been performed in literary salons, others "on commemorative occasions in private houses."[19] Rhetorical works more broadly were "designed for an occasional setting: in church or palace, *oikos*, school-room or street." Rhetors in training would display their skills in inaugural lectures, at the end of the Epiphany speech to the emperor, and in the rhetorical salons or *theatra* of Constantinople. Rhetoric, she concludes, made for the "spectacle of display."[20] Banned by the church as lascivious, idolatrous, and shallow entertainment, *theatron* (theatre) eventually came to designate the hippodrome, but also spectacles and gatherings more generally, including literary groups where "rhetorical works were read aloud."[21] Learned poetry in political verse was aimed at wider audiences, such as "those attending a court ceremonial, a half-educated patroness, or a class of children," in which case it was easy to memorize and thus used for instruction.[22]

We know that in Venetian Cyprus some kind of schooling for the Greek populace became available relatively early. In 1521 the local aristocracy succeeded in launching Greek grammar classes in Nicosia, Kyrenia, and Famagusta with a view to establishing "a 'popular' context within which to forge Greek education."[23] Rodinos, the author of the "Lament for Cyprus," studied in one of

---

17 See Alexiou, *Ritual Lament*, 65–68.

18 M. Mullett, "Rhetoric, Theory, and the Imperative of Performance: Byzantium and Now," in *Rhetoric in Byzantium*, ed. E. Jeffreys (Aldershot, 2003), 151–70, at 152; and M. Mullett, "Do Brothers Weep? Male Grief, Mourning, Lament, and Tears in Eleventh- and Twelfth-Century Byzantium," in *Greek Laughter and Tears: Antiquity and After*, ed. M. Alexiou and D. Cairns (Edinburgh, 2017), 312–37, at 324.

19 M. Mullett, *Theophylact of Ochrid: Reading the Letters of a Byzantine Archbishop* (Aldershot, 1997), 139. On the rhetoric of death in twelfth-century Byzantium, see P. A. Agapitos, "Public and Private Death in Psellos: Maria Skleraina and Styliane Psellaina," *Byzantinische Zeitschrift* 101.2 (2008): 555–607.

20 Mullett, "Rhetoric," 152–53.

21 A. P. Kazhdan, "Theater," in Kazhdan et al., *The Oxford Dictionary of Byzantium*, 3:2031; and W. Puchner, *Greek Theatre between Antiquity and Independence: A History of Reinvention from the Third Century BC to 1830* (Cambridge, 2017), 63.

22 E. Jeffreys, "Poetry," in Kazhdan et al., *The Oxford Dictionary of Byzantium*, 3:1688–89.

23 Grivaud, "Ο πνευματικός βίος," 1112.

those schools, taking classes on Greek grammar and poetry, as well as Italian, in Famagusta.[24] His threnos, which is drafted in rhymed political verse and contains laments for the fall of Nicosia and Famagusta, clearly draws on motifs found in previous threnoi and monodies about the fall of Constantinople, among them "Anakalema." Could Rodinos have come across our poem as part of his schooling in Famagusta? Possibly, although there is no extant information about the performance or teaching of "Anakalema" in Cyprus or elsewhere. As noted earlier, however, a period of oral transmission may have occurred before the poem was written down.

George Hill reports that the sixteenth-century Cypriot Dominican friar and historian Stefano Lusignan "had listened with much emotion to a lament on the ruin of Nicosia, which may have been one of the two dirges on that subject which have survived, and also to a ballad describing the Turkish attack on Malta."[25] In his *Description de toute l'isle de Cypre* (1580), Lusignan, in fact, alludes to Cypriot ritual laments, the "sad and pitiful songs" ("chansons tristes & piteuses") performed by women over the body of the dead "with plenty of tears" ("auec abondance de larmes"), while "adapting their voice according to the subject" ("accommodant la voix semblable au subiect"). The historian warns his reader that "you would break down in tears" ("tu fondrois en larmes") and would not be able "to refrain from crying and grieving" ("abstenir de pleurer & se contrister") if you had "heard" ("tu eusses entendu" and later "si tu pouuois ouyr") the songs of the Ottoman conquest of Nicosia (1570) and the siege of Malta (1565).[26] His use of the auditory verbs *entendu* and *ouyr* is significant because it implies that threnoi for the destruction and fall of cities were in circulation and performed in the sixteenth century. But it is unclear in what context Lusignan, who had left Cyprus for Italy in May 1570,[27] might have listened to those songs, especially the one on the capture of the island's capital, which occurred in September of the same year.[28]

24   Ibid., 1168–69.

25   G. Hill, *A History of Cyprus*, vol. 3, *The Frankish Period, 1432–1571* (Cambridge, 1948), 1110. For the Cypriot poem "Song of the Siege of Malta" ("Asma poliorkias tes Maltas"), composed in political verse, see A. Sakellarios, *Τα κυπριακά: Ήτοι γεωγραφία, ιστορία και γλώσσα της Κύπρου από των αρχαιοτάτων χρόνων μέχρι σήμερον*, 2 vols. (Athens, 1890–91), 2:181–83.

26   S. Lusignan, *Description de toute l'isle de Cypre* (Paris, 1580), 220r–221v.

27   Hill, *History of Cyprus*, 1147; Grivaud, "Ο πνευματικός βίος," 1192.

28   Apart from Rodinos's threnos, a second poem dealing with the Ottoman conquest of Cyprus, composed in rhymed political verse, was discovered in a manuscript in Saint Catherine's Monastery at Sinai in 1957, although its origin has been debated (Grivaud, "Ο πνευματικός βίος," 1189).

The Nahuatl songs draw on the pre-Columbian traditions of the *icnocuicatl* (song of sorrow) and *yaocuicatl* (war song). As already mentioned, they form part of the *Cantares mexicanos* (*Mexica Songs*), a corpus of ninety-one songs largely composed after 1521, although they cling to their preconquest heritage rather tightly. The dating of the songs has been vigorously debated. Among the preconquest camp, we find Fray Ángel María Garibay and his disciple Miguel León-Portilla, both arguing that the greater number of the songs belong to the pre-Hispanic era. Any references in the *Cantares mexicanos* to the Spaniards and Christianity are therefore seen as superficial modifications or "interpolations" mirroring the historical and societal changes ushered in by the conquest.[29] John Bierhorst was the first to put forward a postconquest dating. Although a few songs were possibly devised before the Spanish arrival, he wrote, most of them must come from the early colonial period, as they deal with the conquest and its consequences, adjusting traditional imagery to reflect the crises of the present.[30] James Lockhart seems to bridge the two camps. While acknowledging that we can no longer consider the songs "as virtually pure compositions of the preconquest period, altered only by the word 'God' patched in over the names of indigenous deities," he recognizes that in an oral tradition in which singers reshuffle existing material producing only a slightly different variant, the *Cantares mexicanos* could still be, for the most part, of pre-Hispanic origin.[31] In a more recent article, Bierhorst appears to embrace this view, which was already present, if somewhat understated, in his earlier work, admitting that "a precontact motivation for the songs as we know them is easy to supply."[32]

Unfortunately, little direct information has survived about the context in which the songs of the *Cantares mexicanos* were performed in the sixteenth century. In their majority, says León-Portilla, *cantares* more broadly "were recited or sung at festivals and reunions, accompanied by flutes and drums, the so-called

29 A. M. Garibay K., ed. and trans., *Poesía náhuatl II: Cantares mexicanos, manuscrito de la Biblioteca Nacional de México* (Mexico City, 1965), lvii and passim; M. León-Portilla, *Pre-Columbian Literatures of Mexico*, trans. G. Lobanov and M. León-Portilla (Norman, OK, 1969), 18; and M. León-Portilla, ed. and trans., *Cantares mexicanos*, 3 vols. (Mexico City, 2011), 1:200, 209.

30 Bierhorst, *Cantares*, 4.

31 J. Lockhart, *Nahuas and Spaniards: Postconquest Central Mexican History and Philology* (Stanford, CA, 1991), 143. See also F. Karttunen and J. Lockhart, "La estructura de la poesía náhuatl vista por sus variantes," *Estudios de cultura náhuatl* 14 (1980): 15–64, at 22–23.

32 J. Bierhorst, "Translating an Esoteric Idiom: The Case of Aztec Poetry," in *Born in the Blood: On Native American Translation*, ed. B. Swann (Lincoln, NE, 2001), 370–97, at 390. See also L. Cabranes-Grant, *From Scenarios to Networks: Performing the Intercultural in Colonial Mexico* (Evanston, IL, 2016), 100.

huehuetl and *teponaztli*," and were often complemented with dance[33] and some kind of theatrical performance echoed in their dramatic diction.[34] The performance, Bierhorst tells us, might take place "in a plaza or, in pre-Conquest times, a palace forecourt (*quiahuac*); or it might be held in an inner court (*ithualli*) of the king's palace or of the house of a nobleman," while "sometimes the church (*iglesia*) was used."[35]

Sahagún's description of song activity more generally seems to approximate the songs included in the *Cantares mexicanos* manuscript.[36] Together with other sixteenth-century missionaries like Toribio Benavente (known as Motolinía) and Diego Durán, Sahagún reads this phenomenon against the backdrop of idolatrous ceremonies and festivals in early colonial Mexico. Instead of the terms "music" and "poetry," the Spaniards tend to apply the noun *cantares* or employ the Taino word *areíto* to the typical combination of song, drumming, and dance.[37] Sahagún in particular is very suspicious of this activity. He documents that the indigenous "sing when they wish and celebrate their feasts as they wish and sing the ancient songs they were wont to sing in the days of their idolatry–not all of them but many of them. And no one understands what they say as their songs are very obscure." He continues that even after their conversion, when "they sing some songs they have composed, which deal with the things of God and His saints, they are surrounded by many errors and heresies. And even in the dances and celebrations [areítos] many of their ancient superstitions and idolatrous rituals are practiced, especially where no one resides who understands

33   León-Portilla, *Pre-Columbian Literatures*, 78. Two manuscripts of cantares, or "poems accompanied by music," have survived: *Cantares mexicanos* and *Ballads of the Lords of New Spain* (*Romances de los señores de la Nueva España*), dated about sixty years after the conquest (Bierhorst, "Translating an Esoteric Idiom," 371). Bierhorst says that the events of the conquest are "easier to grasp in the *Cantares*, with its many songs commemorating actual battles, than in the more generalized songs of the *Romances*," where he nevertheless traces "veiled allusions to the siege of Mexico" (J. Bierhorst, ed. and trans., *Ballads of the Lords of New Spain: The Codex* Romances de los Señores de la Nueva España [Austin, TX, 2009], 66–67).

34   Garibay, *Poesía náhuatl*, xl; León-Portilla, *Cantares*, 1:209–10, 257; and A. Segala, *Literatura náhuatl: Fuentes, identidades, representaciones*, trans. M. Mansour (Mexico City, 1990), 125, 202. Bierhorst notes that "one need not assume that different actors played the different roles called for in the texts" (Bierhorst, *Cantares*, 46).

35   Bierhorst, *Cantares*, 70. On this topic, see also D. G. Brinton, *Ancient Nahuatl Poetry, Containing the Nahuatl Text of XXVII Ancient Mexican Poems–with a Translation, Introduction, Notes, and Vocabulary* (Philadelphia, PA, 1890), 20; and G. Tomlinson, *The Singing of the New World: Indigenous Voice in the Era of European Contact* (Cambridge, 2007), 60.

36   Tomlinson, *Singing of the New World*, 57.

37   Ibid., 20.

them."[38] Sahagún's remark about the "ancient songs" and their performance is key because it places them firmly within the framework of pre-Hispanic rituals, as does his comment on the linguistic and semantic obscurity of the areítos, mirrored in the surviving corpus of *Cantares mexicanos*. Although hermetic and incomprehensible to Spanish ears, for many Mexica the production and circulation of the cantares occurred within recognizable contexts.

Unlike "Anakalema," these pieces are heterometric—"they have no regularly recurring rhythm, at least not in the form in which they have been preserved."[39] How then could they be accompanied by a drum cadence? Bierhorst reminds us that it is possible to sing "a heterometric chant while beating out an unrelated regular accompaniment" as long as the cadence is comparatively simple; this phenomenon, he says, "has been recorded again and again by ethnomusicologists working with American Indian materials," and he explains that "the chant has a recitative-like quality, to which the metrical drumbeat gives an accompanying texture, not a counterpoint."[40] The writers of the songs, or *cuicatl*, were referred to as *cuicapicque*, or forgers of songs (from *cuica*, to sing, and *piqui*, to make, as in the Greek *poietes*).[41] According to the *Florentine Codex*, the *calmecac* was a public school where students became well versed in poetry, philosophy, rhetoric, and astrology. As a result, the school attracted the nobility and wealthy, but theoretically it was open to all.[42] There the Mexica, including both the Tenochca, or inhabitants of Tenochtitlan, and the Tlatelolca, or residents of Tlatelolco (fig. 8), memorized their songs.[43] For this reason, Bierhorst views the activity of the cantares as an expression of the Mexica elite.

In theory, "Huexotzincayotl" and "Tlaxcaltecayotl" could have been produced by members of the elite who had attended the calmecac before the conquest and learned songs by heart as part of their training, but the texts were most

38 Sahagún, *Florentine Codex*, intr. vol., 81.

39 Bierhorst, *Cantares*, 43.

40 Ibid., 43–45.

41 León-Portilla, *Pre-Columbian Literatures*, 79; Brinton, *Ancient Nahuatl Poetry*, 12.

42 M. León-Portilla, *Aztec Thought and Culture: A Study of the Ancient Nahuatl Mind*, trans. J. E. Davis (Norman, OK, 1963), 138.

43 León-Portilla, *Pre-Columbian Literatures*, 5. See also Brinton, *Ancient Nahuatl Poetry*, 31. Primary Nahuatl sources "use the terms 'Mexica' and 'Tenochca' interchangeably to identify the Mexica-Tenochca," while "the Mexica-Tlatelolca are often referred to as 'Tlatelolca'" (G. Gutiérrez, "Mexico-Tenochtitlan: Origin and Transformation of the Last Mesoamerican Imperial City," in *The Cambridge World History*, vol. 3, *Early Cities in Comparative Perspective, 4000 BCE–1200 CE*, ed. N. Yoffee [Cambridge, 2015], 491–512, at 494). I use the term "Mexica" with reference to both subgroups.

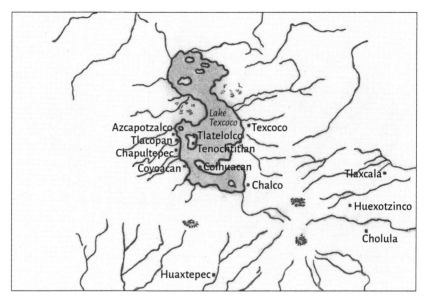

Fig. 8. The Valley of Mexico, ca. 1519. Map by Anthi Andronikou, after I. Clendinnen, *Aztecs: An Interpretation* (New York, 1993), map 2.

likely created by people who were acquainted with that tradition through their collecting of cantares in the second half of the sixteenth century. Ready-made formulas afforded a trove of materials on which to draw in order to fathom, in a familiar language, the trauma of the empire's fall. Unlike "Tlaxcaltecayotl," we shall see that "Huexotzincayotl" is not so full of cantares-style obscurities, which may reflect a strategic decision on the part of the composer to reach younger generations who were less conversant with the tradition of pre-Hispanic songs.

It is generally accepted among theorists of collective trauma that devastating events, however terrible they are for those who experience them, do not automatically qualify as cultural trauma. Jeffrey Alexander argues that societies can undergo momentous disruptions that they do not ultimately regard as traumatic. He explains that for events to emerge as collective traumas, social crises must turn into cultural crises. Trauma is not the result of the pain a group may experience, but the result of that pain "entering into the core of the collectivity's sense of its own identity." Events, he insists, are not intrinsically traumatic. Trauma is socially constructed.[44] In a similar fashion, Neil Smelser points out

---

44 J. C. Alexander, "Toward a Theory of Cultural Trauma," in *Cultural Trauma and Collective Identity*, ed. J. C. Alexander et al., (Berkeley, CA, 2004), 1–30, at 8, 10.

that cultural trauma corresponds to an "invasive and overwhelming event" that is thought to threaten one or more key ingredients of a culture.[45]

The gap between traumatic events and cultural trauma is bridged by means of what Alexander designates the "trauma process" undertaken by "carrier groups," who "represent social pain as a fundamental threat to their sense of who they are, where they came from, and where they want to go."[46] The trauma process, notes Ron Eyerman, requires representation and mediation.[47] Among carrier groups are political leaders, poets, authors, artists, and, more generally, intellectuals, who forge narratives of collective suffering through "meaning-making" processes, while writers and artists in particular fall within what Alexander and Elizabeth Breese call "symbol creators."[48] Alexander posits that when such meaning-making processes occur in the aesthetic sphere, they are channeled through narratives and genres that encourage "imaginative identification and emotional catharsis." Like speakers in speech-acts, he contends, the goal of carrier groups engaging in the trauma process is to successfully project their trauma claim to the target audience. Crucially, in doing so they draw on "the particularities of the historical situation" and on "the symbolic resources at hand."[49]

Besides being the workings of the upper class or, in any case, of the symbol creators of the time, "Anakalema," "Huexotzincayotl," and "Tlaxcaltecayotl" exploit firmly rooted aesthetic traditions that should, in principle, facilitate the reception of their trauma claims. Whether the symbol creators and their audiences had experienced the events themselves or not seems irrelevant from the perspective of cultural trauma theorists, who go so far as to suggest that events considered to be profoundly traumatizing may never have taken place in reality.[50] The trauma, affirms Eyerman, "need not necessarily be felt by everyone in a group or have been directly experienced by any or all."[51] This is a critical point

45 N. J. Smelser, "Psychological Trauma and Cultural Trauma," in Alexander et al., *Cultural Trauma and Collective Identity*, 31–59, at 38.

46 Alexander, "Toward a Theory," 10–11.

47 R. Eyerman, "The Past in the Present: Culture and the Transmission of Memory," *Acta Sociologica* 47.2 (2004): 159–69, at 160.

48 J. C. Alexander and E. B. Breese, "Introduction: On Social Suffering and Its Cultural Construction," in *Narrating Trauma: On the Impact of Collective Suffering*, ed. R. Eyerman, J. C. Alexander, and E. B. Breese (Boulder, CO, 2011), xi–xxxv, at xi–xii, xxii.

49 Alexander, "Toward a Theory," 11–12, 15.

50 Ibid., 8.

51 Eyerman, "Past in the Present," 160.

that is verified by at least one, if not all, of our anonymous authors. Hundreds of miles and perhaps several years away from the events, the "inconsolable sorrow" of the Greek poet does not stem from direct experience.[52] Likewise, the composers of "Huexotzincayotl" and "Tlaxcaltecayotl" were probably children of the Nahua nobility and members of the first generation to grow up in colonial Mexico, and had not witnessed the events of the siege and fall of Tenochtitlan.

A social construct, cultural trauma is dependent on historical circumstances and ideological drifts that can shape, nurse, alter, or obliterate it altogether. Events that are similarly catastrophic in nature, like the conquest of the two imperial cities, may be dealt with in ways that are not only different but also incompatible. In pre- and post-independence Greece and Mexico, the trauma claims of our texts would have strikingly disparate fates.

52 Unless the poem was composed by a Cypriot (or, in any case, someone from Crete or the Dodecanese) who was in Constantinople during the siege.

FOUR

IMPARTING TRAUMA

The Fall of Constantinople

THE FALL OF CONSTANTINOPLE TO THE OTTOMAN TURKS IN 1453 GENERATED a rich body of historiographical and literary materials, and of folk myths and legends, immediately after the events and in the centuries that followed. Perhaps no other single historical event has given rise to so many threnoi and monodies lamenting the loss of the Queen City, which is today strongly established in the Greek popular imagination. "Anakalema tes Konstantinopoles" is an early, eloquent example of the impact that the conquest of Byzantium had on the Greek world and offers a glimpse of the complex mechanisms of cultural trauma construction.

First published by Émile Legrand in 1875, "Anakalema tes Konstantinopoles" appears in the Codex Parisinus Graecus 2873, Bibliothèque nationale de France, Paris (fols. 187r–91r) (fig. 9).[1] The date and provenance of the manuscript do not necessarily disclose those of the poem, as manuscripts are often later copies. This manuscript had made its way to France by the mid-seventeenth century, initially in the personal library of Jean-Baptiste Colbert (1619–1683), the minister of finances under Louis XIV.[2] Based on the owner's note on folio 192v,

---

1   Legrand translates it as "Complainte sur la prise de Constantinople" (*Collection de monuments pour servir à l'étude de la langue néo-hellénique*, 26 vols. [Athens, 1869–75], 5:87).

2   Kehayoglou, "Επίμετρο," 77–78.

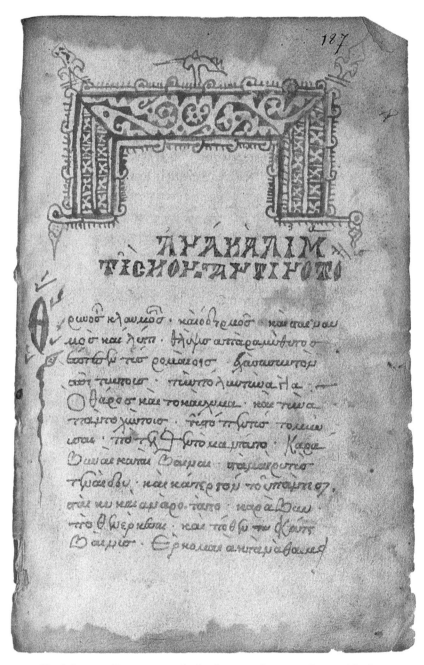

Fig. 9. "Anakalema tes Konstantinopoles," early sixteenth century, Paris, Bibliothèque nationale de France, Codex Parisinus Graecus 2873, fol. 187r. Courtesy of the Bibliothèque nationale de France.

Darrouzès argues that the poem must have been copied around 1509,[3] although there is a broad consensus that it was written relatively close to the events it describes.[4] According to Georgios Zoras, "Anakalema" was possibly drafted in 1453, while for Kehayoglou it was probably composed prior to Mehmed II's death in 1481. Kriaras suggests that it was likely produced well before the end of the fifteenth century because of its lack of rhyme. A Western device, the latter emerges in Greek poetry in the fourteenth and fifteenth centuries and becomes common practice from the sixteenth century on.[5]

"Anakalema" comprises two parts. The first (lines 1–56) is a reflexive threnos, thematizing and dramatizing ritual lamentation and public commemorative activities, while the second (lines 57–118) is a more conventional threnos, with the narrator directly relaying his dismay at the demise of Constantinople and the empire. This division is to some extent reflected in the poem's diction. The first part draws on popular traditions of ritual lament, and the register is generally closer to the vernacular of folk songs, albeit not free of archaisms (as seen, for example, in lines 2, 15, 17, 23, 24, 43, 47, and 48), whereas the second part makes more ample use of archaizing language. Interestingly, an excerpt from the ships' dialogue in the first part has been incorporated rather arbitrarily in several anthologies of folk songs, including one by the Academy of Athens, due to its affinity with the style of folk poetry.[6] From line 48 on, notes Kriaras, the demotic tone of the poem subsides considerably, while the use of archaisms culminates toward the end, where the composition distances itself from the context of folk poetry, at least at the level of language.[7] Like the first half, which is made up of an embedded dialogue and a dramatic monologue, the second half, or lament proper, consists of two sections, a dramatic narration of the events (lines 57–88) and an allegory (lines 89–118).

3   Darrouzès, "Bulletin critique," 260.

4   Kriaras, *To Ανακάλημα*, 19.

5   G. T. Zoras, *Βυζαντινή ποίησις* (Athens, 1956), 38; Kehayoglou, "Επίμετρο," 72–73; Kriaras, *To Ανακάλημα*, 12; and Beaton, *Medieval Greek Romance*, 98.

6   Beaton, *Folk Poetry*, 99. See D. Petropoulos, *Ελληνικά δημοτικά τραγούδια*, 2 vols. (Athens, 1958–59), 1:154, no. 4D; G. Ioannou, *Τα δημοτικά μας τραγούδια* (Athens, 1996), 93; and Academy of Athens, *Ελληνικά δημοτικά τραγούδια*, 2 vols. (Athens, 1962–68), 1:126, where lines 6–13 are reproduced. Iakovos Polylas considers lines 6–8 and 10–13 part of the folk tradition and the rest of the poem a pale imitation of folk poetry (I. Polylas, *Η φιλολογική μας γλώσσα* [Athens, 1892], 70–71).

7   Kriaras, *To Ανακάλημα*, 15. For a list of archaisms in "Anakalema," see ibid., 10.

Ανακάλημα της Κωνσταντινόπολης

Θρήνος, κλαυμός και οδυρμός και στεναγμός και λύπη,
θλίψις απαραμύθητος έπεσεν τοις Ρωμαίοις.
Εχάσασιν το σπίτιν τους, την Πόλην την αγία,
το θάρρος και το καύχημα και την απαντοχήν τους.
Τίς το 'πεν; Τίς το μήνυσε; Πότε 'λθεν το μαντάτο;   5
Καράβιν εκατέβαινε στα μέρη της Τενέδου
και κάτεργον το υπάντησε, στέκει και αναρωτά το:
«Καράβιν, πόθεν έρκεσαι και πόθεν κατεβαίνεις;»
«Έρκομαι ακ τ' ανάθεμα κι εκ το βαρύν το σκότος,
ακ την αστραποχάλαζην, ακ την ανεμοζάλην·   10
απέ την Πόλην έρχομαι την αστραποκαμένην.
Εγώ γομάριν δε βαστώ, αμμέ μαντάτα φέρνω
κακά διά τους χριστιανούς, πικρά και δολωμένα:
Οι Τούρκοι ότε ήρθασιν, επήρασιν την Πόλην,
απώλεσαν τους χριστιανούς εκεί και πανταχόθεν.»   15
«Στάσου, καράβι, να χαρείς, πάλι να σε ρωτήσω:
Εκεί 'λαχε ο βασιλεύς, ο κύρης Κωνσταντίνος,
ο φρένιμος, ο δυνατός, ο περισσά ανδρειωμένος,
ο πράγος, ο καλόλογος, η φήμη των Ρωμαίων;»
«Εκεί 'λαχεν ο Δράγασης ο κακομοιρασμένος.   20
Σαν είδεν τ' άνομα σκυλιά κι εχάλασαν τους τοίχους
κι ετρέξασιν κι εμπήκασιν πεζοί και καβαλάροι
κι εκόπταν τους χριστιανούς ως χόρτο στο λιβάδιν,
βαριά βαριά 'ναστέναξεν μετά κλαυθμού και είπε:
"Ελέησον! Πράγμα το θωρούν τα δολερά μου μάτια!   25
Πώς έχω μάτια και θωρώ! Πώς έχω φως και βλέπω!
Πώς έχω νουν και πορπατώ στον άτυχον τον κόσμον!
Θωρώ οι Τούρκοι 'νέβησαν εις την αγίαν Πόλην
και τώρα αφανίζουσιν εμέν και τον λαόν μου."
Εβίγλισεν ο ταπεινός δεξιά και αριστερά του·   30
θωρεί φεύγουν οι Κρητικοί, φεύγουν οι Γενουβήσοι,
φεύγουσιν οι Βενέτικοι κι εκείνος απομένει.
Ελάλησεν ο ταπεινός με τα καμένα χείλη:
"Εσείς, παιδιά μου, φεύγετε, πάτε να γλυτωθείτε·

Lament for Constantinople

Mourning, weeping, and lamentation and groaning and grief,
inconsolable sorrow has fallen upon the Romaioi.
They have lost their home, the holy City
their courage and pride, and all their hope.
Who said it? Who announced it? When did the news come?   5
A boat was coming down to the region of Tenedos
and a galley met it, stops, and asks it:
"Boat, where do you come from and where are you coming down from?"
"I come from the cursed land and from the heavy darkness,
from lightning and hail, from the swirling storm;   10
I come from the City that has been struck by lightning.
I carry no cargo, but I bear news
evil for Christians, bitter, and grim:
for the Turks came, they took the City,
they destroyed the Christians there and everywhere."   15
"Wait, boat, if you please, I want to ask you again:
did the emperor happen to be there, our lord Konstantinos,
the prudent and strong, and exceedingly brave,
the mild-mannered and affable, the pride of the Romaioi?"
"He was there, the hapless Dragasis.   20
As soon as he saw that the lawless dogs had broken through the walls
and had run and entered, on foot and on horses,
and were slaughtering the Christians like grass in a meadow,
heavily, heavily, he sighed in tears and said:
'Mercy, what a thing my miserable eyes see!   25
How can I still have eyes and look! How can I still have light and see!
How can I still have my mind and walk in this wretched world!
I see the Turks have entered the holy City
and now they are destroying me and my people.'
The wretched man looked to his right and left;   30
he sees the Cretans leaving, the Genoese leaving,
the Venetians leaving, and he remains behind.
With bitter sorrow the poor man said:
'You, my children, you can leave, go and save yourselves;

κι εμέναν πού μ' αφήνετε, τον κακομοιρασμένο;   35
Αφήνετέ με στα σκυλιά κι εις του θεριού το στόμα.
Κόψετε το κεφάλιν μου, χριστιανοί Ρωμαίοι·
επάρετέ το, Κρητικοί, βαστάτε το στην Κρήτην,
να το ιδούν οι Κρητικοί, να καρδιοπονέσουν,
να δείρουσι τα στήθη τους, να χύσουν μαύρα δάκρυα   40
και να με μακαρίσουσιν, ότι ούλους τους αγάπουν·
μηδέν με πιάσουν τα σκυλιά, μηδέν με κυριεύσουν
—ότι ανελεήμονα των ασεβών τα σπλάχνα—,
μηδέν με παν στον αμιρά, το σκύλον Μαχουμέτην,
με το θλιμμένον πρόσωπον, με τα θλιμμένα μάτια,   45
με την τρεμούραν την πολλήν, με τα καμένα χείλη,
και θέσει πόδαν άτακτο εις τον εμόν αυχένα
—εις βασιλέως τράχηλον δεν πρέπει πους ανόμου—,
μη με ρωτήσ' ο άνομος, να πει: 'Πού 'ν' ο Θεός σου;'
να ρίσει ο σκύλος τα σκυλιά να με κακολογήσουν,   50
να παίξουσιν το στέμμα μου, να βρίσουν την τιμήν μου·
απήν με βασανίσουσιν και τυραννίσουσίν με,
να κόψουν το κεφάλιν μου, να μπήξουν εις κοντάριν,
να σκίσουν την καρδία μου, να φαν τα σωτικά μου,
να πιουν από το αίμα μου, να βάψουν τα σπατιά τους   55
και να καυχούντ' οι άνομοι εις την απώλειάν μου." »
Ήλιε μου, ανάτειλε παντού, σ' ούλον τον κόσμον φέγγε
κι έκτεινε τας ακτίνας σου σ' όλην την οικουμένη·
κι εις την Κωσταντινόπολην, την πρώην φουμισμένην
και τώρα την Τουρκόπολην, δεν πρέπει πιο να φέγγεις.   60
Αλλ' ουδέ τας ακτίνας σου πρέπει εκεί να στέλλεις
να βλέπουν τ' άνομα σκυλιά τες ανομιές να κάμνουν,
να ποίσου στάβλους εκκλησιές, να καίουν τας εικόνας,
να σχίζουν, να καταπατούν τα 'λόχρουσα βαγγέλια,
να καθυβρίζουν τους σταυρούς, να τους κατατσακίζουν,   65
να παίρνουσιν τ' ασήμια τους και τα μαργαριτάρια
και των αγίων τα λείψανα τα μοσχομυρισμένα
να καίουν, ν' αφανίζουσιν, στην θάλασσα να ρίπτουν,
να παίρνουν τα λιθάρια των και την ευκόσμησίν των

but as for me, where do you abandon me, me the hapless one?   35
You abandon me to the dogs and to the mouth of the beast.
Cut off my head, Christian Romaioi;
take it, Cretans, carry it to Crete
so that the Cretans may see it and feel the pain in their heart,
beat their breasts and shed dark tears   40
and commemorate me, because I loved them all;
so that the dogs don't capture me, or overcome me,
—for the hearts of the impious ones know no mercy—
or take me to their emir, Mehmed, the dog,
with a sad face, with sad eyes,   45
with so much fright, with painful lips,
who will put his insolent foot on my neck
—the lawless should never put a foot on a regal neck—
and let not the lawless dog ask me and say: "Where is your God?"
and order the dogs to vilify me,   50
and deride my crown and curse my honor;
and after they torment me and torture me,
they cut off my head, they stick it on a pike,
they rip out my heart, they eat my entrails,
they drink from my blood, they dye their swords in it,   55
and they take pride, those lawless ones, in my death.'"
My dear sun, rise everywhere, shine all over the world,
and extend your rays to the entire ecumene;
but upon Constantinople, the once famous city
and now city of Turks, it is no longer proper for you to cast your light. 60
Nor should you send your rays there,
for the lawless dogs to see to commit their crimes,
and turn churches into stables and burn the icons,
and tear and trample on the golden gospels,
and dishonor the holy crosses and break them into pieces,   65
and take their silver and their pearls,
and the fragrant relics of holy men
to burn and destroy, and throw them into the sea,
and take their precious stones and their decoration,

και στ' άγια δισκοπότηρα κούπες κρασί να πίνουν.   70
Άρχοντες, αρκοντόπουλοι, αρχόντισσες μεγάλες,
ευγενικές και φρένιμες, ακριβαναθρεμμένες,
ανέγλυτες πανεύφημες, ύπανδρες και χηράδες
και καλογριές ευγενικές, παρθένες, ηγουμένες
—άνεμος δεν τους έδιδε, ήλιος ουκ έβλεπέν τες,   75
εψάλλαν, ενεγνώθασι εις τ' άγια μοναστήρια—
ηρπάγησαν ανηλεώς ως καταδικασμένες.
Πώς να τες πάρουν στην Τουρκιά, σκλάβες να πουληθούσιν
και να τες διασκορπίσουσιν Ανατολήν και Δύσην
γυμνές και ανυπόλυτες, δαρμένες, πεινασμένες   80
να βλέπουν βούδια, πρόβατα, άλογα και βουβάλια,
παπίτσες, χήνες και έτερα [...]
και το βραδύ να μένουσιν με τους μουσουλουμάνους
και να τες μαγαρίζουσιν, μπαστάρδια να γεννούσιν,
μουσουλουμάνοι να γενού και σκύλοι ματοπίνοι,   85
να πολεμούν χριστιανούς και να τους αφανίζουν!
Μην το πομένεις, ουρανέ, και, γη, μην το βαστάξεις·
ήλιε, σκότασε το φως, σελήνη, μεν τους δώσεις.
Είπω και τίποτε μικρόν αλληγορίας λόγον:
Ήλιον τάξε νοητόν τον Μέγαν Κωνσταντίνο,   90
σελήνη επονόμασε την νέαν του την Πόλην·
μη σου φανεί παράξενο τούτον απού σου λέγω:
κόσμο μέγαν τον άνθρωπον Θεός επονομάζει,
όν έθετο εις τον μικρόν κόσμον, την πάσα κτίση.
Αυτός λοιπόν εκόσμησε ο Μέγας Κωνσταντίνος   95
την Πόλην την εξάκουστην, ήν βλέπεις και ακούεις,
καθώς την κλήσιν έλαβεν και την επωνυμίαν·
ομοίως Ουστινιανός εκόσμησεν μεγάλως,
έκτισεν την Αγιάν Σοφιά, το θέαμαν το μέγα·
παραπλησίον γέγονε Σιών της παναγίας.   100
Εκείνοι ήσαν ήλιος κι η Πόλη 'ν' η σελήνη
—χωρίς ηλίου πούποτε σελήνη ουδέν λάμπει—,
εκείνοι γαρ οι βασιλείς, οι ευσεβείς, οι θείοι,
έλαμπον, εφωτίζασιν την παναγίαν Πόλην,

and drink wine from the holy chalices. 70
Noblemen, children of noble birth, great noblewomen,
gentle and prudent, and raised with care,
unmarried women of good repute, married women and widows,
and gentle nuns, postulants, abbesses
—the wind has not touched them, the sun has not seen them, 75
for they spent their time chanting and reading in the holy monasteries—
were snatched without mercy, as if condemned.
Now they will be taken to Turkey to be sold as slaves,
and scattered from East to West
naked and barefoot, beaten, hungry, 80
to tend oxen, sheep, horses, and buffaloes,
little ducks, geese, and suchlike [...]
and in the evening they will stay with Muslims,
who will defile them, and they will give birth to bastards,
who will become Muslims and bloodthirsty dogs 85
and make war on Christians and annihilate them!
Sky, don't endure this, and earth, don't bear it;
sun, darken your light, moon, don't shine on them.
Let me express it briefly as a kind of allegory:
Suppose that Constantine the Great is the sun, 90
and let's call his new City the moon;
What I am telling you shouldn't baffle you:
God calls mankind a great jewel,
which he placed in the small jewel, the whole created world.
It was therefore Constantine the Great who made beautiful 95
the famous City that you see and hear about,
which took his name and was called after him;
similarly, Justinian adorned it greatly,
he built Hagia Sophia, the great sight,
which was comparable to the all-holy Zion. 100
Those [emperors] were the sun and the City is the moon
—without the sun, the moon can never shine—
because those devout, holy emperors
shone, they lit up the all-holy City,

την Δύσην, την Ανατολήν, όλην την οικουμένην.   105
Όταν εις νουν αθυμηθώ της Πόλεως τα κάλλη,
στενάζω και οδύρομαι και τύπτω εις το στήθος,
κλαίω και χύνω δάκρυα μεθ' οιμωγής και μόχθου.
Ο κόσμος της Αγιάς Σοφιάς, τα πέπλα της τραπέζας
της παναγίας, της σεπτής, τα καθιερωμένα   110
τα σκεύη τα πανάγια και πού να καταντήσαν;
Άρα έβλεπεν ο άγγελος, ως ήτον τεταγμένος,
όστις και έταξεν ποτέ του πάλαι νεανίσκου,
είπεν γαρ «ουκ εξέρχομαι έως ότου να έλθεις»;
Ο νεανίας έρχεται, ο άγγελος απήλθεν·   115
ουχί εκείνος ο ποτέ παίδας των εκτητόρων,
αλλ' άλλος παίδας έφθασε, πρόδρομος Αντιχρίστου,
και άγγελοι και άγιοι πλέον ου βοηθούσι.

"Anakalema": Notes on the Text and Translations

The text follows the most recent critical edition of "Anakalema" in Kriaras, *Ανακάλημα της Κωνσταντινόπολης*, 21–27. For previous editions, see Legrand, *Collection de monuments*, 5:93–100; A. Xirouchakis, *Ο κρητικός πολεμός (1645–1669): Η συλλογή των ελληνικών ποιημάτων Ανθίμου Διακρούση, Μαρίνου Ζανε* (Trieste, 1908), 39–43; F. Bouboulidis, *Κρητική λογοτεχνία* (Athens, 1955), 3–5, and Kriaras, *Το Ανακάλημα*, 29–34 (reprinted in A. Pertusi, ed., *La caduta di Costantinopoli*, vol. 2, *L'eco nel mondo* [Verona, 1999], 366–76). For "Anakalema" and other threnoi in the original Greek, I make use of monotonic orthography (introduced in 1982) as done by Kriaras, Kehayoglou, and other scholars of modern Greek. Excerpts from these poems and their titles, as well as modern Greek texts published before 1982, are romanized following the conventions of transliteration of polytonic Greek, with which the reader is more familiar. All numbers in the text refer to lines in the poem; line 82 is incomplete.

Different parts of the poem have been translated into English by Alexiou, *Ritual Lament*, 88, 98 (lines 6–15); Philippides and Hanak, *Siege of Constantinople*, 218 (lines 109–15); and Karanika, "Messengers, Angels, and Laments," passim (lines 1–15, 21–26,

the West, the East, the entire ecumene.   105
Whenever I call to mind the City's beauties,
I sigh and mourn and beat my breast,
I weep and shed tears with wailing and distress.
The adornments of Hagia Sophia, the consecrated
cloths of the revered holy altar,   110
the all-holy vessels, where did they end up?
Was the angel watching, as he had been ordered to do,
the one who, once upon a time, made a promise to the young man
saying: "I will not leave until you come back"?
The young man is coming back, the angel has gone away;   115
not the young man of the founders,
but another young man has arrived, the forerunner of Antichrist,
and angels and saints no longer help.

34–44, 50–63, 112–15). I borrow these translations and make changes when necessary.
The rest of the translation is mine. John Davis has also translated sections of the poem
(see J. Davis, trans., "Lament on the Fall of Constantinople," in *The Greek Poets: Homer to
the Present*, ed. P. Constantine et al. [New York, 2010], 348–50).

  Both Alexiou and Karanika translate ὅτε in line 14 as "when" (Alexiou, *Ritual
Lament*, 98, and Karanika, "Messengers, Angels, and Laments," 233), thus following
Kriaras's transcription of ἡ τοῦρκοι ὅται as οι Τοῦρκοι ὅτε. On the literacy of the scribe,
who makes numerous spelling mistakes and has difficulties with word separation, see
Legrand, *Collection de monuments*, 5:87–88; Kriaras, *Το Ανακάλημα*, 20; and R. García
Ortega and A. I. Fernández Galvín, *Trenos por Constantinopla: Estudio preliminar, traduc-
ción y comentarios* (Granada, 2003), 132. In the English translation of the poem, I follow
Agamemnon Mourtzopoulos, who has convincingly argued for the replacement of
the temporal conjunction ὅτε with the causal conjunction ὅτι (because, for). See A. T.
Mourtzopoulos, "Διορθωτικό στο Ανακάλημα της Κωνσταντινόπολης,'" *Ελληνικά* 23.2
(1970): 337–46.

Unsurprisingly, threnos is the opening word, immediately followed by five synonyms emphatically announcing the "inconsolable sorrow" of the Romaioi (lines 1–2), as the Byzantines and the Greek-speaking Orthodox Christians living in areas outside the Eastern Roman Empire called themselves. In his fifteenth-century chronicle of Lusignan Cyprus, for instance, Machairas employs the term indistinctly for Byzantines and Greek-speaking Orthodox Cypriots. In Cyprus, he writes, "the entire place was full of Romaioi."[8]

In her discussion of line 1 of "Anakalema," Andromache Karanika observes that the poem opens with an emphasis on the auditory dimension of collective lamentation: "Mourning, weeping, and lamentation and groaning and grief."[9] Intensified through the repetition of the conjunction "and" (polysyndeton), all these words, along with "sorrow" (*thlipsis*) in line 2, are meant to arouse negative feelings in the audience. Affect, says Smelser, is central to the way we understand cultural trauma. Perceived as a threat to the collectivity, cultural trauma triggers negative feelings in those who experience it. Any carrier group looking to fix a situation or an event as traumatic must unavoidably do so in language that will reach the target audience. Affect, he asserts, plays a key role "in alerting individuals to threatening and traumatizing phenomena," and for this reason "experiencing the language of negative affect is a necessary condition for believing that a cultural trauma exists or is threatening."[10] The negative affect prompted by the title and the first two lines serves as a linchpin to project the claim of collective trauma to the audience in a persuasive manner. The link with Greek oral tradition and especially with the ritual lament and popular funeral practices established through the aural imagery alerts readers and audiences to the threatening, "invasive, and overwhelming event" that is about to figuratively unfold.[11]

Kehayoglou also points to a possible connection of the first line of "Anakalema" with *Dioptra* (*Mirror*), an eleventh-century didactic poem in five books by Philippos Monotropos written, for the most part, in fifteen-syllable verse.[12] A text widely disseminated in the late Byzantine period, *Dioptra* features at the beginning of the same manuscript in which "Anakalema" appears (fols. 2–160). Book one, entitled "Weeping and Mourning" ("Klauthmoi

8   L. Machairas, Χρονικόν Κύπρου / Chronique de Chypre, ed. E. Miller and C. Sathas (Paris, 1882), 13 and passim: ὅλος ὁ τόπος ἦτον γεμάτος ʿΡωμαῖοι.

9   Karanika, "Messengers, Angels, and Laments," 232.

10 Smelser, "Psychological Trauma," 40–41.

11 Ibid., 38.

12 Kehayoglou, "Επίμετρο," 79.

kai threnoi"), is a poem of contrition and a mirror image of the first line of "Anakalema," which must have been a stock expression of grief.[13]

"Anakalema" is already fixed in the tradition of ritual lament by dint of its title. We have seen that the noun *anakalema*, a word apparently attested only in the Cypriot dialect, derives from *anakaliemai* or *anakalioumai* (to weep, lament, or mourn) and is associated with "a particularly insistent type of dirge." The ancient Greek verb *anakaleisthai* (to call upon), explains Alexiou, "is used of the persistent calling of the dead by name during the supplication at the tomb, usually accompanied by offerings and libations. Its function was to raise the spirit of the dead from the grave." In this sense it also crops up in Aeschylean tragedy and in epigrams, while *anakalein* was regularly used in the refrain of ancient laments for gods, inviting the dying deity to return to life. Alexiou adds that "the ritual enactment of this *anáklesis* was continued by the women of Megara until Pausanias' day" and that "the verb form is also frequently found in the more popular Byzantine laments, where it is used for the Virgin's invocation to the dying Christ." In the modern Cypriot usage of *anakaliemai* Alexiou rightly sees a remarkable instance of continuity between past and present manifested "in a specific type of lament, the ritual invocation of the dead at the tomb."[14]

The title and first line of "Anakalema" span culturally identifiable "webs of signification," which Alexander and Breese view as the workings of "culture creators" who initiate the process of a trauma claim.[15] These webs of signification weave together the aesthetic, social, and cultural traditions related to lamentation and ritual practice and are at once learned and popular, secular and religious. In the first two lines of the poem, the "trauma drama" is acted out and presented as a "collective trauma experience of massive disruption" and "a dramatic loss of identity and meaning."[16] We learn that the loss of the Romaioi is both material and moral—they are deprived of their city, pride, and hope (lines

13   In our manuscript "Klauthmoi" is placed at the beginning of *Dioptra*, but elsewhere it often appears as book five (E. Afentoulidou-Leitgeb, "The *Dioptra* of Philippos Monotropos: Didactic Verses or Poetry?," in *Poetry and Its Contexts in Eleventh-Century Byzantium*, ed. F. Bernard and K. Demoen [London and New York, 2012], 181–91, at 181). The popularity of *Dioptra* is attested by almost eighty surviving manuscripts (H. Miklas and J. Fuchsbauer, eds., *Die kirchenslavische Übersetzung der Dioptra des Philippos Monotropos* [Vienna, 2013], 405).

14   Alexiou, *Ritual Lament*, 109–10. In addition to "Anakalema," Alexiou provides as an example "the Cypriot version of the folk ballad, *The Song of the Dead Brother*, where the deserted mother raises her dead son Kostandis from the grave with her invocations, weeping first for all her sons: Ούλους στον μνήμαν έκλαιεν, ούλους ανακαλιέτουν (She wept for all at the tomb, all of them she invoked)." Ibid., 110, my emphasis.

15   Alexander and Breese, "Introduction," xxii.

16   Eyerman, "Past in the Present," 160.

3–4)—while their "inconsolable sorrow" is mediated as "a tear in the social fabric."[17] Through a series of rhetorical questions in line 5 reminiscent of folk-song formulas ("Who said it? Who announced it? When did the news come?"), the poet introduces an embedded dialogue between a boat and a galley meeting at the island of Tenedos (lines 6–7). In the exchange between the two vessels (lines 8–15), the fall of the city is announced. The boat warns that instead of "cargo" (*gomarin*) it carries news that is "bitter" and "grim" (lines 12–13). Thanks to the trope of the heavy freight, argues Karanika, the message of the capture of the city takes on physical dimensions.[18] If the ship's figurative cargo mirrors the burden of cultural trauma, the boat itself, whose voice the poetic subject adopts, is a synecdoche for the carrier group, in this case the poet. The conversation of the two ships is part of the meaning-making process, while the poem literally carries the trauma claim in the name of those directly affected.

Collective traumas, insist Alexander and Breese, "are reflections neither of individual suffering nor actual events, but symbolic renderings that reconstruct and imagine them in a relatively independent way." They are the end product of the trauma claim of culture creators.[19] Alexander elaborates that carrier groups need to address four critical questions concerning the type of pain, the identity of the victim, the relation of the victim to the target audience, and the nature of the perpetrator.[20] Threnoi typically tackle all four questions, and so does "Anakalema."[21] The final two lines of the boat's response in particular broadcast the unbearable news, yielding information on the horrendous event ("they took the City"), the victims ("the Christians there"), the perpetrators ("the Turks"), and the relation of the trauma victim to the wider audience ("the Christians . . . everywhere"). The latter point is of great importance. Even when the identity of the victim and the nature of the pain have been determined, observes Alexander, the relationship between the members of the audience and the victimized group must be established. "Only if the victims are represented in terms of valued qualities shared by the larger collective identity will the audience be able to symbolically participate in the experience of the originating trauma."[22] By the end of line 15, the trauma claim has been raised clearly

---

17 Ibid.

18 Karanika, "Messengers, Angels, and Laments," 233.

19 Alexander and Breese, "Introduction," xxvii.

20 Alexander, "Toward a Theory," 12–15.

21 On the range of questions and topics covered in *threnoi*, see G. T. Zoras, Περί την άλωσιν της Κωνσταντινουπόλεως (Athens, 1959), 159–89.

22 Alexander, "Toward a Theory," 14.

and affectively as a shared crisis and a "fundamental threat" to the collective through the device of the boat-cum-messenger, a secularized trumpeting angel (see fig. 1). The city's conquest is a massive disruption not only to the Eastern Roman Empire, but to the entire Christian world.

Contrary to historical folk songs, whose attention to the unfolding of actual events is often contested, "Anakalema" displays a considerable degree of accuracy.[23] Alexiou points out that although the dialogue in the poem adheres to a formula common in Greek folk poetry and threnoi,[24] the meeting of the two boats is a historical fact. She clarifies that "it was at Tenedos that the Venetian galleys on their way to Constantinople had planned to meet an escort from the Greek fleet on 20 May 1453; but anchored at Chios awaiting a favourable wind, Genoese ships from Pera arrived and told them that the city had already fallen" (see fig. 7).[25] Agostino Pertusi similarly mentions that a ship sailing from Constantinople to the west through the Dardanelles would stop at Tenedos.[26] According to Nicolò Barbaro, the Venetian physician and eyewitness of the siege of Constantinople, six Cretan ships, along with another one commanded by Piero Davanzo, left Constantinople on 26 February because they feared that the Turks would attack the city. The ships, reports Barbaro, "went safely as far as Tenedos, without the Turkish fleet seeing them. Once they saw that they had passed through the straits of Gallipoli, they separated from each other, the six ships going to Candia, and Piero Davanzo to Venice."[27] Kehayoglou writes that at least three Cretan ships participated in the sea battles and escaped capture, implying that the boat that bears the news may actually be Cretan, while the galley may be of Cretan or Venetian origin.[28]

---

23 Speaking of the issue of historical accuracy in these folk laments, Alexiou notes that "their value to the historian is almost negligible, since they do not document events, but reflect what has remained in popular consciousness" (*Ritual Lament*, 92–93). See also Beaton, *Folk Poetry*, 90–111, 174–78.

24 See, for instance, the dialogue of Constantinople and Venice in "Lament for Constantinople" ("Threnos tes Konstantinoupoleos") and that of the four patriarchates in "Lament of the Four Patriarchates: Constantinople, Alexandria, Antioch, and Jerusalem" ("Threnos ton tessaron patriarcheion Konstantinoupoles, Alexandreias, Antiocheias kai Ierousalem") in Zoras, *Βυζαντινή ποίησις*, 200–203 and 204–7, respectively. See also García Ortega and Fernández Galvín, *Trenos por Constantinopla*, 38. For the dialogue between the two boats, see Karanika, "Messengers, Angels, and Laments," 232.

25 Alexiou, *Ritual Lament*, 144–45.

26 Pertusi, *La caduta di Costantinopoli*, 484.

27 N. Barbaro, *Diary of the Siege of Constantinople*, trans. J. R. Jones (New York, 1969), 22–23.

28 Kehayoglou, "Επίμετρο," 51–52. Considering that Crete had been under Venetian rule since the early thirteenth century, officially all these ships were "Venetian," regardless of the ethnic origin of their crew.

Folio 1 of the British Museum Add. MS 34060, a collection of Greek theological and historical texts composed probably in Crete in the fifteenth century, provides the following note:

> In the year 1453, June 29th, a Friday, there arrived from Constantinople three Cretan ships, those of Sguros, of Hyalinas, and of Philomates, bringing news that on May 29th, St. Theodosia's day, a Tuesday, at the third hour of the day, the Agarenes, the army of the Turk Chelebi Mehemet, entered Constantinople; and they said that they killed the emperor, the Lord Constantine Dragases Palaiologos. And there was great tribulation and much lamentation in Crete because of the sad news that had come, for nothing worse than this has happened, nor will happen. And may the Lord have mercy on us, and deliver us from his terrible menaces.[29]

Based on evidence culled from the contemporary works of Kritoboulos, Bishop Leonardo Giustiniani of Chios, Jacopo Tetaldi, and Barbaro, Robert Browning specifies that three out of the nine or ten ships guarding the floating chain across the entrance to the Golden Horn (fig. 10) were from Crete. Their captains, according to Barbaro, were "el Filamati de Candia," "ser Zuan Venier da Candia," and "el Guro de Candia."[30] Browning notes that in Barbaro's list we find two of the three commanders whose safe return to Crete is reported in the manuscript of the British Museum. Their ships stayed put during the siege, but left on 29 May, when the city fell to Mehmed II's army. A month later, Philomatis and Sgouros arrived in Crete, spreading the news at Euboea and perhaps at Argos and other Peloponnesian seaports on their way home.[31] Browning reminds us that there was another vessel, that of Hyalinas, the third captain named in the manuscript of the British Museum.[32] Citing another eyewitness of the events, "the 'classical' poet of the siege" Ubertino Pusculo,[33] he suggests that Hyalinas's ship "will have caught up with those from the boom in the

29   In R. Browning, "A Note on the Capture of Constantinople in 1453," *Byzantion* 22 (1952): 379–87, at 381.

30   See N. Barbaro, *Giornale dell'assedio di Costantinopoli 1453*, ed. E. Cornet (Vienna, 1856), 20; idem, *Diary of the Siege of Constantinople*, 69.

31   For more on the Cretan ships and their role in the defense of Constantinople, see Browning, "Note on the Capture of Constantinople," 381–86; and Philippides and Hanak, *Siege of Constantinople*, 471–72.

32   Browning, "Note on the Capture of Constantinople," 382–84.

33   See Philippides and Hanak, *Siege of Constantinople*, 31.

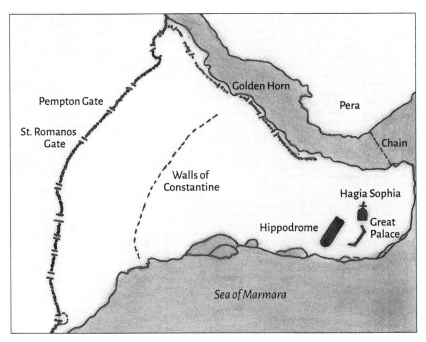

Fig. 10. Constantinople, 1453. Map by Anthi Andronikou, after M. Philippides and W. K. Hanak, *The Siege of Constantinople in 1453: Historiography, Topography, and Military Studies* (Farnham, 2011), map 2, and S. Runciman, *The Fall of Constantinople 1453* (London, 1965), 88.

Sea of Marmara, at Tenedos, where there was a Venetian force, or in Euboea." However, Philippides and Hanak point out that in his text, Barbaro actually refers to Hyalinas as "el Galina." His ship defended the Golden Horn during the siege and left along with those of Philomatis and Sgouros.[34]

The boat bearing news is as much a historical fact as it is a formulaic, albeit slightly revamped, trope shared by literary and folk traditions alike. On the one hand, Karanika considers the ship an *exangelos*, the messenger in ancient Greek tragedy who delivers news "coming from the inside," and as such it is a recognizable reference to misfortune. In "Anakalema," she observes, the boat sails from Constantinople to the outside world. Besides, in Greek antiquity the ship was a frequent metaphor of the state. The topos of a ship in a tempest or a departing ship was a sign of historical change, therefore the personified boat-cum-narrator

34 Browning, "Note on the Capture of Constantinople," 386; Philippides and Hanak, *Siege of Constantinople*, 22, 111, 471; Barbaro, *Giornale*, 59.

in this case is laden with connotations of change.[35] Referring to the symbolism of the ship in folk laments (moirologia) for the dead, Alexiou adds that "when the dead is dressed for the wake before the funeral procession, he is thought of as a ship about to depart for the Underworld," a theme that springs from "the ancient belief that life and death are two stages of a single journey."[36] On the other hand, in folk poetry and especially in historical songs and moirologia, birds often tell the news using human voice or simply lament a human calamity. This is particularly true of funeral laments and laments for klephts.[37] In the Pontic lament "The Capture of the City" ("To parsimo tes Poles"), for instance, a bird whose wings are stained with blood comes from Constantinople, just as birds come from Hades in moirologia.[38]

Gareth Morgan mentions that the meeting of ships in folk poetry is not uncommon, but it is used as "the prelude to battle, not conversation." Similarly, Rosario García Ortega and Ana Isabel Fernández Galvín affirm that although inanimate bearers of news are present in folk songs, the dialogue between two boats seems to be unique to "Anakalema."[39] The substitution of "bird" for "boat" here is more than a literary novelty. In addition to allowing easy identification among erudite and lay audiences by conjuring up ancient tragedy and folk laments, the motif of the ship conforms to historical accuracy. Islands, like Cyprus, Crete, and the Dodecanese, and port cities across the Greek world and beyond learned about the capture of Constantinople from arriving ships. The news carried by the Genoese and Cretan boats that escaped the Ottoman navy, indicates Kehayoglou, had a tremendous impact on the islanders. It is

35 Karanika, "Messengers, Angels, and Laments," 233, 243. For the figure of the angel as messenger (*angelos/exangelos*) in this poem, see ibid., passim.

36 Alexiou, *Ritual Lament*, 191–93.

37 Karanika, "Messengers, Angels, and Laments," 246, and Beaton, *Folk Poetry*, 96.

38 G. Saunier, "Οι αρχές του ιστορικού τραγουδιού και η εθνική συνείδηση," in *Ελληνικά δημοτικά τραγούδια: Συναγωγή μελετών (1968–2000)*, ed. G. Andriomenos and trans. I. Botouropoulou (Athens, 2001), 249–64, at 254. "The Capture of the City" can be found in G. Kehayoglou, "Συνοδευτικά έμμετρα κείμενα," in Kriaras, *Ανακάλημα της Κωνσταντινόπολης*, 102–45, at 129: "A bird, a good bird, fled from the City" (Έναν πουλίν, καλόν πουλίν, έβγαιν' από την Πόλην). For a relevant moirologi, see A. Passow, *Popularia carmina Graeciae recentioris* (Leipzig, 1860), 292, CCCCX.1: "A little bird fled from the underworld; / its nails were red and its wings black / the nails from the blood and the wings from the soil" (Ένα πουλάκι ξέβγαινεν από τον κάτω κόσμο· / είχε τα νύχια κόκκινα και τα φτερά του μαύρα / τα νύχι' από τα αίματα και τα φτερ' απ' το χώμα). Both quotes appear in Saunier, "Οι αρχές," 254.

39 G. Morgan, "Cretan Poetry: Sources and Inspiration," *Κρητικά χρονικά* 14 (1960): 7–68, 203–70, 379–434, at 395; and García Ortega and Fernández Galvín, *Trenos por Constantinopla*, 134.

well known that in Crete and probably in other parts "which had not yet fallen into the hands of the Ottomans, many were alarmed, shocked or deeply moved by the news of the conquest and the death of the last emperor."[40] A dedicatory inscription in the church of Saint George in Apano Symi, in the region of Heraklion (Venetian Candia), eloquently reflects the impact of the news on the Cretans. The painter Manuel Phokas, in his decoration of the church, swapped "anno domini" for "analosei tes Konstantinoupoleos" ("the time of the fall of Constantinople").[41]

Adam Goldwyn reads the opening dialogue of "Anakalema" as one "between a ship of survivors, who stand in here for the dead, and those who have not yet heard of the fall, who stand in for the living," which resonates again with the trope of a bird coming from Hades. Goldwyn draws attention to the verb *katebaineis* in line 8, "a navigational word in the context of sailing," also meaning "to die or to descend to the underworld." In line 9, *anathema* (cursed land) and *skotos* (heavy darkness) are equally associated with death and, metaphorically, with Hades. What we get from the poem is the idea that life after the conquest of Constantinople is "a form of death."[42] The demise of the city is also underpinned by the words *astrapokamene* (struck by lightning), *pikra* (bitter), and *dolomena* (blurry, not clear—here translated as "grim") (lines 11 and 13).[43] In folk laments for the dead, clarifies Guy Saunier, *astrapokamenoi* are those who had a violent death (*biaiothanatoi*), while "bitter" and "blurry" allude to the world of the dead.[44] Besides, the consonant sound "k," repeated twelve times in lines 8 through 11, turns the spotlight on *astrapokamene* and *skotos*, both encapsulating the nature and scale of the destruction.

What follows the initial conversation of the two ships is a symbolic mediation of the horrific events and their aftermath in relative detail through a range

---

40   Kehayoglou, "Ἐπίμετρο," 52.

41   T. Gouma-Peterson, "Manuel and John Phokas and Artistic Personality in Late Byzantine Painting," *Gesta* 22.2 (1983): 159–70, at 170. The English translation is found on page 161. The inscription appears in the narthex of the church (I. Spatharakis, *Dated Byzantine Wall Paintings of Crete* [Leiden, 2001], 203). I would like to thank Michalis Kappas for this reference.

42   A. Goldwyn, "'I come from a cursed land and from the depths of darkness': Life after Death in Greek Laments about the Fall of Constantinople," in *Wanted: Byzantium. The Desire for a Lost Empire*, ed. I. Nilsson and P. Stephenson (Uppsala, 2014), 93–108, at 96–97.

43   For the use of the adjective *pikros* with reference to death, see G. Saunier, "Πικρότητα και θάνατος, πικρός και φαρμάκι στα ελληνικά δημοτικά τραγούδια," in Andriomenos, *Ελληνικά δημοτικά τραγούδια*, 361–85.

44   Saunier, "Οι αρχές," 254.

of themes and imagery that would later resurface in other threnoi, as well as an attempt on the part of the poet to elaborate on the causes of the catastrophic events. Lines 16 to 19 introduce the galley's second question concerning the fate of Emperor Konstantinos XI Palaiologos (r. 12 March 1449–29 May 1453).[45] By using asyndeton, the poet highlights Konstantinos's virtues ("prudent," "strong," "brave," "mild-mannered," and "affable," lines 18–19), which are swiftly contrasted with his fate ("hapless" or *kakomoirasmenos*, line 20) in the boat's response through the rhetorical device of antithesis, which is common in folk songs. The galley's question heralds the drama of the Byzantine emperor as the drama of the collectivity—he is "the pride of the Romaioi," and his misfortune, which is about to be symbolically reenacted, stands in for the misfortune of all.

Similar to a cargo ship carrying weight, says Karanika, the emperor's lament-like monologue in lines 25 to 29 and 34 to 56 "is like a box inside another box, as the voice of the boat will report the voice of the emperor and his words."[46] Konstantinos's words are preceded by a brief description of the events and more specifically of the demolition of part of the city's walls ("[they] had broken through the walls") and the invasion of the Ottoman army ("[they] had run and entered, on foot and on horses"), which ended the nearly two-month-long siege (lines 21–22) (fig. 11).[47] We know that the old city fell around nine in the morning, following a massive attack by Mehmed II's land forces. Marios Philippides and Walter Hanak write that, after a series of failed attempts to capture Constantinople, the inflection point came when the Genoese Giovanni Guglielmo Longo Giustiniani was injured at the Pempton Gate (Fifth Military Gate), part of the western walls not far from the Saint Romanos Gate, which was defended by the emperor (see fig. 10).[48] Just before dawn, a shot struck Giustiniani, perforating his breastplate, writes Steven Runciman, but in fact the exact nature of Giustiniani's wound or wounds remains unclear.[49] When he left the Pempton Gate, possibly in search of

---

45 The poem refers to the emperor by his first name, "Konstantinos," and his maternal surname, "Dragases" (lines 17, 20). Konstantinos's mother, Helena Dragaš, was the daughter of the Serbian nobleman Constantine Dragaš (J. S. Allen, "Constantine Dragaš," in Kazhdan et al., *The Oxford Dictionary of Byzantium*, 1:505–6).

46 Karanika, "Messengers, Angels, and Laments," 233.

47 Although the Moldovita fresco in figure 11 purportedly depicts the Avar siege of Constantinople in 626, it is "clearly inspired by the Turkish siege of 1453" (S. Reinert, "Fragmentation [1204–1453]," in *The Oxford History of Byzantium*, ed. C. Mango [Oxford, 2002], 248–83, at 280). See also D. Nicolle, "Constantinople 1453," in *The Fall of Constantinople: The Ottoman Conquest of Byzantium*, ed. D. Nicolle, J. Haldon, and S. Turnbull (Oxford, 2007), 174–243, at 232, 243.

48 Philippides and Hanak, *Siege of Constantinople*, 568.

49 S. Runciman, *The Fall of Constantinople 1453* (London, 1965), 138.

Fig. 11. *Siege of Constantinople*, fresco, 1537, Romania, Moldovita Monastery, detail of south wall. Artwork in the public domain; photograph by Man vyi, courtesy of Wikimedia Commons.

medical aid, his men followed him thinking that he was retreating, thereby leaving the Pempton Gate unguarded and literally opening the way for the Ottoman sack of Constantinople. "In this inglorious manner," Philippides and Hanak conclude, "the imperial city fell to the *Fatih*, the Conqueror."[50]

The embedded dialogue containing the emperor's dramatic monologue lends the poem an element of immediacy and theatricality. In this Matryoshka-doll narrative, the drama of the fall of Constantinople, known as the *halosis* (sack), is acted out first through the lament of the boat and subsequently through that of the emperor, whose prognosis of his own death makes his narration all the more poignant. "The truth of cultural scripts emerges, not from their descriptive accuracy," argue Alexander and Breese, "but from the power of their enactment. Trauma scripts are performed as symbolic actions in the theaters of everyday collective life." This is what they refer to as "the performative impact of textual enactment."[51] In "Anakalema," enactment and performativity are woven

50   Philippides and Hanak, *Siege of Constantinople*, 523, 568.
51   Alexander and Breese, "Introduction," xxvii, xxx.

into the fabric of the narrative. The emperor's lament begins with an anaphora, a frequent rhetorical figure in moirologia: "How can I still have eyes and look! How can I still have light and see! / How can I still have my mind and walk in this wretched world!" (lines 26–27). The aural imagery of the poem's opening line, connoted here in the anaphora of rhetorical questions evoking ritual lament practices (how ... how ... how), is complemented by the visual imagery ("eyes," "look," "light," "see") that is introduced with the same anaphora. The emphasis on vision is, in fact, already present in the previous line: "Mercy, what a thing my miserable eyes see!" (line 25). Through a barrage of visual, auditory, and kinesthetic images arousing the senses, the audience is invited by the tragic emperor to see, hear, and feel the traumatizing events as the Turks enter the city, destroying the emperor and his subjects (lines 28–29).

The emperor, we learn in the boat's narrative intermission, sees his allies abandoning him. Among them were Genoese, Venetians, and Cretans, who had been under Venetian rule since 1211: "he sees the Cretans leaving, the Genoese leaving, / the Venetians leaving and he remains behind" (lines 31–32). We know that many of the ships at the Golden Horn, including the three Cretan vessels, managed to escape when the crew of the Ottoman fleet joined the sack.[52] In his *Chronicon Maius* (1573–1575), Makarios Melissenos (Pseudo-Sphrantzes) says that the Cretan sailors carried on defending the towers Alexios, Basileios, and Leon while the rest of the city was under Ottoman control. The Cretans, he tells us, "bravely continued the struggle into the sixth and seventh hour and killed many Turks." Once notified of "their bravery," Mehmed "ordered them to come down, under a truce" and "declared that they, their ship, and all their equipment would remain free."[53] Philippides and Hanak, however, stress that Melissenos's account does not match any other "authoritative text" and should thus be read with caution.[54]

In the narrative reimagining of the empire's last stand, the emperor turns to the runaway Cretans, forecasting his own death at the hands of "Mehmed, the dog." He pleads with them not to let the "dogs" (*skulia*) seize him and asks them to cut off his head and carry it to Crete where the "Christian Romaioi" will mourn and "commemorate" (*makarisousin*) his death (lines 34–56). Melissenos

---

52   Browning, "Note on the Capture of Constantinople," 383.

53   In Philippides and Hanak, *Siege of Constantinople*, 469: αὐτοὶ γὰρ γενναίως ἐμάχοντο μέχρι καὶ τῆς ἕκτης καὶ ἑβδόμης ὥρας. . . . Τοῦρκος δὲ τῷ ἀμηρᾷ ἀναφορὰν ποιήσας περὶ τῆς τούτων ἀνδρίας, προσέταξεν ἵνα κατέλθωσι μετὰ συμβάσεως καὶ ὦσιν ἐλεύθεροι αὐτοί τε καὶ ἡ ναῦς αὐτῶν καὶ πᾶσα ἡ ἀποσκευὴ ἣν εἶχον.

54   Ibid., 469–70.

reports three rumors about the emperor's fortune: "he had fled Constantinople; he was in hiding somewhere in the city; or he had died fighting."[55] Historical ambiguity soon gave rise to growing speculation on the emperor's fate both in historiographical texts and in threnoi, monodies, and folk songs for the fall of the city.[56] In his *Turco-Byzantine History* (*Buzantinotourkike historia*) (ca. 1462), the contemporary historian Michael Doukas refers to the emperor's wish to be beheaded by Christians—although not necessarily by Cretans as recorded in the poem—before he is captured by Mehmed II's men: "Is there no one among the Christians who will take my head from me?" The historian adds that the Turks "slew him as a common soldier."[57] Pusculo nevertheless notes that Konstantinos Palaiologos was decapitated by the enemy, while Benvenuto of Ancona apparently heard a trumpet declaring that the emperor was dead and that his head had been taken to Mehmed on a pike.[58] Benvenuto's version is reiterated by Cardinal Isidore, the Greek legate of the pope to Constantinople, though it is not clear whether the latter saw the emperor's head himself or not.[59] Philippides and Hanak assert that the emperor certainly took part in the last stage of the siege close to the Saint Romanos Gate, but the particularities of his final moments remain unknown. It would appear that he died in the conflict, but his death is something of a mystery. They clarify that "no eyewitness author whose work still survives was anywhere near the emperor at this crucial moment," and they speculate that "in the absence of identifiable remains," the sultan may have "selected a severed head and announced that it had been the emperor's."[60]

---

55 A. Papayianni, "*He Polis healo*: The Fall of Constantinople in 1453 in Post-Byzantine Popular Literature," *Al-Masāq* 22.1 (2010): 27–44, at 40.

56 For the controversy over the fate of the emperor, see D. M. Nicol, *The Immortal Emperor* (Cambridge, 1992). On myths, legends, and tales about the fall of Constantinople and the fortune of the emperor in folk history, see Philippides and Hanak, *Siege of Constantinople*, 193–288.

57 M. Doukas, *Michaelis Ducae Nepotis Historia byzantina*, ed. I. Bekker (New York, 2012), 286.c.24–287.c.1 and 287.d.6: οὐκ ἔστι τις τῶν Χριστιανῶν τοῦ λαβεῖν τὴν κεφαλήν μου ἀπ' ἐμοῦ and ὡς κοινὸν στρατιώτην τοῦτον θανατώσαντες. For the English translation, see M. Doukas, *Decline and Fall of Byzantium to the Ottoman Turks*, trans. H. J. Magoulias (Detroit, MI, 1975), 224.13.

58 In Philippides and Hanak, *Siege of Constantinople*, 233–34: "caput abstulit unus / ex humeris" and "inperator Grecorum fuit interfectus, et eius caput super lancea Turcorum domino pr<a>esentatum."

59 Ibid., 236. Other relevant accounts are given by Barbaro (the emperor begs his men to kill him), Leonardo Giustiniani (the emperor asks his attendants to kill him), and Sphrantzes (a laconic note that the emperor was killed) (ibid., 232–34).

60 Ibid., 232, 241.

The author of "Anakalema" seems to have been familiar with the information circulated by Pusculo, Benvenuto, and Cardinal Isidore vis-à-vis the beheading of the last Byzantine emperor. Into Konstantinos's dramatic invocation of the Cretans—the only Orthodox Christians among the escaping allies—the poet injects an element of tragic irony typical of ancient tragedy and folk songs alike.[61] By arousing a sense of dramatic irony in the audience, the emperor's lament becomes a catalyst for the mediation of cultural trauma. His anticipated death at the hands of "Mehmed, the dog" and his soldiers is meant to overwhelm the receptors of his message with negative affect. A frequent motif in learned laments and folk poetry about *halosis*, the canine trope is found in threnoi like "Sack of Constantinople" ("Halosis Konstantinoupoleos," which mentions "the raging dog" [*ton skulon ton lussiaren*]) and "Lament for Constantinople" ("Threnos tes Konstantinoupoleos," which speaks of "the janissaries, the dogs" [*hoi skuloi gianitzaroi*]). Dogs are also mentioned in the folk song "The Sack of Constantinople" ("He halosis tes Konstantinoupoleos"): "so that the dogs don't take it from us and defile it" (*men mas ten paroun ta skulia kai mas ten magarisoun*).[62] Using the dog metaphor (lines 21, 36, 42, 44, 50, 62, 85), the poet of "Anakalema" animalizes the perpetrator and aggravates the threat for the rest of the Romaioi, a process exemplified by the repetition of the word "dog" (*skulos*) in the nominative singular and accusative plural in line 50: "[the dog] order[s] the dogs to vilify me" (*na risei ho skulos ta skulia na me kakologesoun*).

The emperor's projection of his tragic end is enacted in gruesome detail through a series of kinesthetic images mediated by anaphora and asyndeton in the final part of his lament. We are told that the "lawless" Mehmed (who does not accept the law of Christ) will order his "dogs" to vilify, deride, curse, torment, and torture the Byzantine emperor by decapitating him and sticking his head on a pike. The Turks will relish his death by tearing his heart, eating his entrails, and drinking his blood (lines 49–56). The trauma of the conquest culminates in the emperor's final speech-act, which aims to graft the memory of the horrific events onto the audience. Cultural trauma, writes Alexander, erupts when members of a group believe that they have been exposed to a dreadful incident that permanently marks their collective consciousness and irreversibly alters their future identity.[63] Through the emperor's voice, the poet

---

61 Kehayoglou, "Επίμετρο," 55.

62 In Zoras, Βυζαντινή ποίησις, 186.471 and 200.17; and Passow, *Popularia carmina*, 147, CXCVI.13.

63 Alexander, "Toward a Theory," 1.

imaginatively reconstructs the final moments of the empire, casting the trauma-tizing events upon Romaioi "everywhere" (*pantachothen*, line 15).

Cultural trauma theorists underscore the role of imagination in the formu-lation of collective memory and postmemory. Coined by Marianne Hirsch, the term "postmemory" refers to the relationship between subsequent generations and the experiences of those who witnessed collective or cultural trauma—"experiences they 'remember' only by means of the stories, images, and behav-iors among which they grew up." Hirsch stresses that these experiences were conveyed to them in such a profound and affective manner "as to *seem* to con-stitute memories in their own right."[64] No doubt the term is useful when dis-cussing descendants of individuals directly affected by traumatizing events (in this case, those present at the siege of Constantinople), but there is no signifi-cant difference in the *ways* in which cultural trauma and postmemory are medi-ated to audiences with no direct experience of the events more generally. Aware of this, Hirsch would later suggest that postmemory could also describe the relationship "distant contemporary witnesses bear to the personal, collective, and cultural trauma of others."[65] For most contemporary Cretans, Cypriots, Dodecanesians, and other Greeks living outside Constantinople and with no immediate experience of the siege and its aftermath (deaths, plundering, rapes, forced marriages, etc.), collective memory was forged through images, stories, and behaviors, the latter especially in areas like the Lusignan Cyprus of Queen Helena Palaiologina (the emperor's niece), where several Constantinopolitans, among them monks and artists, found shelter in the months and years follow-ing the fall. Accommodated in the monastery of Saint George of Mangana in Nicosia, the monks established a scriptorium, contributing significantly to the production of Greek manuscripts on the island. Apart from the monastery, the queen granted these Constantinopolitan monks "villages and revenues that exceeded the amount of 1,500 ducats."[66] The prevailing atmosphere of "Anakalema," observes Kehayoglou, would resonate strongly within the circles of Helena Palaiologina.[67]

---

64   M. Hirsch, *The Generation of Postmemory: Writing and Visual Culture after the Holocaust* (New York, 2012), 5, original emphasis.

65   M. Hirsch, "Connective Histories in Vulnerable Times," *PMLA* 129.3 (2014): 330–48, at 339.

66   C. Kaoulla, "Queen Helena Palaiologina of Cyprus (1442–1458): Myth and History," *Επετηρίς του Κέντρου Επιστημονικών Ερευνών* 32 (2006): 109–50, at 141–44.

67   Kehayoglou, "Επίμετρο," 98.

Postmemory, according to Hirsch, is mediated "by imaginative investment, projection, and creation."[68] Similarly, Alexander highlights the pivotal role of imagination in the construction of trauma, whether actual or perceived. "It is only through the imaginative process of representation," he says, "that actors have the sense of experience."[69] Drawing on relevant rumors circulating at the time, the poet's imaginative reconstruction of the emperor's death transmits the memory of the trauma to those who have not witnessed it so that they "remember." This memory is channeled through literary devices (dialogue, dramatic monologue, tragic irony) that create immediacy and encourage identification and, more importantly, through recognizable aesthetic traditions and themes (folk songs, threnoi, ancient tragedy) and deep-seated popular practices (ritual lamentation and funerary practices).

Karanika points out that, in addition to voicing a death wish, the emperor communicates his desire for lamentation by stipulating specific practices of ritual lament, such as weeping (*na chusoun maura dakrua*; line 40), breast-beating (*na deirousi ta stethe tous*; line 40), and the memorial act of *makarismos* (*na me makarisousin*; line 41).[70] The link between weeping and breast-beating with ritual lament is self-evident. In preclassical times, indicates Alexiou, the term *goos* was used to refer to the spontaneous dirge of the female relatives of the dead, whereas *threnos* was reserved for the lament of professional mourners. The threnoi of Simonides and Pindar, for instance, were "characterised by a calm restraint, gnomic and consolatory in tone rather than passionate and ecstatic," while the goos was "less restrained."[71]

Mullett points out that even though threnoi have been traditionally associated with female mourning, surviving examples from the eleventh and twelfth centuries are by men, like Theophylact of Ochrid's two poetic laments for the death of his brother Demetrios in 1107, composed in anacreontics and iambics.[72] Theophylact, writes Mullett, had access to the "traditions of heroic ascetic weeping and of imperial weeping." The apostles' mourning of the Virgin in depictions of the *Koimesis* (Dormition of the Virgin) in Byzantine art was commonplace, and King David's weeping for Jonathan was a widely available biblical model of male-for-male lamentation. About fifty years after Demetrios's death, Emperor

68 Hirsch, *Generation of Postmemory*, 5.

69 Alexander, "Toward a Theory," 9.

70 Karanika, "Messengers, Angels, and Laments," 235.

71 Alexiou, *Ritual Lament*, 103.

72 Mullett, *Theophylact of Ochrid*, 141, 244–45.

Manuel I (r. 1143–1180) "cries at Myriokephalon that his water is mixed with blood because King David . . . did the same."[73]

Male lamentation is prominent in "Anakalema," initially in the emperor's encased lament and subsequently in the poet's lament proper, and so is goos, whose agency is rhetorically degendered since the Cretans as a whole, not just women, are asked to perform it through weeping and breast-beating, both reenacted by the narrator in lines 107 and 108. Read by the symbol creator as a historical transgression, the loss of the Eastern Roman Empire, or Romania, necessarily called for transgressive gender acts. Karanika first traced features of goos in the emperor's lament, but with a twist. Contrary to ritual lamentation, in which the death wish of the mourners does not come true but instead serves as a lyrical representation of physical death, in our poem the emperor's death wish is actually fulfilled. Crucially, Konstantinos also "iconizes" his head, which "is meant to be viewed and to be memorialized."[74] Like the miraculous portrait of Christ the king of heaven (*basileus ton ouranon*) on the lost Mandylion of Edessa,[75] the discursively reconstructed image of the head of the Byzantine emperor is to be revered and commemorated. Like the Mandylion, the textual visualization of the emperor's head somehow becomes a powerful icon in absentia.

The emperor requests that the Cretans "see" his head and grieve for him (line 39). His threnos becomes theirs through imaginative investment and a "public act of commemoration"—*makarisousin*.[76] Commemorative practices, note Alexander and Breese, aim to convey the trauma to those who have not experienced it and present it as "the trauma of all."[77] One way to mold collective memory, according to Peter Burke, is through "rituals of commemoration," which he labels "reenactments of the past" and "acts of memory."[78] Similarly, Paul Connerton posits that social memory can be found in "commemorative ceremonies," which are fundamentally performative. His understanding of "performative memory" as bodily makes him speak of "bodily social memory." Reenactments of the past, argues Connerton, hinge as much on their rhetorical potency as they do "on prescribed bodily behaviour," both markedly present

73   Mullett, "Do Brothers Weep?," 328–29.

74   Karanika, "Messengers, Angels, and Laments," 235–36.

75   See A. Cameron, "The History of the Image of Edessa: The Telling of a Story," in *Okeanos: Essays Presented to Ihor Ševčenko on His Sixtieth Birthday by His Colleagues and Students* (*Harvard Ukrainian Studies* 7 [1983]): 80–94. A depiction of the Mandylion is seen in fig. 11 (center left).

76   Alexander, "Toward a Theory," 7.

77   Alexander and Breese, "Introduction," xxviii.

78   P. Burke, *Varieties of Cultural History* (Ithaca, NY, 1997), 48.

in the poem.[79] The titular anakalema (for Constantinople) and the embedded goos (for the emperor) are, in fact, the two versions of the same commemorative act. Like the emperor, a synecdoche for Romania, the Cretans, here called "Christian Romaioi," metonymically stand for the Greeks "everywhere."[80] Their makarismos and goos—literally, examples of bodily social memory, or "mnemonics of the body"[81]—are rituals of commemoration to be reenacted across the Greek-speaking world in order to fashion collective memory in time and space. The Mandylion-like image of the emperor's head functions as a mnemonic prompt for the remembrance of the traumatic events that have abruptly and negatively impacted collective identity.[82]

The scene is encapsulated in the twentieth-century drawing by Fotis Kontoglou "Lament for Konstantinos Palaiologos" ("Ho threnos Konstantinou tou Palaiologou") (fig. 12). Produced in 1949 and published in the May/June 1953 issue of the magazine *Kibotos*, which commemorated the fifth centenary of the fall of Constantinople, Kontoglou's visual lament for the tragic death of the emperor reflects the relevance of the cultural trauma to contemporary Greeks.[83] Borrowing from the iconography of the Crucifixion, the Descent from the Cross, and the Lamentation of Christ, the artist puts Konstantinos in the place of Christ and substitutes the Virgin Mary and Mary Magdalene with Orthodoxy (Orthodoxia) and Greece (Hellada) under the caption: "Brothers, let us give a parting farewell to the one who has died."[84] The quote from the funeral service or *akolouthia nekrosimos* extends the invitation to Orthodox Greeks to lament the loss of the sanctified emperor and postpones the closure of the threnos, placing the trauma of his death (and the fall of the city) in a time loop. Like the death of the King of Heaven, the ritual lament and funeral procession for the last

---

79 P. Connerton, *How Societies Remember* (Cambridge, 1996), 71–72.

80 The Emperor Konstantinos Palaiologos, Hagia Sophia, and Constantinople are frequent metonymies of the empire in the threnoi, folk songs, and monodies for the fall of the city. Referring to the threnos "The Death of Konstantinos Dragases" ("Ho thanatos tou Konstantinou Dragaze"), for example, Goldwyn notes that "much as Hector is a metonym and symbol for all the citizens of Troy, and as his death presages the fall of the city, so too does Constantine's death represent the death of the city's inhabitants, even the metaphorical death of its survivors" (Goldwyn, "'I come from a cursed land,'" 95).

81 Connerton, *How Societies Remember*, 74.

82 Alexander, "Toward a Theory," 10.

83 F. Kontoglou, "Θρηνητικὸν συναξάριν Κωνσταντίνου τοῦ Παλαιολόγου," *Κιβωτός* 17–18 (1953): 193.

84 Δεῦτε τελευταῖον ἀσπασμὸν δῶμεν ἀδελφοὶ τῷ θανόντι.

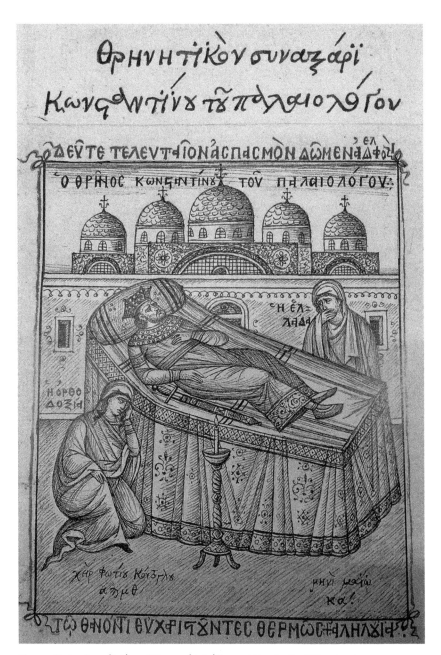

Fig. 12. Orthodoxy (left) and Greece (right) lament the death of Konstantinos Palaiologos. Drawing by Fotis Kontoglou, *A Synaxariun of Laments for Konstantinos Palaiologos*, ink and sepia, 1949, 16 × 23 cm, D. Kontoglou-Martinou Collection. Courtesy of Fotis Martinos.

basileus of Byzantium is to be reenacted in perpetuity.[85] Kontoglou's remodeling of Byzantine iconography, steeped in the texts and subtexts of the Byzantine rite, enables a passage from the profane to the sacred and from a historical to a transhistorical trauma.

By the end of the first part of the poem (lines 1–56), the trauma claim has been established with a view to shaping collective memory through prescribed commemorative rituals. I have pointed out that contrary to the reflexive lament of the first part, the second part of "Anakalema" (lines 57–118) is a more conventional threnos made up of a dramatic narration of the events by the lyric subject in the first person (lines 57–88) and an allegory (lines 89–118). The poet begins by describing the pillage of the city through a series of formulas common in the threnoi, monodies, and folk songs for the sack of Constantinople. These stock images are related to the defiling and destruction of all things sacred, including churches, icons, gospels, crosses, chalices, and holy relics (lines 63–70),[86] and to the rape of women and their subsequent enslavement in the Ottoman hinterland. There they are forced to take care of livestock and give birth to "bastards" who will become janissaries, here dubbed "bloodthirsty dogs" (lines 71–86).[87]

On the morning of 29 May, write Philippides and Hanak, when the Ottoman troops entered through the Pempton Gate, a three-day sack of the city began,

85   Historically, the lament for the last Byzantine emperor (and metonymically for Constantinople) may or may not have been accompanied by the notion of symbolic resurrection in the form of recapturing the lost empire. The idea of the liberation of Byzantium, which was manifested in prophetic texts, threnoi, and folk songs, culminated in the ideology of the *megali idea* (literally, great idea or grand vision) in the nineteenth and early twentieth centuries. See "Texts and Their Afterlife," below.

86   The theme of desacralization is present, for instance, in the monodies of Manuel Christonymos (in S. P. Lambros, *Νέος Ελληνομνήμων*, vol. 5 [Athens, 1908], 237.1–6) and Andronikos Kallistos (ibid., 205.3–5, 211.23–25), and in folk songs about Hagia Sophia, such as the numerous variants of "The Capture of the City" ("To parsimo tes Poles") (Kehayoglou, "Συνοδευτικά έμμετρα κείμενα," 125.7–10, 126.12–16).

87   This particular point on the suffering of captured women in the rural areas of the Ottoman Empire suggests that some time must have elapsed between May 1453 and the composition of "Anakalema," during which the news about their misfortunes reached places like Cyprus and Crete. Kehayoglou observes that information about cruelties and crimes perpetrated by the Ottomans are reported in Cypriot texts not immediately after the events but a few years later, providing as an example Boustronios's (known as Tzortzes Boustrous) *Chronicle of Cyprus* (*Diegesis Kronikas Kuprou*) (Kehayoglou, "Επίμετρο," 72), which covers the years 1456–1501 with a particular focus on the period 1456–1474. A contemporary of the poet of "Anakalema," Boustronios probably started writing his chronicle before 1489 and completed it by 1501, the year of his death (Kehayoglou, "Το γραμματειακό 'πολυσύστημα,'" 97). As already mentioned, the year 1509 is the latest possible date for the creation of "Anakalema."

corroborated in eyewitness accounts by Benvenuto, Leonardo Giustiniani, and the Genoese *podestá* of Pera, Angelo Giovanni Lomellino.[88] Even Mehmed II's biographer Kritoboulos recorded in his *History* (known as *History of Mehmed the Conqueror*, 1467) that the Ottoman army "emptied and deserted, and despoiled and blackened the entire City as if by fire."[89] Soon after the sack followed a series of executions of Greek notables, among them the Notara family,[90] a fact the poem seems to allude to in line 71, with the reference to the noblemen and their children.[91]

In book 1 of his *History*, Kritoboulos dedicates a relatively long and, for him, atypically dramatic passage to the rape of women and children, in which he mentions "young and chaste women of noble birth and well to do, accustomed to remain at home and who had hardly ever left their own premises," and "handsome and lovely maidens of splendid and renowned families, till then unsullied by male eyes," who were "dragged by force from their chambers and hauled off pitilessly and dishonorably." He also speaks of "well-born and beautiful young boys [who] were carried off" and of "consecrated virgins who were honorable and wholly unsullied, devoted to God alone and living for Him to whom they

---

88 Philippides and Hanak, *Siege of Constantinople*, 93–94.

89 Michael Kritoboulos, *Critobuli Imbriotae Historiae*, ed. D. R. Reinsch (Berlin, 1983), 75, 67.3.14–15: πᾶσαν ταύτην ἐκένωσε καὶ ἠρήμωσε καὶ πυρὸς δίκην ἠφάνισε καὶ ἠμαύρωσε. For the English translation, see Kritoboulos, *History*, 76.254. Here, I have slightly altered Charles Riggs's translation. See also E. Zachariadou, "Η επέκταση των Οθωμανών στην Ευρώπη ως την άλωση της Κωνσταντινουπόλεως (1354–1453)," in *Ιστορία του ελληνικού έθνους: Βυζαντινός ελληνισμός, μεσοβυζαντινοί χρόνοι (1071–1204), υστεροβυζαντινοί χρόνοι (1204–1453)*, vol. 9 (Athens, 1979), 184–213, at 213.

90 Philippides and Hanak, *Siege of Constantinople*, 246–65.

91 Ἄρχοντες, αρκοντόπουλοι. Philippides and Hanak speculate that the executions may have taken place at the Vefa Meidan. They point out that information on the executions of Greek captives is provided by Cardinal Isidore, who, at that point, was hiding in Pera. In a letter dated 6 July 1453 and sent from Crete to his friend Cardinal Bessarion, Isidore "devotes a few words on the fate of some of their acquaintances: 'A few days later the Turk [sc. Mehmed II] pretended that it was his wish to settle the city and ransomed all noblemen of high rank, whose lives, he led them to hope, would be spared. Three days later, by his first decree and command, he beheaded the two sons of [Loukas] Notaras (while his third son had of course perished gloriously in the fight), before the eyes of their father, whom he then decapitated. Then he executed the three very handsome, excellent sons of the grand domestic along with their father. Next he executed the illustrious lord Nikolaos Goudeles and very many other famous men'" (in Philippides and Hanak, *Siege of Constantinople*, 248–49). Notaras's execution is also mentioned in Pusculo's poem: "Your end was even more cruel Notaras. You saw that your daughter and your boy were raped by the tyrant [= sultan]. Before your own eyes you saw your beloved two sons slaughtered and you were sprinkled with their blood. Then you were also executed" (ibid., 252–53).

had consecrated themselves." Kritoboulos tells us that "some of these were forced out of their cells and driven off, and others dragged out of the churches where they had taken refuge and driven off with insult and dishonor."[92] The historian's description reverberates throughout the poet's lament proper, which appears to employ an almost identical imagery and phraseology:

> Noblemen, children of noble birth, great noblewomen,
> gentle and prudent, and raised with care,
> unmarried women of good repute, married women and widows,
> and gentle nuns, postulants, abbesses
> —the wind has not touched them, the sun has not seen them,
> for they spent their time chanting and reading in the holy monasteries—
> were snatched without mercy, as if condemned.[93]

Both Kritoboulos's text and "Anakalema" emphasize noblewomen as well-born and prudent, virgins as being of noble extraction, and nuns or postulants as chaste and upstanding, having devoted themselves to God. In both texts, the women are out of the sight of men and the public sphere, figuratively embodied by the sun and the wind. Through the use of hyperbole, the women's chastity is contrasted with their ruthless seizing and rape. Note also in both texts the allusion to the rape of young children. These parallels are not mere accidents, they are rooted in shared vocabulary.[94]

92 Kritoboulos, *Historiae*, 71–72, 61.5.26–61.6.20, and Kritoboulos, *History*, 72.240, 73.242–43: γυναῖκας νέας καὶ σώφρονας, εὐγενεῖς τε καὶ τῶν εὖ γεγονότων τὰ πολλὰ οἰκουρούσας καὶ οὐδὲ τὴν αὔλειον προελθούσας ποτέ ... παρθένους εὐπρεπεῖς καὶ ὡραίας, λαμπράς τε καὶ λαμπρῶν οἰκιῶν καὶ μέχρι τότε ἀρρένων ὀφθαλμοῖς ὅλως ἀψαύστους ... βίᾳ τῶν θαλάμων ἐξελκομένας ἀπηνῶς τε ἅμα καὶ ἀναιδῶς ἁρπαζομένας ... παῖδας εὐγενεῖς καὶ ὡραίους ἀπαγομένους ... παρθένους μοναζούσας σεμνάς τε καὶ ἀπροίτους τὸ ὅλον καὶ τῷ θεῷ μόνῳ προσανεχούσας καὶ ζώσας, ᾧ καθιέρωσαν ἑαυτάς ... τὰς μὲν τῶν δωματίων βιαίως ἐξαγομένας καὶ συρομένας, τὰς δὲ τῶν ἱερῶν ἀποσπωμένας, ἐν οἷς κατέφευγον, καὶ ἀπαγομένας σὺν ὕβρει καὶ ἀτιμίᾳ.

93 Lines 71–77: Ἄρχοντες, αρκοντόπουλοι, αρχόντισσες μεγάλες, / ευγενικές και φρένιμες, ακριβαναθρεμμένες, / ανέγλυτες πανεύφημες, ύπανδρες και χηράδες / και καλογριές ευγενικές, παρθένες, ηγουμένες / —άνεμος δεν τους έδιδε, ήλιος ουκ έβλεπεν τες, / εψάλλαν, ενεγνώθασι εις τ' άγια μοναστήρια— / ηρπάγησαν ανηλεώς ως καταδικασμένες.

94 Excerpts from Kritoboulos's text are followed here by those from "Anakalema": εὐγενεῖς / ευγενικές; σώφρονας / φρένιμες; παρθένους εὐπρεπεῖς / ανέγλυτες πανεύφημες; λαμπράς τε καὶ λαμπρῶν οἰκιῶν / πανεύφημες and ακριβαναθρεμμένες; παρθένους μοναζούσας / καλογριές ... παρθένες; σεμνάς / ευγενικές; τῷ θεῷ μόνῳ προσανεχούσας καὶ ζώσας / εψάλλαν, ενεγνώθασι εις τ' άγια μοναστήρια; οὐδὲ τὴν αὔλειον προελθούσας ποτέ and ἀρρένων ὀφθαλμοῖς ὅλως ἀψαύστους / άνεμος δεν τους έδιδε, ήλιος ουκ έβλεπεν τες; βιαίως ἐξαγομένας καὶ συρομένας / ηρπάγησαν ανηλεώς; παῖδας εὐγενεῖς / αρκοντόπουλοι.

Kritoboulos's graphic remarks on sexual violence are immediately followed by an equally emotive commentary on the looting of the churches. We learn, for instance, that "icons and reliquaries and other objects from the churches . . . [were] thr[own] in dishonor on the ground" and that "they were stripped of their decoration, and some were given over to the fire while others were torn to shreds and scattered at the crossroads."[95] We are also told that "the last resting-places of the blessed men of old were opened, and their remains were taken out and disgracefully torn to pieces, even to shreds, and made the sport of the wind while others were thrown on the streets" and that "chalices and goblets and vessels to hold the holy sacrifice, some of them were used for drinking and carousing, and others were broken up or melted down and sold." Finally, we read that "holy and divine books, and others mainly of profane literature and philosophy, were either given to the flames or dishonorably trampled under foot."[96]

"Anakalema" once again mirrors Kritoboulos's passage, only in reverse order, in its representation of the looting of churches (lines 63–70) just before the rape scenes (lines 71–77):

[A]nd [they] turn churches into stables and burn the icons,
and tear and trample on the golden gospels,
and dishonor the holy crosses and break them into pieces,
and take their silver and their pearls,
and the fragrant relics of holy men
to burn and destroy, and throw them into the sea,
and take their precious stones and their decoration,
and drink wine from the holy chalices.[97]

95 Riggs translates "the crowd snatched some of these" instead of "they were stripped of their decoration." I follow Diether Roderich Reinsch and Fotini Kolovou's reading of κόσμος as "decoration." See M. Kritoboulos, Ιστορία, ed. and trans. D. R. Reinsch and F. Kolovou (Athens, 2005), 243.

96 Kritoboulos, Historiae, 72–73, 62.1.26–62.3.8, and Kritoboulos, History, 73.244–74.246: κατεβάλλοντο μὲν ἀτίμως εἰς γῆν εἰκόνες καὶ ἀφιδρύματα καὶ τἆλλα τῶν ἱερῶν . . . ἀπεσπᾶτο δὲ κόσμος ὁ τούτων, ἐδίδοτο δὲ τὰ μὲν αὐτῶν τῷ πυρί, τὰ δὲ ἐς λεπτὰ τεμνόμενά τε καὶ συντριβόμενα ἐπὶ τῶν τριόδων ἐρριπτεῖτο . . . ἠνοίγοντο δὲ θῆκαι τῶν παλαιῶν καὶ μακαρίων ἀνδρῶν καὶ τὰ τούτων ἐξήγετο λείψανα καὶ ἀτίμως λεπτυνόμενα καὶ λυόμενα εἰς ἀέρα ἑλίκματο, τὰ δὲ καὶ ἐπὶ τῶν ἀμφόδων ἐρριπτεῖτο . . . κρατῆρές τε καὶ φιάλαι καὶ ἃ τὴν παναγεστάτην θυσίαν ἐδέχετο, αἱ μὲν ἐς προπόσεις ἦσαν καὶ μέθην αὐτοῖς, οἱ δὲ συντριβόμενοί τε καὶ χωνευόμενοι ἀπεδίδοντο . . . βίβλοι τε ἱεραὶ καὶ θεῖαι, ἀλλὰ δὴ καὶ τῶν ἔξω μαθημάτων καὶ φιλοσόφων αἱ πλεῖσται, αἱ μὲν πυρὶ παρεδίδοντο, αἱ δὲ ἀτίμως κατεπατοῦντο.

97 Lines 63–70: να ποίσου στάβλους εκκλησιές, να καίουν τας εικόνας, / να σχίζουν, να καταπατούν τα 'λόχρουσα βαγγέλια, / να καθυβρίζουν τους σταυρούς, να τους κατατσακίζουν, / να παίρνουσιν

Both texts put an emphasis on the burning of icons, the trampling on holy books, the dishonoring and shattering of holy objects that are stripped of their precious decoration, the opening of reliquaries and the destruction of holy relics, and the defiling of holy chalices.[98]

Even though the sack of the churches and the rape of civilians are staple themes in the literature on the fall, none of the contemporary Greek historians, perhaps with the exception of Doukas, affords such a scrupulous account. Doukas's passage on the plundering of the churches is relatively close to that of Kritoboulos, but not nearly as extensive or striking. The former's comments on the stripping of decoration in particular are suggestive and so is his mention of women who have never been exposed to the sun, a common image in folk songs that is also found in "Anakalema" (line 75):

> The rapine caused the tugging and pulling of braids of hair, the exposure of bosoms and breasts, and outstretched arms. . . . Virgins, who had never been exposed to the sun and hardly ever seen their own fathers, were dragged about, forcibly pushed together and flogged. . . . The dogs hacked the holy icons to pieces, removing the ornaments. As for the chains, candelabra, holy altar coverings, and lamps, some they destroyed and the rest they seized. All the precious and sacred vessels of the holy sacristy, fashioned from gold and silver and other valuable materials, they collected in an instant, leaving the temple desolate and naked; absolutely nothing was left behind.[99]

τ' ασήμια τους και τα μαργαριτάρια / και των αγίων τα λείψανα τα μοσχομυρισμένα / να καίουν, ν' αφανίζουσιν, στην θάλασσαν να ρίπτουν, / να παίρνουν τα λιθάρια των και την ευκόσμησίν των / και στ' άγια δισκοπότηρα κούπες κρασί να πίνουν.

98 As before, Kritoboulos's text is followed here by that of "Anakalema": ἐδίδοτο δὲ τὰ μὲν αὐτῶν τῷ πυρί / να καίουν τας εικόνας; βίβλοι τε ἱεραὶ καὶ θεῖαι . . . κατεπατοῦντο / να καταπατούν τα 'λόχρουσα βαγγέλια; ἀτίμως / καθυβρίζουν; κατεβάλλοντο μὲν ἀτίμως εἰς γῆν and συντριβόμενα ἐπὶ τῶν τριόδων ἐρρίπτειτο / να τους κατατσακίζουν; ἀπεσπᾶτο δὲ κόσμος ὁ τούτων / να παίρνουσιν τ' ασήμια τους και τα μαργαριτάρια and να παίρνουν τα λιθάρια των και την ευκόσμησίν των; τὰ τούτων ἐξήγετο λείψανα καὶ ἀτίμως λεπτυνόμενα καὶ λυόμενα εἰς ἀέρα ἑλίκματο, τὰ δὲ καὶ ἐπὶ τῶν ἀμφόδων ἐρρίπτειτο / και των αγίων τα λείψανα . . . να καίουν, ν' αφανίζουσιν, στην θάλασσαν να ρίπτουν; φιάλαι . . . ἐς προπόσεις ἦσαν καὶ μέθην αὐτοῖς / στ' άγια δισκοπότηρα κούπες κρασί να πίνουν.

99 Doukas, *Historia byzantina*, 291.b.16–22, 292.d.11–17, and Doukas, *Decline and Fall*, 227.20, 227.21: ἡ δὲ τῆς ἁρπαγῆς καὶ τοῦ ἑλκυσμοῦ αἰτία πλόκαμοι τριχῶν, στηθέων καὶ μασθῶν ἀποκαλύψεις, βραχιόνων ἐκτάσεις . . . παρθένους ἃς οὐχ ἑώρα ἥλιος, παρθένους ἃς ὁ γεννήσας μόλις ἔβλεπεν, ἑλκόμεναι, εἰ δὲ καὶ βία ἀντωθοῦντο, καὶ ῥαβδιζόμεναι . . . οἱ κύνες τὰς ἁγίας εἰκόνας

"Anakalema" is no doubt closer to Kritoboulos's narrative, displaying semantic, lexical, and structural affinities, sometimes even in the unfolding of imagery, to the extent that lines 63 to 77 feel like a paraphrase or a poetic remake of the historical text. And yet, as far as we know, Kritoboulos's *History*, like Doukas's, has survived in just one manuscript discovered in the archives of the Topkapı Palace in the mid-nineteenth century. This fact implies that the poet most likely had not consulted Kritoboulos.[100] As it happens, we do not know whether "Anakalema" was written before or after these histories. The only fairly safe conclusion we can reach is that the authors drew on common oral and written sources, including accounts of the Latin sack of Constantinople in 1204, which would have yielded a pool of formulas.[101] They likely also consulted early

---

κατέκοψαν τὸν κόσμον ἀφελόντες, τὰς ἁλύσεις, μανουάλια, ἐνδυτὰς τῆς ἁγίας τραπέζης, τὰ φωτοδόχα ἀγγεῖα, ἄλλα φθείροντες, ἕτερα λαμβάνοντες. τὰ τοῦ ἱεροῦ σκευοφυλακίου τίμια καὶ ἱερὰ σκεύη χρυσᾶ τε καὶ ἀργυρᾶ καὶ ἐξ ἄλλης τιμίας ὕλης κατασκευασθέντα ἅπαντα ἐν μιᾷ ῥοπῇ συνήγαγον, ἀφέντες τὸν ναὸν ἔρημον καὶ γυμνὸν, μηδ᾽ ὁτιοῦν καταλείψαντες. The historian makes use of the formulaic expression "it was a pitiful sight to behold" (καὶ ἦν ἰδεῖν θέαμα ἐλεεινὸν) (Doukas, *Historia byzantina*, 296.d.8, and Doukas, *Decline and Fall*, 229.29), also found in Kritoboulos as an introductory comment to the passage on rape ("there was a further sight, terrible and pitiful" [καὶ ἦν ἰδεῖν θέαμα δεινὸν καὶ ἐλεεινὸν], Kritoboulos, *Historiae*, 71, 61.5.25, and Kritoboulos, *History*, 72.240), in Christonymos (καὶ ἦν ἰδέσθαι θέαμα ἐλεεινὸν in Lambros, *Νέος Ἑλληνομνήμων*, 237.1), and others. Christonymos makes a similar reference to virgins who are forced out of maidens' apartments: παρθένους ἐκ παρθενώνων ἐξερχομένας (ibid., 237.23). As already noted, Doukas "reports" the emperor's final words as, "Is there no one among the Christians who will take my head from me?"

100 Kritoboulos's manuscript was first edited in 1870 (B. Braude, "The Success of Religion as a Source for Compromise in Divided Empires: Ottoman and Safavid, Past and Present," in *Power Sharing in Deeply Divided Places*, ed. J. McEvoy and B. O'Lear [Philadelphia, PA, 2013], 176–97, at 180, 195). For a somewhat similar description but with different phraseology and less detail, see Christonymos (in Lambros, *Νέος Ἑλληνομνήμων*, 237.1–21). Contrary to Laonikos Chalkokondyles's *Histories*, which "survives in about thirty manuscripts, far outpacing his potential Greek rivals," Kritoboulos "survived in one copy in the sultan's private library" and Doukas "survives (effectively) in one copy too" (A. Kaldellis, *A New Herodotos: Laonikos Chalkokondyles on the Ottoman Empire, the Fall of Byzantium, and the Emergence of the West*, Dumbarton Oaks Medieval Library Suppl. [Washington, DC, 2014], 238).

101 In his description of the Latin sack of Constantinople, the historian Niketas Choniates writes: "O, the shameful dashing to earth of the venerable icons and the flinging of the relics of the saints, who had Alexios Doukas suffered for Christ's sake, into defiled places! How horrible it was to see the Divine Body and Blood of Christ poured out and thrown to the ground! These forerunners of Antichrist..." (N. Choniates, *O City of Byzantium, Annals of Niketas Choniates*, trans. H. J. Magoulias [Detroit, MI, 1984], 314–15). Likewise, in his funeral oration for his brother, the metropolitan of Ephesus, Nikolaos Mesarites, who was an eyewitness of the sack of Constantinople by the Crusaders, laments the plundering and atrocities perpetrated by

narratives of the conquest, like the "Letter to all Christians" by Cardinal Isidore, who defended the city, and was wounded, captured, and eventually ransomed on the same day. This was possibly Isidore's most famous letter, dated 8 July 1453 and recorded in nine manuscripts, eight of them from the fifteenth century. The letter, which survives in Latin, may have been drafted in Greek and then translated, as the cardinal "never managed to master Latin."[102] Morgan, in fact, argues that the poem was composed with Isidore's letter "in mind, if not in hand," as the two of them reveal significant similarities.[103] At any rate, if Kritoboulos's *History* is a biography of "the Great Sultan Mehmed," praising, to some degree at least, the conqueror's bravery and wit, "Anakalema" is surely an antibiography, a diatribe against "Mehmed, the dog."[104] At the same time, it becomes clear that the poet's trauma claim relies, according to Alexander, as much on available symbolic resources as it does on the specificities of the historical moment.

The dramatic description of the three-day sack of the city and its aftermath is introduced (lines 57–62) and concluded (lines 87–88) with apotropaic

the Crusaders. They "sacked the sacred places and trampled on the divine things [and] ran riot over the holy vessels... they tore children from their mothers and mothers from their children, and they defiled the virgins in the holy chapels" (D. J. Geanakoplos, *Byzantium: Church, Society, and Civilization Seen through Contemporary Eyes* [Chicago, IL, 1984], 369). In both these texts we come across some of the stock images found in "Anakalema," Kritoboulos, Doukas, and others.

102 Philippides and Hanak, *Siege of Constantinople*, 27–28. For Cardinal Isidore's text, see J.-B. L'Écuy, ed., *De capta a Mehemethe II Constantinopoli, Leonardi Chiensis et Godefridi Langi narrationes, sibi invicem collatae* (Paris, 1823), 76–91. His letter is addressed to *universis Christi Fidelibus*.

103 Compare lines 71–78 of "Anakalema" to *tam nobiles quam populares, tam monachos et monachas consecratos, quam etiam alios simplices populares. Et feminas virtute praeditas et nobilitate, vituperose et indecorate detractas.... Adolescentulos vero et adolescentulas, pueros et puellas, a parentibus segregabat, et divisim eos vendebat*. Also compare να καίουν τας εικόνας, / να σχίζουν, να καταπατούν τα 'λόχρουσα βαγγέλια (lines 63–64) to *imagines... pedibus conculcarunt, deturparunt et diripuerunt*; να καθυβρίζουν τους σταυρούς, να τους κατατσακίζουν (line 65) to *et crucem Christi... dejecerunt et diripuerunt*; και των αγίων τα λείψανα (line 67) to *sacris corporibus Sanctorum, quae laniabant et vastabant*; and την ευκόσμησίν των (line 69) to *sacras et sanctas stolas*. Morgan mentions another similarity between the two texts. See τα πέπλα της τραπέζας / της παναγίας, της σεπτής, τα καθιερωμένα / τα σκεύη τα πανάγια (lines 109–11) and *Similia his, et in sacra pepla, hoc est, paramenta Ecclesiae egerunt* (Morgan, "Cretan Poetry," 397–99, and L'Écuy, *De capta a Mehemethe II Constantinopoli*, 80, 84). Kritoboulos is vague about his sources, which, he tells us, were oral in nature (both Greek and Turkish) (D. R. Reinsch, "Εισαγωγή," in Kritoboulos, Ιστορία, 7–19, at 14, and L. Neville, *Guide to Byzantine Historical Writing* [Cambridge, 2018], 309).

104 Kritoboulos, *Historiae*, 11, 3, and Kritoboulos, *History*, 7: Μεχεμέτι μεγίστου αυτοκράτορος. "Anakalema": το σκύλον Μαχουμέτην (line 44).

invocations of the sun and the moon. Kehayoglou notes that the invocation of celestial bodies as "witnesses of suffering and injustice" is a stock element of monodies and supplications (*deeseis*).[105] The poet pleads with the sun and the moon not to shed light on Constantinople so that the Turks cannot see to commit their crimes, and asks the sky and earth not to bear their wrongdoings. Invocations of nature were employed in the ancient ritual lament for the dying god, as, for instance, in the *Epitaphios of Adonis*, where Aphrodite calls "on the mountains, valleys, and streams to join her lament for Adonis." Alexiou has traced the history of such invocations from antiquity to Byzantine learned literature and folk songs, where the sun and the moon in particular play prominent parts.[106] García Ortega and Fernández Galvín specify that the poem's invocation of the celestial bodies is a leitmotiv in threnoi, monodies, and folk songs about the fall of cities.[107]

Eschatological narratives are also known for being attuned to cataclysmic events. Book one of *Dioptra* ("Weeping and Mourning"), for instance, makes reference to the day "when the sun does not shine nor does the moon cast light / when the stars fall like tree leaves," a point that takes us back to the Byzantines' anxious anticipation of the end of the world or *synteleia* (see fig. 1).[108] The death of Byzantium is presented eschatologically as a threat to the entire Greek, if not the entire Christian, world, and the trauma is projected as an indelible catastrophe threatening the existence of Romaioi everywhere.[109] Evidently the numerous allusions to darkness and death throughout the poem furnish the backdrop against which this trauma process is played out.

---

105 Kehayoglou, "Ἐπίμετρο," 69. Karanika similarly observes that the use of the imperative at this point gives this part of the poem "a prayer form" (Karanika, "Messengers, Angels, and Laments," 236).

106 Alexiou, *Ritual Lament*, 56, 67. The *Epitaphios of Adonis* is attributed to Bion (early third century BCE).

107 García Ortega and Fernández Galvín, *Trenos por Constantinopla*, 135. See, for instance, the threnos "Sack of Constantinople" (in Zoras, Βυζαντινή ποίησις, 186.406–412) and the monodies of Kallistos (in Lambros, Νέος Ἑλληνομνήμων, 216.7–8), Christonymos (ibid., 239.3–6), and Ioannis Eugenikos (ibid., 245.9–14).

108 In Miklas and Fuchsbauer, *Die kirchenslavische Übersetzung*, 370.118–119: ὅταν οὐ λάμπῃ ἥλιος οὐδ' ἡ σελήνη φέγγει / ὅταν τὰ ἄστρα πίπτωσιν ὥσπερ φύλλα τῶν δένδρων. On the end of the Byzantine Empire in connection with the end of the world, see "Sack of Constantinople": "This is the destruction of the world and a great *synteleia* / the end of the Christians, the poor Romaioi" (Ἔνι του κόσμου χαλασμός και συντελειά μεγάλη / συντελεσμός των χριστιανών, των ταπεινών Ρωμαίων) (in Zoras, Βυζαντινή ποίησις, 180.130–131).

109 Smelser, "Psychological Trauma," 44.

The poet's claim of the existence of a massively disruptive trauma culminates in the "allegory" injected in line 89. Foundational myths of Constantinople and beliefs of the time concerning the advent of the Antichrist and *synteleia* come together here in a way that is vital to the meaning-making process.[110] While eschatology heightens the threat, the allegory presupposes a degree of dissociation between signifier and signified as the audience is admonished that what is about to be uttered should be construed allegorically, not literally, and in this case historically, not metaphysically.[111] This enables a semantic slippage between an eschatological account that heralds the end of the world and one that warns of the presence of a threat that could bring about the end of the community at any moment. Such an interpretive shift from fact to possibility and from occurrence to risk is key to establishing the events of the fall as a cultural trauma. For culture creators and audiences in Lusignan Cyprus, Venetian Crete, Hospitaller Rhodes, and other parts of the Greek world not yet under Ottoman rule, the end has not come but *could* come soon. The threat of cultural trauma needs to be imminent.

The allegory begins with the equation of Constantinople with the moon and of the emperors Constantine the Great and Justinian I—the founders of the city and Hagia Sophia, respectively, who are depicted in a mosaic in the southwest vestibule of the latter (fig. 13)—with the sun (lines 90–91, 98–105). These parallelisms lend continuity to the threnos while casting the foundational myth of the city upon the bleak canvas of the poem, populated, as we have seen, with frequent juxtapositions of light and darkness and with invocations of celestial bodies. The attention soon moves to Hagia Sophia as a synecdoche for Constantinople. The centrality of the church to the representation of trauma here and elsewhere in the poem resonates with the role it plays in the foreboding narratives of the fall. Whenever he "call[s] to mind" Hagia Sophia and the "beauties" of the city (line 106), the poet tells us, he "sigh[s] and mourn[s] and beat[s his] breast, / [he] weep[s] and shed[s] tears with wailing and distress" (lines 107–8), which is matched, as Morgan points out, by Cardinal Isidore's "polished horror," expressed in his letter of 8 July 1453.[112]

A degendered rhetorical reconstruction of a proper ritual lament, the poet's remembrance of the "all-holy City" (line 104) is an act of commemoration and

---

110 On the topic of the Antichrist, see Kehayoglou, "Επίμετρο," 74–75.

111 We shall see that this reading is supported by the fact that, contrary to other threnoi and particularly those written by the clergy, there is no sign of theodicy in "Anakalema."

112 Morgan, "Cretan Poetry," 399; Cardinal Isidore writes: *Sed cum memoriae tradidero, totus tremo* (in L'Écuy, *De capta a Mehemethe II Constantinopoli*, 84).

Fig. 13. Emperors Justinian I (left) and Constantine (right) offering models of Hagia Sophia and Constantinople to the Virgin. Mosaic, tenth century, Istanbul, Hagia Sophia, southwest vestibule. Artwork in the public domain; photograph by Myrabella, courtesy of Wikimedia Commons (CC0 1.0).

an accurate enactment of the emperor's earlier instructions, which involved weeping and breast-beating (lines 39–40). The aesthetic realm has already allowed for the trauma process to unfold and the claim to be made. Now, thanks to the poem's reflexivity, the cultural trauma is also commemorated in the poet's ritual lament. "Anakalema," in fact, emerges as a circular and connotatively infinite poem of lamentations. The author's anakalema contains the boat's threnos within which we find embedded the emperor's lament, which, in turn, includes the Cretans' prescribed ritual lamentation that the poet, in a circular maneuver, reenacts toward the end of the composition, just before the allegorical finale. At the epicenter of these concentric circles of lamentation lies the cultural trauma.

The city lament is among the oldest types of public commemoration. Early surviving examples of such laments come from the ancient Near East. They are laments about cities abandoned by their gods and originate in the first half of the second millennium BCE.[113] God's departure from Constantinople, an

113   A. Suter, "Introduction," in Bachvarova, Dutsch, and Suter, *Fall of Cities*, 1–12, at 2–4; and J. Jacobs, "The City Lament Genre in the Ancient Near East," in Bachvarova, Dutsch, and Suter, *Fall of Cities*, 13–35.

idea raised in Nestor-Iskander's description of the towering flame over Hagia Sophia during the siege (see fig. 3), is narrated here in the form of a "historiola,"[114] which encapsulates one of the foundational myths of Hagia Sophia. The story is reported in *Patria Konstantinoupoleos* (*Patria of Constantinople*), a tenth-century collection of texts on the history, topography, and monuments of the imperial city, and is cited by the Castilian historian Pero Tafur, who had visited Constantinople in the 1430s.[115] Legend has it, recounts Tafur, that "when Constantine built his church, he used many people as his laborers and one day the master-builder ordered a child who was there to guard the implements." The boy did as he was instructed, until "a very handsome man on a horse appeared to him and said: '. . . Go without fear and I promise you that I will guard the church and the city until you return.'" The child, continues Tafur, "did so, and a very handsome man on horseback appeared and the child left but did not return at all, because he feared punishment. And so the horseman remained in accordance with the promise that he had made. And they say that he was an angel." Tafur goes on to compare the two Ottoman sieges of Constantinople—the first, unsuccessful, by Murad II in 1422 and the second by Mehmed II in 1453—before he concludes: "Yet it can be said now that the child had come back and that the angel has left his post, for the city has been captured and is under occupation; but back then the Turk departed."[116] Tafur's familiarity with the legend, asserts Karanika, shows that it was circulated orally around the time of the conquest.[117] Philippides and Hanak confirm that the story was known widely throughout Christendom and that the angel was very often thought to be the archangel Michael, adding that echoes of the legend are present in "Anakalema."[118]

After reciting the theme of the desacralization, this time in relation to Hagia Sophia (lines 109–111), the poet introduces the finale with the rhetorical question, "Was the angel watching, as he had been ordered to do?" (line 112). A few lines later the response is given in the emphatic antithesis: "The young man is coming back, the angel has gone away." In the angel's place arrives a young man;

114   Karanika, "Messengers, Angels, and Laments," 237.
115   For the relevant quote in *Patria*, see T. Preger, ed., *Scriptores originum Constantinopolitanarum*, 2 vols. (Leipzig, 1901–7), 1:83–88, also cited in Karanika, "Messengers, Angels, and Laments," 240–41.
116   In Philippides and Hanak, *Siege of Constantinople*, 217–18.
117   Karanika, "Messengers, Angels, and Laments," 239.
118   Philippides and Hanak, *Siege of Constantinople*, 218.

not that of the "founders," we are told, "but another young man." The young man of lore is swapped for the twenty-one-year-old Mehmed, who becomes the "forerunner of Antichrist" (lines 115–18). Appearing in the epistles of John, the Antichrist finds an early manifestation in Paul's Second Epistle to the Thessalonians, where he is referred to not as Antichrist but as "the lawless one" (*anomos*) who will precede the coming of Christ. He will act "with the power of Satan" and mislead the flock "with false signs and wonders."[119] Mehmed is called *anomos* in "Anakalema" (line 49). So too are his men, "those lawless ones" (*anomoi*, line 56) and "the lawless dogs" (*anoma skulia*, line 21) who commit "unlawful acts" or "crimes" (*anomies*). Their wrongdoings against the Romaioi are foregrounded by the repetition of both words (a case of polyptoton) in line 62: "for the lawless [*anoma*] dogs to see to commit their crimes [*anomies*]."[120] Of course, neither Mehmed nor his men are interested in deceiving the Byzantines with false signs and wonders. Their role as conquerors is clear, a point that takes me back to my earlier argument about the interpretive shift from the metaphysical to the historical. The poet of "Anakalema" turns the Antichrist of the allegory into a secular historical figure through the perpetrators of the trauma, the "bloodthirsty dogs" (line 85). In this way Christian eschatology collapses into history and the cultural trauma is fixed as an imminent threat to all those who regard themselves as Romaioi. The poem here seems to draw on Cardinal Isidore's letter, where Morgan finds the first reference to Mehmed as the forerunner of Antichrist, a further indication that the poet may have been familiar with that narrative.[121]

The angel's departure from Hagia Sophia, with its obvious overtones of divine abandonment, signals the end of Byzantium. But contrary to other threnoi, where theodicy is a staple, "Anakalema" moves away from moralizing subtexts. When the trauma process takes place in the religious realm, observes Alexander, trauma is linked to theodicy. He cites as an example the story of Job, which asks why God allows evil to happen. Any attempt to answer this

---

119 2 Thess. 2:3–12: κατ' ἐνέργειαν τοῦ σατανᾶ ... σημείοις καὶ τέρασι ψεύδους. See L. J. Lietaert Peerbolte, "Antichrist," in *Dictionary of Deities and Demons in the Bible*, ed. K. van der Toorn, B. Becking, and P. W. van der Horst (Leiden and Grand Rapids, MI, 1999), 62–64, at 63.

120 There is a further reference to Mehmed as "lawless" in the genitive, *anomou* (line 48).

121 Morgan, "Cretan Poetry," 398, 401. Cardinal Isidore writes: *Quoniam jam prope Anti-Christi praecursor, Teuchrorum princeps et dominus, cujus nomen est Machometta* ... (in L'Écuy, *De capta a Mehemethe II Constantinopoli*, 79). As seen in n. 101 above, the same expression was used by Choniates for the Latins who sacked the city in 1204.

question "will generate searching discussions about whether and how human beings strayed from divinely inspired ethics and sacred law."[122] There are several threnoi that engage in relevant discussions, mainly (but not exclusively) those devised by members of the clergy, who typically attribute the events to sinfulness. "It is because of bad Christians that the city was lost," we learn in "Sack of Constantinople,"[123] a contemporary threnos composed, according to Günther Steffen Heinrich, by Emmanuel Georgilas Limenitis, a cleric who also wrote "The Plague of Rhodes" ("Thanatikon tes Rodou") (1498).[124] Similarly, Goldwyn points out that in "Lament and Weeping for Constantinople" ("Threnos kai klauthmos peri tes Konstantinoupoleos"),[125] the bishop of Myra, Matthaios, reads the fall of Constantinople, "a new Sodom and Gomorrah," as part of a divine plan to destroy cities of sinners,[126] while the anonymous poet of "Lament for Constantinople" ("Threnos Konstantinoupoleos"),[127] a redraft of Matthaios's lament, rehearses "the Biblical view of historical causation" by arguing that God punished Constantinople for its sinful emperors.[128]

We know that for the Russians, as well as for many Greek Orthodox, the conquest was a divine sanction for the Palaiologan royal family's barely concealed romance with Catholicism, which may have also prompted Nestor-Iskander's vision described earlier. The politically driven efforts at the Council of Ferrara-Florence (1438–1439) to unite the Western Catholic and Eastern Orthodox churches, separated since 1054, were meant to draw Western military support against the advancing Ottomans, but for much of the Greek Orthodox

---

122 Alexander, "Toward a Theory," 15. García Ortega and Fernández Galvín remind us that the topos of theodicy found in threnoi is present in the *Book of Lamentations* (García Ortega and Fernández Galvín, *Trenos por Constantinopla*, 19).

123 In Zoras, Βυζαντινή ποίησις, 190.662: διά κακούς χριστιανούς εχάθη τέτοια χώρα.

124 See G. S. Heinrich, "Ποιος έγραψε το ποίημα Άλωσις της Κωνσταντινουπόλεως *(BB 1, 177–197),*" in *Constantinopla: 550 años de su caída / Κωνσταντινούπολη: 550 χρόνια από την άλωση*, 3 vols., ed. E. Motos Guirao and M. Morfakidis Filactos (Granada, 2006), 2:405–14, at 412.

125 In Zoras, Βυζαντινή ποίησις, 207–16.

126 Goldwyn, "'I come from a cursed land,'" 103–4.

127 In Zoras, Βυζαντινή ποίησις, 220–21.

128 Goldwyn, "'I come from a cursed land,'" 102. For specific examples of theodicy in threnoi, see "Sack of Constantinople" ("Halosis Konstantinoupoleos") (in Zoras, Βυζαντινή ποίησις, 190.661–672); "Lament for Constantinople" ("Threnos tes Konstantinoupoleos") (ibid., 201.70–71); "Lament of the Four Patriarchates: Constantinople, Alexandria, Antioch, and Jerusalem" ("Threnos ton tessaron patriarcheion Konstantinoupoles, Alexandreias, Antiocheias kai Ierousalem") (ibid., 207.100); "Lament and Weeping for Constantinople" ("Threnos kai klauthmos peri tes Konstantinoupoleos") (ibid., 210.2477–2480); and "Lament for Constantinople" ("Threnos Konstantinoupoleos") (ibid., 220.13–24).

populace the move simply signified capitulation to the Latin church. As a result, some Byzantines read the Ottoman rule both as divine punishment and protection from the Latins,[129] while the church of Hagia Sophia, where the union was formally celebrated in December 1452, was seen by antiunionists as contaminated, a heretical place they should avoid at all costs. And so they did, until the dramatic day of the fall when ironically many sought refuge there.[130]

Such antiunionist sentiments are alien to "Anakalema," and the absence of theodicy in the poem has its correlate in popular tradition. The clergy's moral narrative, asserts Saunier, does not seem to have taken root in folk songs. In the Greek imagination, responsibility falls virtually always on the masters (*aphentades*), whereas common people are usually portrayed as innocent victims of overwhelming catastrophes, whether personal, as in folk laments (moirologia), or collective, as in historical folk songs. In Pontic songs about the fall of Trebizond, God is identified as the perpetrator of the tragedy. The scope of the disaster is such that divine involvement must be assumed. In these compositions, adds Saunier, people explicitly blame God for their ordeal, acquitting themselves of any wrongdoing. He concludes that "lamentation and the unshaken belief in the innocence of Hellenism" are leitmotivs in the otherwise diverse corpus of folk city laments.[131]

For all the archaizing language of the finale, "Anakalema" once again aligns itself with folk tradition and, crucially, with the collective consciousness. Theodicy is exchanged for divine betrayal in the final line—"angels and saints no longer help" (line 118), and they, along with the "lawless dogs," are responsible for the cultural trauma. The poem's strong ties with folk tradition are confirmed by the appearance of the threnos in several anthologies of Greek folk songs, among them that of the Academy of Athens. Symbolic sources pertaining to folk poetry serve as an interpretive vehicle through which the poet can powerfully and widely disseminate his trauma claim.[132] That the poem is mostly written in the standard Greek of the time, the Byzantine *koine*, with only some idiomatic variants, may reflect the author's effort to make his text intelligible to the broader community.

129   K. E. Fleming, "Constantinople: From Christianity to Islam," *The Classical World* 97.1 (2003): 69–78, at 71–76; D. Stathakopoulos, Μικρή ιστορία της Βυζαντινής Αυτοκρατορίας (Athens, 2017), 331.

130   Philippides and Hanak, *Siege of Constantinople*, 227–31.

131   Saunier, "Οι αρχές," 260–62. There is no blame on the masters in "Anakalema," where the Byzantine emperor is described in the most positive terms.

132   Alexander, "Toward a Theory," 27.

We have seen that the trauma claim of "Anakalema" drew on familiar cultural and aesthetic traditions, such as threnoi, monodies, supplications (*deeseis*), lore, ritual lamentation, and folk songs, as well as on the historical situation recorded in contemporary texts by Doukas, Pusculo, Benvenuto, Cardinal Isidore, Kritoboulos, and others. By addressing a series of key questions (what happened, who suffered, who did it, and what is the relationship between the victim and the target audience?), the poet imaginatively reconstructed the fall of Constantinople as a massive disruption to the Greeks within and outside the borders of Byzantium. He was aided by a number of rhetorical devices, including rhetorical questions and repetition (e.g., anaphora and polyptoton), and by visual, auditory, and kinesthetic imagery, all of which encouraged affective and cognitive engagement with the collective trauma claim. The exoneration of the victims from any wrongdoing makes the poet's claim all the more compelling and heartbreaking.

Now what about the songs of the *Cantares mexicanos*? Was the siege and fall of the Mexica Empire seen as divine abandonment? Did the Mexica blame their gods or did they assume responsibility for their defeat? Does the trauma claim in the two Nahua songs follow paths of meaning-making similar to those of "Anakalema," and are compositions like these common in Nahua tradition? How did the indigenous see the transfer to Spanish rule?

Emblematic of the encounter of two worlds, the conquest of Mexico is documented in Spanish and indigenous accounts of the sixteenth century. Among the most significant are Cortés's letters to Emperor Charles V (1519–1526) and Díaz del Castillo's *True History of the Conquest of New Spain* (*Historia verdadera de la conquista de la Nueva España*) (1550s–1584), two classic narratives written from the viewpoint of the Spaniards, and book 12 of the *Florentine Codex* (ca. 1540–1585) and the *Annals of Tlatelolco* (*Anales de Tlatelolco*) (1540s), which convey the events from the perspective of the Mexica. The siege and fall of Tenochtitlan-Tlatelolco in 1521 are movingly reenacted in "Huexotzincayotl" and "Tlaxcaltecayotl," the two songs from *Cantares mexicanos* that, like "Anakalema," draw on the historical events and precontact symbolic resources to articulate their trauma claim.

Cantares mexicanos is preserved on folios 1r to 85r of the manuscript 1628 bis, Biblioteca Nacional de México, Mexico City, which contains texts in Nahuatl and Spanish. "Huexotzincayotl" (fig. 14) and "Tlaxcaltecayotl" are found on folios 6v–7r and 54r–55v respectively, with a variant of the latter recorded on folios 83r–85r. All songs are rendered in alphabetized Nahuatl following the rules of Castilian orthography.[133] Bierhorst observes that *Cantares mexicanos* is a Jesuit copy of a lost Franciscan original, or perhaps originals. The songs were largely collected from the 1550s to the 1570s (one or two were taken in the 1580s) from indigenous informants, most of them from Tenochtitlan and Tlatelolco, and some possibly from Mexico's close ally, Azcapotzalco (see fig. 8); according to Gary Tomlinson, *Cantares mexicanos* was likely copied from 1582 to 1597 from previous alphabetized sources.[134]

"Huexotzincayotl" and "Tlaxcaltecayotl" exploit the long tradition of pre-Hispanic cantares, or "poems accompanied by music."[135] Mexica singers who had received professional training before the conquest, argues Bierhorst, would be in their forties and fifties by the mid-sixteenth century, when work on the *Cantares mexicanos* is first reported. This activity appears to fade after 1585, which suggests that it may have relied on "these older singers, who, during the third quarter of the century, would have had ample opportunity to display the phraseology, if not the song forms, that they had learned in their youth."[136]

133 Tomlinson, *Singing of the New World*, 28.
134 Bierhorst, *Cantares*, xii, 9; Tomlinson, *Singing of the New World*, 28.
135 Bierhorst, "Translating an Esoteric Idiom," 371.
136 Bierhorst, *Cantares*, 106–9.

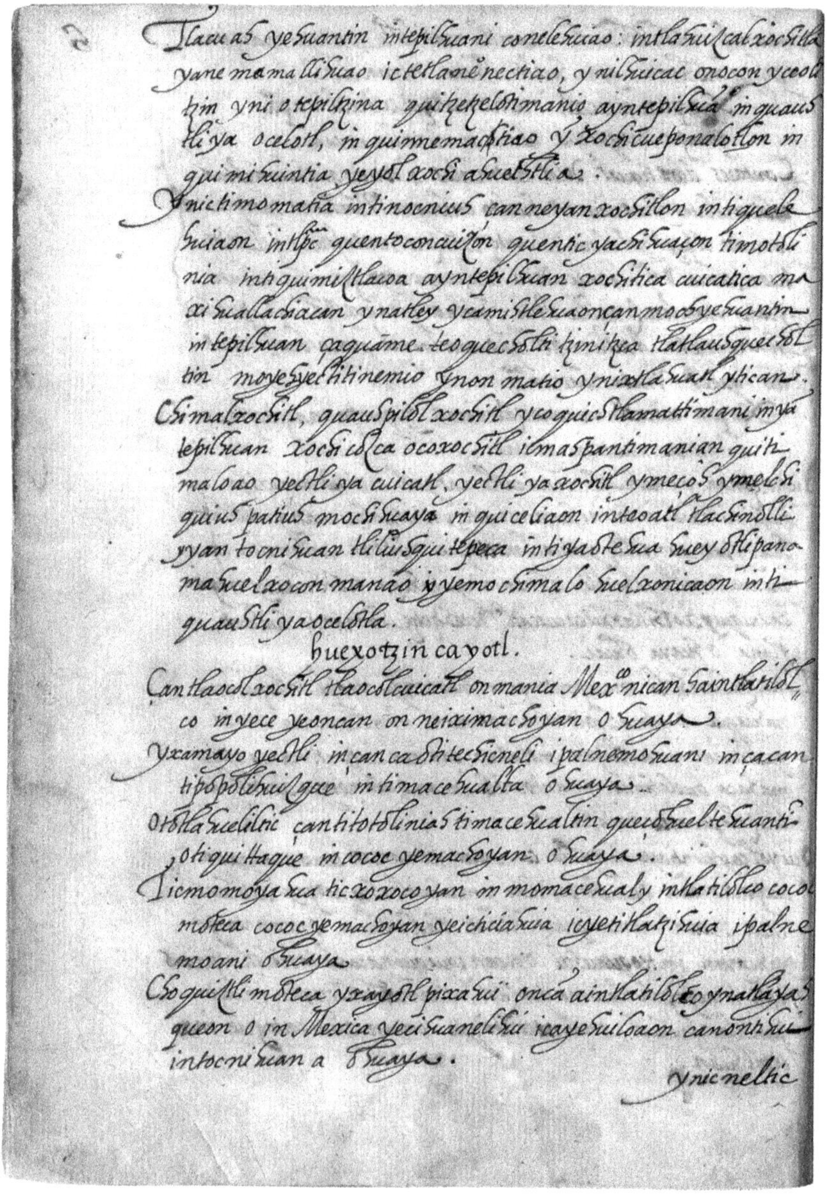

huexotzin cayotl.

Fig. 14. "Huexotzincayotl," in *Cantares mexicanos*, sixteenth century, Mexico City, Biblioteca Nacional de México, MS 1628 bis, fols. 6v–7r. Courtesy of the Biblioteca Nacional de México.

ynic neltic oyacatia atloyantepetl o m̄ Mex̄ inpocti etia
toc ayahuilon mantoc intoconyacah tieaya ipalnemoani
o tieaya.

ynan mexica maxiquilhia miquican oya cantopinguik
mohtia y ellelon imateuco yetian can yetian Dios yetia
anguinyeoncan incoyonacalco o tieaya.

Cacanyeoncan canguincho quit tlapaloa o anguituik manatl
incan yeicó motelchiuh bruya oanguinyemochin ha intlaylo
tlaqui, asintlacotzin, asintlacateuctli in oquichtin y tiichia
ica caye conya causqui intenochtitlan o tieaya.

ynantocnitican matai tocacan aya maxoconmatica ycaye
hiccausque Mexicayotl tieita can yeyatl chichix tiela nocan
ye tlagualli etieti eaya can con aysae tiuhqui nipalnemoani
ha in tlatiloteo y o tieaya.

Iel ahcan y tiian tiuco que ton in Motelchiuhtzin ha intlacotzin
can mocuica ellagtiauh toque Acachinanco in ab iguac inte
pan quixiloto in coyoticacan o tieaya.

✝ . I H S .

Nican ompehua in cuicatl intlatentia melatiuac tiuexotzinca
yotl icmoquittitoaya in tlatoque tiuexotzinca manimecat,
ca: yexian guica micttlatlamantitica, Teucuicatl ahno
ao quautiuicatl, xochicuicatl, icnocuicatl. Auh iniemo
tlotioha tiuetiuetl: cencamatl mocautiuitih, auh y nocen
camatl ipan tietzi yetetl ti: auh in tiuel icompehua ca
antetl ti, Auh iniemo ucepa quin yguac yticpetiue
tzi y tiuetiuetl can mocemana in maitl, auhtquini
guac yeinepantla occeppa iteneotiualetioloa in tiue
tiuetl: iel ye tiuatl iteotinotital, yniima ynaquin
cuicani guimati inictomohtlotioha. auhya
cuican yenoceppa ynincuicatl yehua D. Diego
deleon Gouer nador Azcapotaleo: yetiatl oquitho
tzon in D. H̄o Plauda y pan acitiuik 1551.
y pan metcalilitzin H̄o feu etiito.

Huexotzincayotl

Çan tlaocolxochitl tlaocolcuicatl onmania Mex^co nican ha in tlatilolco
in yece ye oncanon neiximachoyan ohuaya.

Yxamayo yectli in çan ca otitechicneli ipalnemohuani in ça can
tipopolihuizque in timacehualta ohuaya.

Ototlahueliltic çan titotoliniah timacehualtin queçohuel tehuantin
otiquittaque in cococ ye machoyan ohuaya.

Ticmomoyahua ticxoxocoyan in momacehualy in tlatilolco cococ
moteca cococ ye machoyan yeic ticiahuia ic ye titlatzihuia
ipalnemoani ohuaya.

Choquiztli moteca yxayotl pixahui oncã a in tlatilolco yn atlã yahqueon o
in Mexica ye cihua nel ihui ica ye huiloaon canon tihui in tocnihuan
a ohuaya.   5

Ynic neltic oyacahua atlo yan tepetl o in Mex^co in poctli ehuatoc
ayahuitl onmantoc in toconyachihuaya ipalnemoani ohuaya.

Yn anmexica ma xiquilnamiquican oya çan topan quitemohuia yellelon
imahuiço yehuan çan yehuan Dios yehua anquin ye oncan in
coyonacazco ohuaya.

Ça can ye oncan çan quinchoquiztlapaloa o anqui huitzmanatl in çan
ye iuh motelchiuh onya o anquin ye mochin ha in tlaylotlaqui,
ah in tlacotzin, ah in tlacateuctli in oquihtzin y hui hui ica çã ye
conyacauhqui in tenochtitlan ohuaya.

Yn antocnihuan ma xachocacan aya ma xoconmaticã yca ye ticcauhque
Mexicayotl huiya çan ye y atl chichix huiya no çan ye tlaqualli
chichix aya çan conayachiuhqui in ipalnemoani ha in tlatilolco y
ohuaya.

Tel ah çan yhuian huicoquehon in Motelchiuhtzin ha in tlacotzin çan
mocuicaellaquauhque Acachinanco in ah iquac in tlepan quixtiloto
in coyohuacan ohuaya.   10

Huexotzinca Piece

Only sad flowers, sad songs, lie here in Mexico, in Tlatelolco. Beyond is
    the place where recognition is achieved.
O Life Giver, it's good to know that you favored us, and we commoners
    will perish.
How unfortunate are we, we poor ones, we commoners! How favored are
    we? We've seen it: it's misery, yes, it is known.
In Tlatelolco you disperse your underlings, you rout them. Misery
    spreads, misery is known, because we were weary, because we were
    lax. O Life Giver!
Tears are pouring, teardrops are raining there in Tlatelolco. The Mexica
    have gone into the water; along with the women they go. There we
    go, our friends.   5
True it is. They forsake the city of Mexico. The smoke is rising,
    the haze is spreading. This is your doing, O Life Giver.
Mexicans, remember that he who sends down on us his agony, his fear, is
    none but God, alas, there in Coyonacazco.

There the captain, Motelchiuh, addresses them tearfully, all of them, ah!
    the Arbiter, ah! Tlacotzin, ah! Commander Oquiztzin, alas, alas.
    And so he's abandoned Tenochtitlan.

You friends of ours, weep and acknowledge that we have abandoned all
    that is Mexicaness. The water is bitter, also the food is bitter. This is
    the doing of Life Giver in Tlatelolco.

Yet peacefully were Motelchiuh and Tlacotzin taken away. They fortified
    themselves with song in Acachinanco when they went to be
    delivered to the fire in Coyohuacan.   10

Tlaxcaltecayotl

Otacico ye nican Tenochtitlan y ximochicahuacã antlaxcalteca ye
　　huexotzinca quen concaquiz teuctlo xicotencatly y nelpiloniya
　　ximochicahuacan netlaya.　　　　　　　　　　　　　　　　　　1
Hualtzatzia in tachcauh in quauhtencoztli çan conilhuia in capitani
　　ya o tonã ye malintzin y xacaltecoz acachinanco otacico huel
　　ximochicahuacã netlaya.　　　　　　　　　　　　　　　　　　2
Tlaoc toconchiacã ynacal capitan aya huel ye oqui hualaci yn iquachpã
　　in tepepolli çan ye ixpã aya ye ixpolihuio in macehualtin Mexicame
　　hue ximochicahuacan netleya.　　　　　　　　　　　　　　　3
Xiquinpalehuican totecuiyohuan a ayahue tepoztlahuiceque quixixinia
　　atlon yan tepetl quixixinia Mexicayotl ximochicahuacã netlaya.　　4
. . .

　　　　　　　　　　　Yc ontetl huehuetl
Tla huel xiquimottacan a yehuantin chimaltica mittotia, a, otonnexineque
　　in tehuetzquiti yn tecoatzin tlehnoço anyezque mayecuele ma
　　onnetotilo in tla xicuica anicahuan, Ma cecen otlipan ximochicahuacã
　　ticohuayhuitl in tiitzpotonqui tle'noço anyezque maocyecuele ma
　　õnehtotilo yn tla xicuicacan annicahuan.　　　　　　　　　　10
Onel ticyacauhque tla xicaqui ye nocuic in tauh totepeuh in tenochtitlã
　　o Mex^{co}nican in huel nelli, a, niquittohua niqueehua yeehua ye
　　tonacizquia inn izta nanauhca in tlatelolco ma çan tlapic ye mochiuh
　　Tlaxcalteca aya yn tla xicuicacan annicahuan.　　　　　　　11
Çan nicyaittac nicmahuiço ye oncã Nanahuacalteuctli chimaltica y
　　expalatica yequene quihualtocaya in Tlaxcalteca aya in caxtillan
　　tlaca Atitlan quincahuato ya tacitoya ma çan tlapic ommochiuh
　　Tlaxcalteca aya in tla xicuicacã anicahuan.　　　　　　　　12

　　　　　　　　　　　Yc yey huehuetl
. . . tlaxcalteca ỹ meetlo ye huexotzinca y meetla　　　　　　　13
. . .

Tlaxcala Piece

A

We've arrived here in Tenochtitlan! "Be strong, Tlaxcalans!
  Huexotzincans!" And what will Nelpiloni be hearing from Lord
  Xicotencatl? "Be strong! Hail!" 1
The leader, Cuauhtencoztli comes shouting. The captain, Doña
  Marina, says, "Disembark! We've arrived in Acachinanco!" Be
  strong! Hail! 2
"Let's keep watch for the captain's boats. And ah, his banner is just
  coming in from Tepepol. Beneath it the commoners, the Mexica
  are ravaged." Woe! Be strong! Hail! 3
Give aid to our lords! Those with metal weapons are wrecking the city,
  they're wrecking Mexicaness! Be strong! Hail! 4
. . .

B
Second drum-*cadence*

See them dancing with their shields! We've cut off our hair, O
  Tehuetzquiti, O Tecoatzin! What else would you do? Onward!
  Let there be dancing! Sing, brothers! Everybody on the road!
  Be strong! O Coaihuitl, O Itzpotonqui, what else would you do?
  Onward! Let there be dancing! Sing, brothers! 10
Truly we've abandoned—hear my songs!—this, our city, this Tenochtitlan,
  here in Mexico. Oh I sing them in earnest, I utter them, ah! And we
  would have arrived in Tlatelolco from the four directions. May it not
  be in vain that it has happened, Tlaxcalans! Aya! Sing, brothers! 11
I only saw Lord Anahuacatl there and marveled at him. Finally, with
  shields and swords they were chasing him, they the Tlaxcalans, aya!
  and they the Castilians. Off he goes, into the water, leaving them
  behind. And off we go—to arrive! May it not be in vain that it has
  happened, Tlaxcalans! Sing, brothers! 12

C
Third drum-*cadence*

. . . Tlaxcalans, hey! Huexotzincans, hey! 13
. . .

Yc nahui huehuetl

Yn huel ximotzomoco ma xõmicalita çan titlacateccatl a yn temilotzin
  ỹ ye oquiçaco in imacal caxtilteca chinanpã,neca yaoyahualolo in
  tenochcatlaya yaoyahualolo in tlatelolcatl.   19
Ỹ oc tlatzatzaquatoa in tlacochcalcatl in coyohuehuétzin a ye on
  oquiçaco in Acolihua o in Tepeyacac o in huey otli ypan
  yaoyahualolo in Tenochcatla yaoyahualolo in Tlatelolcatla.   20
In ye huel patiohuay in Tenochtitlan y ye ixpolihuio ye ipilhuã in ye
  çan yehuan Tiox chalchiuhcapitan yehuan Guzma Mex^co nicã
  yaoyahualolo in Tenochcatla yaoyahualolo Tlatelolcatla.   21
Y xiuhhualcapoztica tla'tlahtlatzinia ayahuitl moteca y no conanque
  ya in quauhtemoctzin a yahue cém atl onmantia ỹ Mexica in
  tepilhuan aya yaoyahualolo in Tenochcatl in Tlatelolcatla.   22

Yc macuilli huehuetl

Ma xiquilnamiquican Tlaxcalteca tomachhuã yn iuhqui ticchiuhque
  Coyonacazco Neiçoquihuiloc in Mexica ye cihua ye tepepenalo
  in tlacahuaque ayahue.   23
… yahue yn iuhqui oticchiuhque coyonacazco neiçoquihuiloc in
  Mexica ye cihua ye tepepenalo ỹ tlacahuaque ayahue.   24
. . .
In chiucnahuilhuitica onteaxitilo in Coyohuacã in Quauhtemoctzin
  in Coanacoch tetlepanquetzatzin ye neculilolo in ãteteuctin ayyo.   27
Quimonellaquaya, a, in Tlacotzin ye quimonilhuia o Ahua tomachvane
  ximochihuacan aya teocuitlatepozmecatica ya onilpiloque ỹ
  ayahue ye neculilolo ỹ anteteuctin ayyo.   28
I yn quihualittohua o in tlatoani o in Quauhtemoctzina, Ahua
  nomatzine can tonanaloc tontzitzquiloc ac ynahuac timotlalia
  Genelal Capitan ahuaye nella toya yxapeltzina ahuaya
  nomachticatzine ayaya nella aye neculilolo in teteuctin ayyo.   29
… ahua nomatzine can analoc tontzitzquiloc aqu inahuac aya
  timotlalia in Genelal Capitan ahuaye nella toya yxapeltzina yahue
  ye neculilolo ya teteucti aayo ye neculilolo ya teteuctin ayyo.   30

D
Fourth drum-*cadence*

Gather your strength and go fight, O Commander, O Temilotzin.
Castilians and Chinampanecs are coming in with boats. Tenochcans
are surrounded, Tlatelolcans are surrounded.   19
Meanwhile the troop chief Coyohuehuetzin throws up barricades.
Acolhuans are coming down the Tepeyacac causeway! Tenochcans
are surrounded, Tlatelolcans are surrounded.   20
He who might serve as a payment for Tenochtitlan, he who's destroyed,
is one of the children of God the jade captain: it's Guzmán, here in
Mexico! Tenochcans are surrounded, Tlatelolcans are surrounded. 21
It thunders and thunders from out of a turquoise harquebus, and the
vapor rolls. They've even seized Cuauhtemoc. All the Mexica lords go
off through the water. Tenochcans are surrounded, Tlatelolcans are
surrounded.   22

E
Fifth drum-*cadence*

My dear Tlaxcalan nephews, now remember how we did it in
Coyonacazco: the Mexica women muddied their faces, and all the
masters made their choices.   23
. . . Ah! This is how we did it in Coyonacazco: the Mexica women
muddied their faces, and all the masters made their choices.   24
. . .
After nine days Cuauhtemoc, Coanacoch, and Tetlepanquetzatzin were
brought to Coyohuacan. Yes, all you lords are seized!   27
Tlacotzin cheers them, saying, "Nephews, be strong!" Aya! They've
been bound with golden chains! Yes, all you lords are seized!   28

The ruler Cuauhtemoc says, "O my little niece! You're seized, you're taken!
Who are you sitting beside? The Captain General. Truly it's Doña
Isabel!" "O my little niece!" Aya! It's true. And lords are seized. 29

. . . "O my little niece! You're seized, you're taken! Who are you sitting
beside? The Captain General. Truly it's Doña Isabel!" And lords are
seized. Yes, lords are seized.   30

"Huexotzincayotl" and "Tlaxcaltecayotl": Notes on the Texts and Translations

The Nahuatl texts and their corresponding translations are found in Bierhorst, *Cantares*, 150–53 ("Huexotzincayotl") and 318–23 ("Tlaxcaltecayotl").

I have modified Bierhorst's translation of "Huexotzincayotl" as follows. The second part of stanza 5 of "Huexotzincayotl" follows the rendition in León-Portilla, *Cantares*, 2.1:85, while in stanza 9, I translate "Mexicayotl" as "Mexicaness" instead of "Mexican nation." The following changes have also been made thanks to the insightful observations of the anonymous reviewer, with Bierhorst's original translation in parentheses: "you favored us" ("you will favor us") and "perish" ("die") in stanza 2; "commoners" ("underlings") in stanzas 2 and 3; "it is known" ("it is felt") in stanzas 3 and 4; "spreads" ("is pouring") in stanza 4; "You friends of ours, weep and acknowledge that we have abandoned all that is Mexicaness" ("Weep and be guilty, friends. You've forsaken the Mexica nation, alas") in stanza 9.

For the sake of brevity and balance, only the parts of "Tlaxcaltecayotl" that are analyzed in this chapter are reproduced here. In "Tlaxcaltecayotl," the Nahuatl text makes reference to "huehuetl" (drum). The word "cadence" has been added by Bierhorst "in order to complete the meaning for readers of English." For this reason, in the translation the word appears in italics (Bierhorst, *Cantares*, 128). I have also modified Bierhorst's translation of "Tlaxcaltecayotl" as follows. In stanza 2, Bierhorst translates "quauhtencoztli" as "Chief Yellow-Beak Eagle," whereas I report the original name as León-Portilla does (*Cantares*, 2.2:793). In stanza 3, I render "Mexicame" as "the Mexica" instead of "the Mexican people." The same applies to the "Mexica" of stanza 22.

Bierhorst, together with Burkhart, Tomlinson, and Amos Segala, among others, see the *Cantares mexicanos* as an upshot of the colonial encounter, a mirroring of the early postconquest experience.[137]

137 See L. M. Burkhart, "Introduction," in *Words and Worlds Turned Around: Indigenous Christianities in Colonial Latin America*, ed. D. Tavárez (Boulder, CO, 2017), 4–26, at 7; Tomlinson, *Singing of the New World*, 26–27; Segala, *Literatura náhuatl*, 250. In 1985, Bierhorst was the first to translate the entire corpus of *Cantares mexicanos* into any language. Although his work is a momentous contribution to the field, he has been harshly criticized for his "ghost-song" theory (Lockhart, *Nahuas and Spaniards*, passim; León-Portilla, *Cantares*, 1:193–94; Tomlinson, *Singing of the New World*, 26). Bierhorst claims that *Cantares mexicanos* contains ghost songs, which he describes as "a musical performance in which warrior-singers summon the ghosts of ancestors in order to swell their ranks and overwhelm their enemies." In his view, we are "confronted with the evidence for a Mexican revitalization movement," one that "appeals to the supernatural when the opportunity for open rebellion has since passed" (Bierhorst, *Cantares*, 3–4, 60, and idem, "Translating an Esoteric Idiom," 391). I do not subscribe to this theory and make every effort to avoid any manipulations in

Similarly, in stanza 4, I translate "Mexicayotl" as "Mexicaness" instead of "Mexican nation." In stanzas 11 and 27–30, I follow León-Portilla, who translates "Mex^{co} nican" as "here in Mexico" instead of Bierhorst's "this Mexico-on-earth," and "necuilolo" as "seized" instead of Bierhorst's "delineated," respectively (ibid., 799, 811, 813). Likewise, the following changes to Bierhorst's translation were made with thanks to the anonymous reviewer: the word "princes" has been replaced with "lords" throughout; "We've arrived" ("You've arrived") in stanzas 1 and 2; "The leader, Cuauhtencoztli comes shouting. The captain, Doña Marina, says, 'Disembark!'" ("Chief Yellow-Beak Eagle comes shouting. And Captain, or Mother Marina, says, 'Yellow Beak, my lookout!'") in stanza 2; "the commoners" is added, as "macehualtin" was omitted by Bierhorst in stanza 3; "Those with metal weapons" ("With iron weapons") in stanza 4; "Truly we've abandoned" ("This we've abandoned") and "And we would have arrived in Tlatelolco from the four directions" ("And we would arrive. From the four directions they move toward Tlatelolco!") in stanza 11; "May it not be in vain that it has happened" ("Let it not be done in vain") in stanzas 11 and 12; "I only saw" ("Alone I saw") and "they were chasing him" ("they come to chase him") in stanza 12; "the Mexica women" ("the women of Mexico, all of them") in stanzas 23 and 24; "nine days" ("nine months") in stanza 27; "golden chains" ("iron ties of gold") in stanza 28; "O my little niece!" (for both "My darling, hail!" and "My dearest darling!") in stanzas 29 and 30; "Who are you sitting beside? The Captain General" ("Who is she that sits beside you, O Captain General?") in stanzas 29 and 30.

That idolatrous past and Christian present are intertwined in these texts is important because it challenges the Spanish reading of the conquest as a rupture between colonial and precolonial Mexico and reflects the wider sociopolitical and cultural context of early colonial Nahua society.[138] But what exactly was this context within which the two songs were created? Are these laments typical or exceptions to early colonial Nahua production? Who might have been the actual authors? When did they compose them, and what kind of diction did they use and why? Addressing these questions is key to reconstructing the

---

the translation by cross-checking it against the Nahuatl original in Bierhorst's transcription, as well as against the translations of León-Portilla, *Cantares*, 2.1:82–87 ("Huexotzincayotl") and 2.2:792–813 ("Tlaxcaltecayotl"), and A. M. Garibay K., ed. and trans., *Poesía indígena de la altiplanicie: Divulgación literaria* (Mexico City, 1940), 55–56 ("Huexotzincayotl") and 57–62 ("Tlaxcaltecayotl").

138 Burkhart, *Slippery Earth*, 57.

contextual framework of early colonial Mexico within which "Huexotzincayotl" and "Tlaxcaltecayotl" should be read and understood.

Contrary to the traditional Spanish narrative, the conquest was the result not of the exceptionality of Cortés, but of a massive rebellion of indigenous city-states, including the Tlaxcalteca and Huexotzinca, fighting to topple the Mexica Empire.[139] Matthew Restall treats the Spaniards, or Caxtilteca (people from Castile), as one faction in a coalition that helped bring the empire of Moctezuma Xocoyotzin (r. 1502–1520), variously called Montezuma or Moteuczoma, to its knees. Nahua leaders, he writes, were active agents in the game and "came closer to being in control" than Cortés, who was only one of the players.[140]

At the time of the Spaniards' arrival, alliances across groups with different languages were rare. Ethnic, cultural, and sociopolitical fragmentation did not allow for a concerted indigenous response to the Spanish invasion, and siding with the invaders was a common survival strategy in preconquest Mesoamerica. Aligning with the aggressor historically involved partial loss of autonomy, but also "the preservation of the status, the protection of the expanding power, and the opportunity for advancement by joining new imperial expeditions."[141] For the Tlaxcalteca, the fall of Tenochtitlan was their heyday. They perceived themselves as conquerors, showcased their achievements within the Spanish–indigenous alliance in the *History of Tlaxcala* (*Lienzo de Tlaxcala*), a pictorial manuscript originally painted in 1550 (fig. 15), and cashed in on that alliance for several generations.[142] Other Nahuas (including Mexica) as well as Maya also became conquistadors, following the precontact tradition of militarism, and boasted of their feats. In the invasion of Guatemala during the 1520s, Spanish conquistadors were outnumbered by their native counterparts "by at least ten to one, sometimes thirty to one," while certain battles were wholly indigenous enterprises.[143]

139 Restall, *Seven Myths*, 26.

140 Restall, *When Montezuma Met Cortés*, 145, 174, 180.

141 S. Wood, *Transcending Conquest: Nahua Views of Spanish Colonial Mexico* (Norman, OK, 2003), 8; M. Restall and F. Asselbergs, *Invading Guatemala: Spanish, Nahua, and Maya Accounts of the Conquest Wars* (University Park, PA, 2007), 17.

142 F. Asselbergs, "Stories of Tlaxcalteca and Quauhquecholteca Conquistadors," in *Indian Conquistadors: Indigenous Allies in the Conquest of Mesoamerica*, ed. L. E. Matthew and M. R. Oudijk (Norman, OK, 2007), 65–101, at 65–66. Interestingly, in "Tlaxcaltecayotl," as will become clear, the Mexica imagine, with bitter humor, the Tlaxcalteca rejoicing in the conquest of Moctezuma's empire.

143 Wood, *Transcending Conquest*, 104–6, 142–44; Restall and Asselbergs, *Invading Guatemala*, 4, 16. See also Matthew and Oudijk, *Indian Conquistadors*, and Restall, *Seven Myths*, 44–63.

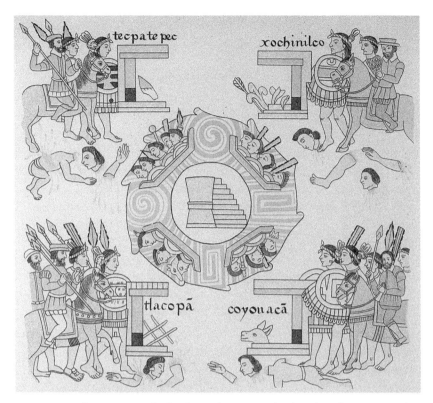

Fig. 15. Siege of Mexico-Tenochtitlan (center), in *Lienzo de Tlaxcala*, cell 42, nineteenth-century copy of ca. 1550 original, Mexico City, Biblioteca Nacional de Antropología e Historia. Secretaría de Cultura.-INAH.-Mex. Courtesy of the Instituto Nacional de Antropología e Historia.

Though Mesoamerican sources from the early years of the conquest are scarce and indirect, there is no evidence in the surviving native corpus that Spaniards appeared as a uniform group of loathed invaders extorting intolerable labor dues and taxes from the locals.[144] Lockhart mentions that the conquest itself barely figures in indigenous-language histories relating to community lands (*títulos primordiales*) from the region of Chalco, which had joined the Spanish–indigenous coalition. It simply appears as the arrival of Cortés or of faith: as a "cosmic event." These local histories betray no sign of regret or sadness that the conquest represented the twilight of an era.[145] Later in

144 Wood, *Transcending Conquest*, 136, 141.
145 Lockhart, *Nahuas and Spaniards*, 59.

the colonial period, the Spanish threat was embodied not in the political and religious elite but in the settlers, who gradually seized lands belonging to native communities.[146]

Elizabeth Boone observes that, with the exception of the *Codex Mendoza*, all the Nahua pictorial annals report the conquest and then carry on with "the colonial story," integrating Spanish rulers like Cortés and eminent figures like Juan de Zumárraga, Mexico's first bishop, as well as new events along with traditional ones.[147] The end of the Mexica Empire, says Burkhart, "was not the end of the world"; in Nahua time, events "could not be watersheds." The shift to Spanish rule and the accompanying conflict and epidemic diseases were merely seen as more events in the historical sequence of wars and natural disasters.[148] This may not have meant exactly business as usual, but it did reflect the reality of the Nahua elite (little is known of the common people), who found inventive ways to absorb the events and carve out a place for themselves in early colonial society by negotiating and accommodating difference.[149]

Looking at a range of provincial, non-Mexica sources from Mesoamerica, both graphic and textual and spanning the colonial era, Stephanie Wood argues that indigenous people usually do not view themselves as conquered, vanquished, or helpless. Of course, in early native testimonies originating in places close to the Mexica capital, or the capital proper, it was more common to lament the fall of the empire, but the story changes the further we move from Tenochtitlan-Tlatelolco and from the moment of the events. Wood concludes that the European narrative of the conquest as a rupture is nowhere visible in these provincial Mesoamerican testimonies. Their authors "transcended any memory of mass destruction and loss of life, seeing only distant transfers of power, if any at all." Battles between the Spaniards and their ancestors occurred either far away or very briefly close to home.[150] As a result, colonial Nahuas developed what Jorge Klor de Alva has called a "counternarrative of continuity,"

---

146 Wood, *Transcending Conquest*, 148–49.

147 E. H. Boone, "Aztec Pictorial Histories: Records without Words," in *Writing without Words: Alternative Literacies in Mesoamerica and the Andes*, ed. E. H. Boone and W. D. Mignolo (Durham, NC, 1994), 50–76, at 67–68.

148 L. M. Burkhart, "Introduction," in *Aztecs on Stage: Religious Theater in Colonial Mexico*, ed. L. M. Burkhart, trans. L. M. Burkhart, B. D. Sell, and S. Poole (Norman, OK, 2011), 3–29, at 4; Burkhart, *Slippery Earth*, 79.

149 Restall, *Seven Myths*, 74. On negotiations of cultural difference in Latin America more generally, see also E. Kefala, ed., *Negotiating Difference in the Hispanic World: From Conquest to Globalisation* (Oxford, 2011).

150 Wood, *Transcending Conquest*, 136, 142–43, 149.

which, contrary to the Spanish rhetoric of discontinuity between pagan past and Christian present, asserted a cultural and historical continuum before and after 1521. The Nahua "rotational ordering scheme," according to which one thing is regularly substituted by another, helped conceptualize the conquest not as imposition or break, but simply as a rotating shift.[151] Besides, the notion of an absolute "other" was hardly part of Nahua sociopolitical thought. Its inscription within the familiar and concomitant assimilation were a standard precontact strategy, which eventually allowed Nahuas to track down "precedents in their past for all of this newness" and read the Spanish colonial paradigm in habitual terms.[152] The incorporation of the European epistemic system into their own world let them protect local interests to a substantial degree throughout the colonial years.[153]

Epistemic reinterpretation, of course, is not a one-way process. Cultural interaction between Nahuas and Spaniards was characterized by what Lockhart refers to as "double mistaken identity," where each party assumes that "a given form or concept is functioning in the way familiar within its own tradition and is unaware of or unimpressed by the other side's interpretation." Each side read the other through the prism of its own culture, a process that yielded a practicable model "minimally acceptable to both." In this way, many aspects of preconquest Nahua culture endured for an indefinite period, and reciprocal misreadings fostered "an illusion of sameness."[154] Though Lockhart's major focus is on Nahua sociopolitical organization related to the *altepetl*, or city-state, religion is another area where false assumptions were rife.[155] Burkhart confirms that the friars ultimately satisfied themselves with a barely orthodox Nahua Christianity, while the Nahuas managed to "become just Christian enough" to carry on in the colonial era "without compromising their basic ideological and moral

151 Klor de Alva, "Nahua Colonial Discourse," 17, 21–22, 26.

152 Ibid., 16, 18–19, 31; Burkhart, *Holy Wednesday*, 96–97.

153 Klor de Alva, "Nahua Colonial Discourse," 26. Klor de Alva, however, argues that this narrative was counterproductive in the long term for the indigenous communities in their entirety because it generated "asymmetrical sociopolitical and cultural effects" (ibid., 17).

154 J. Lockhart, *Of Things of the Indies: Essays Old and New in Early Latin American History* (Stanford, CA, 1999), 98–99; Burkhart, *Holy Wednesday*, 41.

155 Lockhart, *Of Things of the Indies*, 112. Here Lockhart also draws attention to the different ways in which "double mistaken identity" was functioning in the realm of religion, compared with the "world of sociopolitical organization." On "double mistaken identity" in religion, see ibid., 112–18. On the *altepetl* in the early colonial period, see ibid., 99–103.

orientation." In the ensuing hybridized Christianity, Nahua elements persisted dressed in Christian cloth.[156]

The fall of Tenochtitlan-Tlatelolco, however traumatic for the Mexica, did not prevent them from reorganizing and running their city, save for the Spanish administrative center in the middle. The Spaniards themselves acknowledged, made use of, and profited from indigenous polities, even though they did not essentially understand them. The result was that the Nahuas continued to have considerable self-governance locally.[157] In densely populated areas in particular, higher tribute meant that the native leaders who collected it had a greater chance to be recognized officially as governors by the Spanish colonial administration, while both Spaniards and Nahuas found mutual interest in paving the path of sociopolitical reorganization. In the meantime, Nahua towns across central Mexico defended their rights and lands vigorously. Some Nahuas learned Spanish, but Nahuatl itself, aside from its lexicon, which borrowed massively from Spanish (mainly nouns), remained little changed until around 1650.[158] In fact, Spaniards were not preoccupied with the "wholesale Hispanization" of the indigenous peoples beyond the realm of religion.[159]

If cultural trauma has to be first projected publicly by a carrier group as a fundamental threat to collective identity and then sustained continuously, Nahuas, including the Mexica, preferred not to do much of this. With few exceptions, laments in the mode of "Anakalema" do not appear in the surviving corpus. In early colonial Mexico there was a tendency to elide, rather than lament over, the transfer to Spanish rule, and this is why songs like "Huexotzincayotl" and "Tlaxcaltecayotl" are so unique. They are intriguing deviations from that pattern, but also striking examples of what in the end turned out to be a failed attempt to disseminate the trauma claim in the long term. They were seeds sown on barren ground by certain members of the Nahua elite who ran counter to prevailing attitudes, openly lamenting the loss of the empire and its rulers ("openly" here does not suggest that their names as authors were necessarily divulged in

156 Burkhart, *Slippery Earth*, 184, 187. See also Burkhart, *Holy Wednesday*, 79–80.

157 Lockhart, *Of Things of the Indies*, 101, 103; Restall, *Seven Myths*, 73. For a concise discussion of Nahua political and religious life in early colonial Tenochtitlan-Tlatelolco, see Burkhart, *Holy Wednesday*, 73–80.

158 Wood, *Transcending Conquest*, 122; R. Horn, *Postconquest Coyoacan: Nahua-Spanish Relations in Central Mexico, 1519–1650* (Stanford, CA, 1997), 142; J. Lockhart, *The Nahuas after the Conquest: A Social and Cultural History of the Indians of Central Mexico, Sixteenth through Eighteenth Centuries* (Stanford, CA, 1992), 261.

159 Restall, *Seven Myths*, 75.

sixteenth-century Mexico, since they may have maintained their anonymity). For them the invasion and conquest of Mexico was a major disruption.

Despite the fact that the Nahua elite generally did not embrace a conquest narrative, the fall of Tenochtitlan, like that of Constantinople, is emblematic of radical destruction and social transformation. Book 12 of the *Florentine Codex* is critical in this respect, providing a poignant account of the conquest of Mexico from the indigenous perspective. As we will soon see, at least one of the songs, if not both, belongs to the circle of Nahua intellectuals at the Real Colegio de Santa Cruz de Tlatelolco, who were involved, among others, in the composition of the *Florentine Codex*.

It should be evident by now that the title of this book, *The Conquered*— which would have alienated most colonial Nahuas, especially those who took an active part in the coalition against Moctezuma and saw themselves as conquistadors—adopts the viewpoint of the laments and their authors. It mirrors their trauma claims and amplifies what seem to have been largely ignored cries in a society that was rushing to adapt, subtly or not so subtly, to a new context. But who were the authors of the songs?

León-Portilla points out that "Huexotzincayotl" "was probably composed in 1523," but Bierhorst appears to disagree on linguistic grounds. He considers this lament, along with songs 1–4, 6–9, and 12 in *Cantares mexicanos*, part of what he calls "missionary Nahuatl." Bierhorst uses this phrase to describe the songs' diction, which, although "correct," is not "noticeably idiomatic" (or rather, as mentioned earlier, not so full of cantares-like obscurities) and translates into "Spanish (or English) with suspicious ease." He adds that even though the "subject matter is in keeping with other . . . songs," it is "somewhat deritualized." He further speculates that these compositions may have been the work of "a bilingual Indian whose repertoire was filled out" with songs 5, 10, and 11, all three "picked up from unacculturated singers."[160] León-Portilla's early dating allows

---

160 León-Portilla, *Pre-Columbian Literatures*, 145; Bierhorst, *Cantares*, 47. Bierhorst calls the "typical" or "basic unit" of the cantares a "stanza." A typical stanza is made up of verse (advancing narrative), refrain (of "lyric value"), and litany. Litany consists of "a short phrase or two, invariably interruptive, and almost always reduced to a meaningless vocable," such as *ohuaya* (see also n. 245, below). Sometimes stanzas are paired, in which case they share the same refrain and litany. Bierhorst calls "canto" the combination of "two or more pairs." He emphasizes that his description of the stanza "is typical only in the abstract" because "many stanzas have no refrain at all" (ibid., 42–43), as is the case with "Huexotzincayotl," which has litany but not a refrain. The lack of refrain does make the song feel "somewhat deritualized," but it does not indicate a divergence from what is, in Bierhorst's terms, an already highly "heteromorphic" body of songs (ibid., 43). "Tlaxcaltecayotl" has both litany and refrain. On "missionary Nahuatl" in texts sponsored by the Church, see Burkhart, *Slippery Earth*, 27–28.

little space for a bilingual songwriter as it predates the opening of the Colegio de San José de los Naturales (1527) and the Colegio de Santa Cruz in Tlatelolco (1536), where members of the native elite studied under the Franciscans. The Colegio de Santa Cruz in particular became a haven for the cultivation and documentation of indigenous knowledge and culture.[161] We have seen that among its renowned instructors was the Franciscan missionary Sahagún, whose most illustrious Nahua students would participate, under his supervision, in the collection of materials incorporated in the *Florentine Codex* and, possibly, in *Cantares mexicanos*. The collector of the songs, postulates Bierhorst, "was an acculturated Indian, probably in the service of Sahagún," maybe "the well-known Indian writer and political leader Antonio Valeriano," who was from Mexico's ally, Azcapotzalco; alternatively, there may have been a group of collectors that included Valeriano.[162]

León-Portilla attributes "Huexotzincayotl" to a Tlatelolca composer, perhaps someone who had studied at the Colegio.[163] We know, for example, that among Sahagún's Nahua scholars, Martín Jacobita, Andrés Leonardo, Diego de Grado, and Bonifacio Maximiliano were from Tlatelolco.[164] But the mention of Tlatelolco in this song may have to do more with the historical particularities of the conquest (that is, where the Tenochtitlan rulers eventually surrendered) and less with the identity of the composer. Although the Tlatelolca author of the *Annals of Tlatelolco* distinguishes repeatedly between the residents of Tenochtitlan (Tenochca) and those of Tlatelolco (Tlatelolca), who were purportedly more valiant than their neighbors, there is no such distinction in "Huexotzincayotl," whose *cuicapicqui*, or songwriter, could have come from any of the constituent cities of the island of Mexico, or even from Azcapotzalco.[165]

To return to Bierhorst's argument on the authorship and dating of the song, there is no reason why a member of the Mexica elite and student at the calmecac prior to 1521 could not have been "a bilingual Indian" by the time the *Cantares mexicanos* were collected in the second half of the sixteenth century. As noted before, some members of the Mexica aristocracy, who found

161 D. Magaloni Kerpel, *The Colors of the New World: Artists, Materials, and the Creation of the Florentine Codex* (Los Angeles, CA, 2014), 2. See also Burkhart, *Holy Wednesday*, 55–73.

162 Bierhorst, *Cantares*, 4, 9, 12.

163 León-Portilla, *Cantares*, 1:232.

164 Sahagún, *Florentine Codex*, intr. vol., 55, and León-Portilla, *Pre-Columbian Literatures*, 16.

165 The intratextual presence of Tlatelolco in "Huexotzincayotl" resonates with that of the Cretans in "Anakalema." Both references reflect historical reality and should not necessarily be associated with the identity of the author. Like the *Annals of Tlatelolco*, book 12 of the *Florentine Codex* has a Tlatelolca bias.

their niche in the incipient power networks of the early colonial era, became bilingual. But, as we shall see, "Huexotzincayotl" was most likely created not by a former calmecac singer who had become bilingual, but by one of the indigenous intellectuals at the Colegio in Tlatelolco. These scholars were Christian but were also children of the Nahua elite growing up under the colonial administration. The composer of "Huexotzincayotl," having assimilated the tradition of the cantares as a collector, produced a number of his own songs. Instead of an "acculturated" songwriter, we should view him as a broker mediating between different cultural systems and as heir of an imperial past whose "abandonment" he laments. The same possibly applies to the author of "Tlaxcaltecayotl." Both texts were composed by educated songwriters who employed traditional modes of expression to disseminate the trauma claim in or close to the second half of the sixteenth century. The absence of a direct reference to the Spaniards in "Huexotzincayotl" and the shift of responsibility from Cortés to the indigenous warriors in "Tlaxcaltecayotl" may allude to the composers' position in early colonial society, or, more likely, to their view of the conquest as an anti-imperial rebellion, or both.

Meanwhile, the less difficult language of "Huexotzincayotl" is connected to the development of alphabetic writing in Nahuatl, and more specifically to "missionary" or "reduced" Nahuatl, in the sense of William Hanks's "Maya reducido." Speaking of colonial written Maya, Hanks explains that this "reduced," codified language, which was used by the Franciscans in the Yucatán Peninsula partly to eliminate "ritual speech," was "a sort of neologistic register of Maya, purged and realigned to suit the needs of Christian practice, governance, and civility."[166] The composition of grammars, dictionaries, and doctrinal texts regularized usage of the native languages in written sources to some extent,[167] and made songs like "Huexotzincayotl" comprehensible to Nahuas and others untrained in this speech register. The language of the song could therefore signal a conscious effort on the part of its author to reach wider audiences, particularly younger generations who were born after 1521 and were less familiar with the register and typology of pre-Hispanic cantares.

The issue of authorship has been a subject of dispute among scholars, some of them ascribing certain cantares to famous pre-Hispanic poets-cum-rulers, like Nezahualcoyotl of Texcoco and his son Nezahualpilli, Tecayehuatzin of

---

166 W. F. Hanks, "Birth of a Language: The Formation and Spread of Colonial Yucatec Maya," *Journal of Anthropological Research* 68.4 (2012): 449–71, at 449, 453.

167 Ibid.

Huexotzinco, and Ayocuan of Tecamachalco.[168] Bierhorst has forcefully contested this view. The fact that historical rulers are frequently invoked in the cantares through the "I am" formula, he says, has led to one of the most widespread misconceptions about these songs. The "I am" formula, common since Mesopotamian times in the so-called Old World, need not denote the author. It is a narrative device that may simply point to the singer acknowledging celebrated poets as his muse, thus heightening the dramatic effect of the songs.[169] On the same point, Lockhart suggests that the actual people referred to in these cantares are largely thought to be speaking not in the present of the song but in their own time, and that the events mentioned are the real historical ones. Such a reading, he notes, both makes the cantares more credible and moving and concurs with contemporary observers, who relate that their main intention was to recall bygone feats.[170]

The geographical provenance of the songs of *Cantares mexicanos* has also generated controversy. On the one hand, Garibay and León-Portilla see them as the cultural legacy of a range of communities in the valley of Mexico, namely Tenochtitlan-Tlatelolco, Texcoco, and Tlacopan (also known as the Triple Alliance), Azcapotzalco, Colhuacan, Huexotzinco, Cholula, and Tlaxcala (see fig. 8). On the other, Bierhorst, as mentioned before, insists that the songs were collected in Tenochtitlan-Tlatelolco and, perhaps, in its ally and Valeriano's hometown, Azcapotzalco, on the western shores of Lake Texcoco. "It seems quite possible," he adds, that most of the songs "belong to the city of Mexico," except for a few of them, which may have been composed in Azcapotzalco.[171] The controversy over provenance is important because it has a direct impact on interpretive approaches. This is particularly true of songs classified under the category "toponym + *cayotl/cuicatl*," among them "Huexotzincayotl" and "Tlaxcaltecayotl," considering that before the conquest Huexotzinco and Tlaxcala, along with Cholula, were Mexico's rivals.

Befuddled by such titles, scholars often take an ambivalent attitude toward these songs. Garibay argues that the geographical designation is either related to provenance (i.e., the songs were produced in Huexotzinco and Tlaxcala) or

---

168 Garibay, *Poesía náhuatl*, xlix–l, and León-Portilla, *Pre-Columbian Literatures*, 17, 78. In this case, León-Portilla is referring to songs included in *Cantares mexicanos, Romances de los señores de la Nueva España* (see "Tradition and Theory," n. 33) and "another collection of songs preserved at the National Library of Paris."

169 Bierhorst, *Cantares*, 101.

170 Lockhart, *Nahuas and Spaniards*, 155.

171 Garibay, *Poesía náhuatl*, xlv–xlviii; León-Portilla, *Cantares*, 1:196–97; Bierhorst, *Cantares*, 98–99.

performance (the singers imitated the Huexotzinca and Tlaxcalteca by disguising themselves with the "trappings proper to those peoples").[172] Correspondingly, León-Portilla perceives "Tlaxcaltecayotl" as a song "probably" drafted by the Tlaxcalteca, who recount their participation in the sack of Tenochtitlan, while, as we have seen, he reads "Huexotzincayotl" "a la manera de huexotzinca," that is, as a composition sung "in the manner of Huexotzinco" but devised by the Tlatelolca, who were defeated by the Huexotzinca. The latter, like the Tlaxcalteca, played a crucial role in the conquest of Mexico.[173] These titles, affirms Daniel Brinton, show that "the song, or its tune, or its treatment was borrowed from another locality or people."[174] Sahagún says that "if the song were to be intoned after the manner of Uexotzinco, they were adorned like men of Uexotzinco, and spoke even as they did; they were imitated with the song and in their adornment and their equipment." He states further that "if a song were to be intoned after the manner of Anauac, the speech of the men of Anauac was imitated, and their adornment as well as their equipment. Likewise, if a song were to be intoned after the manner of La Huaxteca, their speech was imitated."[175]

Deliberating on the songs' geographical provenance, Bierhorst reasons that if Sahagún's report were accurate, the *Cantares mexicanos* "with its numerous national pieces ought to be a prime source for the study of regional dialects. Unfortunately, though the *Cantares* does include dialect words, they are not confined to the national pieces in which they ought to be heard."[176] Sahagún, of course, may not necessarily speak of idiomatic lexicon and syntax but of different accents and intonations of Nahuatl, or even of variations in drum beat, pitch, and dance during performance. In fact, this is exactly what the physician Francisco Hernández, who had visited Mexico from 1571 to 1577 on the order of King Philip II,[177] relates in his *Antiquities of New Spain* (*Antigüedades de la Nueva España*): "What shall I say about *Cuextecayotl*, in which they imitated the mode of dancing, the adornment and the aspect of the people of the Huaxteca region, and represented the war in which they conquered them with varying sound and modulated martial uproar?"[178]

172 Garibay, *Poesía náhuatl*, xii.

173 León-Portilla, *Cantares*, 1:223–25, 232.

174 Brinton, *Ancient Nahuatl Poetry*, 16.

175 Sahagún, *Florentine Codex*, book 8, ch. 14, 45.

176 Bierhorst, *Cantares*, 94.

177 P. Burke, *A Social History of Knowledge: From Gutenberg to Diderot* (Malden, MA, 2000), 79.

178 F. Hernández, *Obras completas*, vol. 6, *Escritos varios*, ed. E. C. del Pozo et al. (Mexico City, 1984), 106: "¿Qué diré del *cuextecayotl*, en el cual imitaban el modo de bailar, el ornato y la

Hernández's remark about Cuextecayotl as a mise-en-scène of the Mexica's triumphant war against the Huaxteca is critical and resonates with Bierhorst's view that the songs are part of a genre developed by the Mexica to poke fun at their opponents. In several songs, writes Bierhorst, the traditional enemies of Mexico, notably Huexotzinco, Tlaxcala, and Chalco, are "humiliated," hence the existence of the subgenres Huexotzincayotl, Tlaxcaltecayotl, and Chalcayotl. Such songs, he continues, often observe historical battles.[179] Crucially, Hernández furnishes a further example that supports this reading: "Huexotzincayotl, that is, the song of those of Huexotzinco, in which they [the Mexica] celebrated the victory they achieved over them; it was mainly sung when they [the Huexotzinca] were taken to be sacrificed to the gods." He continues:

> Chichimecayotl, in which they remembered the beginnings and origin of those people. . . . Also: Otoncuicatl, Cuitlatecayotl, Michoacayotl, Tlaxcaltecayotl, Coyxcayotl, Tlacahoilizcuicatl, Cempoaltecayotl, Temazcalcuicatl, Anahoacayotl, Cozcatecayotl, Oztomecayotl, and others, where honorable mention was made of the trophies and the arts of those people, as the names themselves indicate.[180]

What Hernández is telling us is that the songs of this type are not *from* the areas they name, but *about* those areas.[181] They could either honor their accomplishments, as in the Tlaxcaltecayotl subgenre, or heap scorn on the defeated, whose skulls may later be displayed on the *tzompantli*, or skull rack, during sacrificial rituals at the Plaza Mayor, the heart of Tenochtitlan, as is the case with the subgenre of Huexotzincayotl.[182] Hernández's reference to the "honorable

---

aparicencia de la gente huasteca, y representaban la guerra en que los vencieron, con sonido vario y tumulto marcial muy bien acomodado?"

179 Bierhorst, *Cantares*, 4.

180 Hernández, *Obras completas*, 106: "El *huexocincayotl*, o sea canto de los de Huexocingo, en el que celebraban la victoria que habían alcanzado sobre ellos; se cantaba principalmente en el tiempo en que eran arrastrados para ser inmolados a los dioses" and "El *chimimecayotl*, en el cual recordaban los principios y origen de aquella gente. . . . Además el *otoncuícatl, cuitlateca-yotl, michoacayotl, tlaxcaltecayotl, coyxcayotl, tlacahoilizcuícatl, cempoaltecayotl, temazcalcuícatl, anahoacayotl, cozcatecayotl, oztomecayotl*, y otros donde se hacía mención honorífica de los trofeos y de las artes de esa gente, tal como indican los propios nombres."

181 This, however, does not mean that the Mexica could not have borrowed the songs, or their tune and treatment, from those localities and altered them according to their needs.

182 Most evidence of sacrifice has been found west of the Plaza Mayor. From 1948 to 2013, 153 sacrificial victims were identified in the Templo Mayor, among them 100 adults and 53 children. Almost two-thirds were decapitated. All victims correspond to the period

mention" of Tlaxcalteca feats in relation to Tlaxcaltecayotl as a subgenre is nevertheless perplexing. In *Cantares mexicanos*, Tlaxcala and Huexotzinco, together with Chalco, are the "principal scapegoats."[183] As we have seen, the Mexica's preconquest rivals joined Cortés in his march to Mexico. "All the dwellers in cities beyond the mountains—those of Tlaxcala, of Tliliuhquitepetl, of Uexotzinco," the *Florentine Codex* reports, "sped along at the rear. They came girt for war, with their cotton armor, their shields, their bows."[184] Bierhorst notes that in the songs, responsibility for the conquest shifts from the Spaniards to these usual suspects, especially Tlaxcala and Huexotzinco.[185] *Cantares mexicanos* is laden with relevant references that reprimand the indigenous peoples for allying with Cortés.[186] So why would the Mexica praise the "trophies" (*trofeos*) or victories of their long-term antagonists either before or after the conquest? Did "Tlaxcaltecayotl," after all, originate in the Tlaxcalteca tradition, as León-Portilla suggests?

Even if we agree that the subgenre did come from Tlaxcala, which is not what Hernández seems to imply in his discussion of songs about other localities, the "Tlaxcaltecayotl" in the *Cantares mexicanos* manuscript is certainly not a Tlaxcalteca creation. The song, as I will later argue, is a Mexica composition that laments the siege and fall of Tenochtitlan and the capture of its leaders, while emphatically reminding the Tlaxcalteca of the forced union between Mexico's women and the Spanish conquistadors. Therefore, if we were indeed faced with a subgenre used by the Tlaxcalteca to showcase their own triumphs, the song in *Cantares mexicanos* should be understood as a *Mexica borrowing* from that tradition. In a tragicomic move, the latter now project themselves as the trophy of the foe.

If instead we consider the subgenre part of the Mexica cultural tradition and accept as accurate Hernández's argument that "honorable mention was made of the trophies and the arts of those people [i.e., the Tlaxcalteca]," there emerge

---

1440–1502 (X. Chávez Balderas, "Bioarqueología del sacrificio humano: La ofrenda de vida," *Arqueología mexicana* 24.143 [2017]: 56–61, at 59, 61). Interestingly, in the ancient Greek tradition it was common to perform poetic works dedicated to both the victor and the vanquished, sometimes with irony, sometimes with sympathy. Such examples are Phrynichus's lost play *Phoenician Women* (ca. 476 BCE) and Aeschylus's *Persians* (472 BCE). For a short discussion of the Persians in Greek tragedy, see R. Scodel, *An Introduction to Greek Tragedy* (New York, 2010), 72–84.

183 Bierhorst, *Cantares*, 4.

184 Sahagún, *Florentine Codex*, book 12, ch. 15, 39.

185 Bierhorst, "Translating an Esoteric Idiom," 375.

186 Bierhorst, *Cantares*, 57.

two further, and rather different, understandings of the Tlaxcaltecayotl type. We could take Hernández's observation at face value and read the subgenre as a Mexica eulogy of the Tlaxcalteca. But in what context and why would the Mexica lionize their competitors? We know that enemy leaders were invited to attend sacrificial rituals in Tenochtitlan. David Carrasco, for instance, informs us that Moctezuma commissioned the erection of Coateocalli, where the images of Huitzilopochtli and all the gods worshiped in the imperial territory were held, including those belonging to enemy city-states like Tlaxcala. Prior to the dedication of the temple, writes Carrasco, Moctezuma waged war against the rebellious city of Teuctepec. Those seized were brought to Tenochtitlan to be sacrificed in a ritual initiated by the emperor himself. Several rulers of enemy and allied towns were summoned to observe the sacrifices.[187]

Speaking of one of the greatest religious spectacles in Tenochtitlan, the annual "Flaying of Men Ceremony" or Tlacaxipehualiztli, which went on for over half a month, Patrick Hajovsky similarly reports that its most spectacular element was the gladiatorial sacrifice, in which the most competent enemy fighters were set against experienced Mexica warriors in one-on-one combat. The captives, we learn, "were tethered by a rope to the center of a circular stone (*temalacatl*) on a raised platform and given mock weapons to defend themselves" as Mexica warriors "battled" them "with obsidian-edged clubs."[188] Hajovsky notes that, according to Durán, Mexica kings would make invited leaders watch the gladiatorial sacrifice and the humiliating ordeal of their fighters in order to scare and subdue them. During the same festival the captors paraded through Tenochtitlan together with their victims, achieving fame in proportion to the standing of their captive. Citing Sahagún, Hajovsky points out that at the end of the twenty-day period, the Mexica warriors gathered in the *cuicacalli*, or house of song, and sang "in praise of their gods" for an extra twenty days. This gathering would be an occasion to recall the "transformational experience of the ritual" and the feats of the warriors.[189] Could this, then, be the time when the captive's exploits were mentioned with the intention of ultimately extolling the military prowess of the Mexica warrior? While there is no way to answer this question with certainty due to the lack of relevant sources, we cannot rule out the possibility that in this or other contexts the

187 D. Carrasco, *City of Sacrifice: The Aztec Empire and the Role of Violence in Civilization* (Boston, MA, 1999), 76.

188 P. T. Hajovsky, *On the Lips of Others: Moteuczoma's Fame in Aztec Monuments and Rituals* (Austin, TX, 2015), 31, 33.

189 Ibid., 31–33.

Mexica heaped praise on the military and cultural conquests of their adversaries as a means of *self-praise*.

It is only half a step from this interpretation of Hernández's comment to a slightly different understanding of the subgenre of Tlaxcaltecayotl. This alternative approach is consistent with Bierhorst's earlier proposition that many songs in the *Cantares mexicanos* manuscript humiliate Mexico's habitual opponents. Satire and mimicry, the scholar argues, are present in *Cantares mexicanos* in a range of subtypes, among them the "female song" (*cihuacuicatl*) and the "old man song" (*huehue cuicatl*). Men in women's attire performed the former, while in the latter the singers would imitate elderly men. An example of the first subtype is the "Chalca Female Song" ("Chalcacihuacuicatl") (fols. 72–73v), a composition about the conquest of the Chalca by Moctezuma I (r. 1440–1468) and his allies. In the guise of a Chalca woman, notes Bierhorst, the singer "satirizes the agony of the conquered Chalcans by pretending to submit sexually to the Mexican king Axayacatl."[190] Taking into account the presence of satire and mimicry in the volume as a whole as well as Hernández's remark that in the areítos the indigenous would sing, dance, and perform some of their deeds in the form of tragedy or comedy,[191] we could think of the Tlaxcaltecayotl subgenre as a spoof of the accomplishments of the people of Tlaxcala and a mimicry of their victories. Following this reading, the Mexica did not exalt but scoffed at the feats of their antagonists.

We cannot know for sure whether the subgenre of Tlaxcaltecayotl was a Mexica loan from the Tlaxcalteca tradition or a Mexica invention, in which case it should be construed either as a hidden form of self-praise or an open travesty. In my opinion the subgenre belongs to the tradition of the Mexica. What is pretty obvious, however, is that the song that appears in *Cantares mexicanos* under the same name displays an interpretive reshaping of this subgenre. Whatever the provenance of the latter, in the song there is a semantic slippage from praise to lament and a dramatic, if satirical, projection of the self as the trophy of the enemy. In "Tlaxcaltecayotl" the Mexica imagine the Tlaxcalteca gloating over the humiliation of their historical rivals; it is a bitter humor, written from sufficient temporal distance to afford such a view.

Like "Anakalema," both "Tlaxcaltecayotl" and "Huexotzincayotl" indicate a semantic shift, but of a different kind this time. Where there used to be a travesty of the other, there is now the trauma of the collective self. As victors (fig. 16) become victims (fig. 17) and vice versa, traditional webs of signification are rewoven to unlock new layers of meaning. Similar to the poets of threnoi, the

190 Bierhorst, *Cantares*, 95, 502.
191 Hernández, *Obras completas*, 105.

Fig. 16. Sacrificial ritual, in *Codex Magliabechiano*, ca. 1566, Florence, Biblioteca Nazionale Centrale, Magl. XIII, 3, fol. 70r. Courtesy of the Ministero per i beni e le attività culturali e per il turismo / Biblioteca Nazionale Centrale, Firenze.

composers of cantares exploit readily available symbolic resources, which, in this case, are sheathed in the cultural and ritual contexts of precontact Mexico. Of particular interest is the ironic twist they give to these subgenres: they identify their people as the trophies of the foe and put themselves in the place of those whom they used to deride and sacrifice.

León-Portilla considers "Tlaxcaltecayotl" a yaocuicatl, or war song, and refers to "Huexotzincayotl"—a ritual war song according to Hernández—as an icnocuicatl, or song of sorrow, whereas Garibay reads both of them as "epic poems."[192] Songs of war and sorrow are ubiquitous in the Mexica tradition.

192 León-Portilla, *Cantares*, 1:232, 244; León-Portilla, *Cantares*, 2.1:568; and Garibay, *Poesía indígena*, 32, 55–62. A wealth of relevant terms has survived in contemporary texts. The terms generally fall into four categories: stylistic, thematic, instrumental, and "national" (Bierhorst, *Cantares*, 92). Both *icnocuicatl* and *yaocuicatl* are thematic titles, whereas "Huexotzincayotl" and "Tlaxcaltecayotl" are obviously what Bierhorst refers to as "national" titles. For more on *icnocuicatl* and *yaocuicatl*, see Garibay, *Poesía náhuatl*, xi–xii; León-Portilla, *Pre-Columbian Literatures*, 15; Bierhorst, *Cantares*, 94–95; Segala, *Literatura náhuatl*, 138; and P. Correa, *La cultura literaria de los aztecas* (Madrid, 1994), 120, 123, 128. For a criticism of Garibay and

Fig. 17. Spaniards attacking a temple, in *Florentine Codex*, 1577, Florence, Biblioteca Medicea Laurenziana, MS Med. Palat. 220, fol. 408r. Courtesy of the Ministero per i beni e le attività culturali e per il turismo.

A "song of sadness," icnocuicatl was a reflection of the Mexica's awareness of their own limits, "of the melancholic vision of life," which is "irremediably condemned to an end, of the ephemerality of joy" and of the sense of mortality. Most Mexica songs, confirms Pedro Correa, seem "to follow this trend and recreate [themselves] in it."[193] Likewise the theme of war is omnipresent in the cantares, and echoes of the conquest are found in several compositions.[194] The subgenres of Huexotzincayotl and Tlaxcaltecayotl serve as interpretive frameworks in the

León-Portilla's use of Western typological categories, see Tomlinson, *Singing of the New World*, 22, 24, 27, and J. Lee, "*Mestizaje* and the Creation of Mexican National Literature: Ángel María Garibay Kintana's Nahuatl Project," *Bulletin of Spanish Studies* 91.6 (2014): 889–912.

193 Correa, *La cultura*, 123.

194 Bierhorst, "Translating an Esoteric Idiom," 390–91. Bierhorst notes that in addition to "Huexotzincayotl" and "Tlaxcaltecayotl," references to the conquest are found in songs 60 ("Fish Song") and 68 ("Water-Pouring Song"), among others (Bierhorst, *Cantares*, 58, and idem, *Ballads of the Lords of New Spain*, 66).

hands of culture creators, who put a subversive spin on them in the second half of the sixteenth century. A raft of stylistic and conceptual formulas ingrained in the pre-Hispanic traditions of icnocuicatl, yaocuicatl, and satire are cast into these frameworks and read anew with a view to ritualizing and commemorating traumatic events. The corpus of *Cantares mexicanos*, Bierhorst reminds us, represents "not salvage ethnography but a living genre observed in public performance by various writers," adding that the cantares are essentially ritualistic.[195] But how exactly is the cultural trauma articulated in the two songs?

A relatively brief song comprising ten stanzas,[196] "Huexotzincayotl" reconstructs the siege of Mexico by arousing negative affect right from the opening stanza: "Only sad flowers [*tlaocolxochitl*], sad songs [*tlaocolcuicatl*], lie here in Mexico, in Tlatelolco."[197] Like "Anakalema," whose opening line sets in motion the trauma process through the parataxis of five synonyms denoting sorrow ("Mourning, weeping, and lamentation and groaning and grief"), the Nahuatl song starts off with an emphasis on grief conveyed through repetition of the word *tlaocolli* (sadness, misery, suffering), and more specifically through the parataxis of the composite nouns *tlaocolxochitl* (sad flower) and *tlaocolcuicatl* (sad song), followed by the thrice repeated *cococ* (misery, affliction) in stanzas 3 and 4.

A polysemic term, *xochitl* (flower) can be used as a substitute for song, but also as a symbol of sacrificial blood. Garibay and others have argued that the metaphor "flower-and-song" (*in xochitl in cuicatl*) means "poem,"[198] but Bierhorst, Lockhart, and Tomlinson insist that *Cantares mexicanos* contains songs, not poetry,[199] accepting *xochitl* as an alternative for "song" (*cuicatl*).[200] For all that from a modern viewpoint we could think of *Cantares mexicanos*

195 Bierhorst, "Translating an Esoteric Idiom," 390; see also 372.

196 See n. 160, above.

197 As mentioned earlier, the original Nahuatl text of "Huexotzincayotl" and its English translation can be found in Bierhorst, *Cantares*, 150–53. For the Spanish translation, see León-Portilla, *Cantares*, 2.1:82–87, and Garibay, *Poesía indígena*, 55–56. All references from here on are made to stanzas. I generally follow Bierhorst's rendition, occasionally adopting León-Portilla's or my own, especially when Bierhorst's "ghost-song" theory exercises an explicit influence on the translation (see n. 137, above).

198 A. M. Garibay K., *Llave del náhuatl* (Mexico City, 1961), 116; León-Portilla, *Pre-Columbian Literatures*, 8, 77; León-Portilla, *Cantares*, 1:285; and B. Ortiz de Montellano, "Ghosts of the Imagination: John Bierhorst's Translation of *Cantares mexicanos*," *Tlalocan: A Journal of Source Materials on the Native Cultures of Mexico* 11 (1989): 469–79, at 477.

199 Bierhorst, *Cantares*, 17; Lockhart, *Nahuas and Spaniards*, 393; and Tomlinson, *Singing of the New World*, 24–27.

200 Bierhorst, *Cantares*, 24, and idem, *Ballads of the Lords of New Spain*, 37–38.

as poetry, says Bierhorst, "the definition 'xochitl/cuicatl = poetry' is a flaccid concept at best and at worst a misnomer."[201] According to Bernardo Ortiz de Montellano, flowers often appear in sculpture and codices "in conjunction with the *zacatapayolli* (a sacrificial grass bundle), *uitztli* [*sic: huitztli*] (a sacrificial thorn), and/or an *omitl* (a sacrificial bone awl)."[202] Song and sacrifice meet and merge in Hernández's description of the subgenre of Huexotzincayotl as well as in the eponymous *cantar* of the corpus. The latter, it will later transpire, closes as a sacrificial ritual, thus conforming to what the Spanish physician claimed to be the convention of the subgenre.[203]

The emphatic use of the pronoun *tehhuantin* and the subject prefix *ti-*, both meaning "we,"[204] in stanzas 2 and 3 clearly positions the audience members as participants and, by extension, as victims—"we commoners [*timacehualta*][205] will perish [*tipopolihuizque*]"[206] and "how unfortunate are we, we poor ones [*titotoliniah*],[207] we commoners [*timacehualtin*]!"[208] Similar to "Anakalema," the traumatic events are tied up with divine involvement, but contrary to the Greek poem, the indelible trauma here seems to be linked, albeit loosely, to human negligence: "In Tlatelolco you disperse your underlings, you rout them. Misery spreads, misery is known [*macho*], because we were weary [*ticiahuia*], because we were lax [*titlatzihuia*]. O Life Giver!" (4).[209] The use of the verb *macho* (from

201 Bierhorst, *Cantares*, 4, 17–18.

202 Ortiz de Montellano, "Ghosts of the Imagination," 476.

203 Hernández, *Obras completas*, 106.

204 J. Bierhorst, *A Nahuatl-English Dictionary and Concordance to the* Cantares Mexicanos: *With an Analytic Transcription and Grammatical Notes* (Stanford, CA, 1985), 301, 320. *Ti-* can refer both to the first-person plural and second-person singular.

205 *Macehualli* (pl. *macehualtin*) = vassal, subject, underling (ibid., 187) in the possessed form, as in stanza 4, while the unpossessed form means "commoner" (R. Horn, "Indigenous Identities in Mesoamerica after the Spanish Conquest," in *Native Diasporas: Indigenous Identities and Settler Colonialism in the Americas*, ed. G. D. Smithers and B. N. Newman [Lincoln, NE, 2014], 31–78, at 41).

206 *Pohpolihui* = to be wasted, to be destroyed (Bierhorst, *Nahuatl-English Dictionary*, 270).

207 *Tolinia* = to be poor, to suffer (ibid., 362).

208 Stanza 3 reads as follows: "Ototlahueliltic çan titotoliniah timacehualtin queçohuel *tehuantin* otiquittaque in cococ ye machoyan ohuaya" (my emphasis).

209 On the one hand, Bierhorst translates *ciahui* (to be tired or weary) and its synonym *tlatzihui* (to be tired or worn out) (Bierhorst, *Nahuatl-English Dictionary*, 86, 352) in the first person plural, thus rendering the prefix *ti-* as "we." He also comments that the verb *ticiahuia* here appears to be in the imperfect tense (ibid., 712). On the other hand, Garibay and León-Portilla attribute *ticiahuia* and *titlatzihuia* to Life Giver, interpreting *ti-* as "you" (singular): "te has cansado" / "te cansas" (you are tired) and "estás hastiado" / "sientes fastidio" (you are/feel annoyed/weary) respectively (Garibay, *Poesía indígena*, 56, and León-Portilla,

mati = to know, realize)[210] here and in the previous stanza—"it's misery, yes, it is known [macho]" (3)—along with the employment of anaphora—"misery spreads [*cococ moteca*], misery is known [*cococ ye macho*]"—call for affective and cognitive engagement with the trauma claim made by the symbol creator.

The song's apparent reference to ritual negligence or laxity ("because we were weary, because we were lax") is matched by a similar reference in the Sahaguntine *Colloquios* (*Debates*), whose Nahuatl version was composed by Valeriano, Jacobita, Leonardo, and Alonso Vegerano, all scholars at the Colegio de Santa Cruz in Tlatelolco.[211] Written in 1564, the text is a fictional dialogue between Nahua priests and wise men and the first Franciscans who arrived in Mexico to evangelize them. The former, represented in "reverential and heroic tones," are allegedly convinced by the friars of Christianity's superiority, but the deferential, if nostalgic, way in which Nahua religion and culture are portrayed by the collegians may have been the cause for the book's withdrawal from publication, likely by Sahagún himself, in the late 1570s and early 1580s.[212] In *Colloquios* the native priests and nobles hint at their possible negligence as a reason for their defeat: "Indeed, we are merely insignificant common people, we are covered with dirt, we are covered with mud, we are bruised, we are poor, we are afflicted, we are sorrowful. . . . Have we, perhaps, been negligent in doing things [*aço titlatlatziujtique*]?" Note that the verb *tlatzihui*, meaning to be tired, lazy, or worn out, is used in both texts.[213]

Cantares, 2.1:83). On the prefix *ti-*, see n. 204, above. Despite his different rendition, Garibay understands that people bear responsibility for their sufferings. In stanza 3 he reads "we have erred and we suffer" ("hemos errado y sufrimos"), whereas Bierhorst and León-Portilla simply make reference to the Mexica as "unfortunate"/"desdichados" (poor wretches). In all three translations, Life Giver is clearly responsible for the situation. See for instance, "you disperse, you harm your vassals" ("dispersas, dañas a tus vasallos"), "this is your doing, Life Giver" ("es tu obra, Dador de la vida"), and "so has Life Giver done in Tlatelolco" ("así lo ha hecho el Dador de la vida en Tlatelolco") in stanzas 4, 6, and 9 (León-Portilla, *Cantares*, 2.1:83, 85, 87); "you did it, oh, you for whom we all live" ("tú lo hiciste, oh por quien todos viven") and "this is what the one for whom we all live did in Tlatelolco" ("esto hizo en Tlatelolco aquel por quien todos viven!") in stanzas 6 and 9 (Garibay, *Poesía indígena*, 55–56).

210 Bierhorst, *Nahuatl-English Dictionary*, 205.

211 J. Klor de Alva, "The Aztec-Spanish Dialogues of 1524," *Alcheringa: Ethnopoetics* 4.2 (1980): 52–55, at 53.

212 Burkhart, *Holy Wednesday*, 68. See also L. M. Burkhart, "Doctrinal Aspects of Sahagún's *Colloquios*," in *The Work of Bernardino de Sahagún: Pioneer Ethnographer of Sixteenth-Century Aztec Mexico*, ed. J. Klor de Alva, H. B. Nicholson, and E. Quiñones Keber (Albany, NY, 1988), 65–82.

213 B. de Sahagún, *Colloquios y doctrina christiana*, ed. and trans. J. Klor de Alva, *Alcheringa: Ethnopoetics* 4.2 (1980): 56–193, at 117–18.

In the Nahua belief system, notes Burkhart, sanctions in the shape of illnesses were imposed by the gods when rituals were breached. "The earth was a slippery place where misfortunes easily befell," and therefore observing rituals was crucial to maintaining tenuous order.[214] Between two orderly periods there was a disorderly one, but this was only temporary. "Order had to be forcibly wrested from chaos and then paid for periodically through ritual sacrifices."[215] Both *Colloquios* and "Huexotzincayotl" seem to suggest that a disorderly period between Mexica and Spanish rule may have been caused by failing to perform the appropriate rituals.[216] The confluence between the two texts also supports the theory that "Huexotzincayotl" comes from the same context of indigenous scholars at the Colegio de Santa Cruz in Tlatelolco.

Divine intervention can be invoked when the trauma process unfolds within the realm of religion, as is the case with "Huexotzincayotl"—Hernández has linked the subgenre to sacrificial rituals. According to the Nahua pantheon, Ometeotl (Lord of Duality or Dual Divinity) was the god-creator who engendered the four Tezcatlipocas associated with the four cardinal directions. The Black Tezcatlipoca was known as the god Tezcatlipoca, the most feared and revered of all. His opposite was White Tezcatlipoca, or Quetzalcoatl, and the two of them were locked in an eternal cosmic struggle. Huitzilopochtli, the god of war and the sun, was the Blue Tezcatlipoca, while Xipe Totec, to whom the Flaying of Men Ceremony was dedicated, was the Red Tezcatlipoca, the god of natural renewal and vegetation.[217] In our song, Life Giver (or "Dador de la vida" in León-Portilla's translation) appears as "Ipalnemoani" (2, 4, 6, 9), literally "he-by-whom-one-lives."[218] The name Ipalnemoani or Ipalnemohuani, among other spellings, is present in indigenous prayers to Tezcatlipoca recorded in the *Florentine Codex*.[219] Bierhorst clarifies that this "supreme spirit" should not be interpreted as monotheism. "Sometimes the god Tezcatlipoca was preeminent in Aztec cultic activities, sometimes the sun." In Mexico Huitzilopochtli was often acknowledged "as first among equals."[220] Jongsoo Lee points out that while

214 Burkhart, *Slippery Earth*, 31, 193.

215 Ibid., 38, 78.

216 Ibid., 78.

217 M. Aguilar-Moreno, *Handbook to Life in the Aztec World* (New York, 2007), 138; Hajovsky, *On the Lips of Others*, 31.

218 Bierhorst, *Nahuatl-English Dictionary*, 168.

219 Sahagún, *Florentine Codex*, book 6, ch. 3 and 4, 11–20.

220 Bierhorst, *Cantares*, 38.

the Tlatelolca venerated Tezcatlipoca, the Tenochca served Huitzilopochtli,[221] although the *Annals of Tlatelolco* contains several allusions to Huitzilopochtli in the passage dedicated to the events of the conquest.[222]

The composer of the song utilizes a generic deity epithet such as Ipalnemohuani along with the word "Dios" in stanza 7, so that native concepts of divinity could appear to be compatible with Christianity and indigenous morality could be adjusted fairly easily to Christian contexts. In colonial Nahuatl texts, writes Burkhart, terms like "Ipalnemohuani," "Ilhuicahua Tlalticpaque" (possessor of earth or heaven), and "Tloque Nahuaque" (possessor of the near) are attributed to the Christian god, and Nahua notions are built into the core of Christian moral education. The friars, she argues, may have relegated the Nahuas' illustrious forefathers "to the abyss of hell," but in *Cantares mexicanos* past and present are united. The preconquest values of sacrifice and militarism persist, the influence of Christian moral teaching is trivial, and the Spanish narrative of the conquest is rejected.[223] In "Huexotzincayotl," as will become clear, the hybridized Christian god sends fear and affliction to his subjects, but the song deflects the colonizing rhetoric that the Christian god allowed the conquest because of the sins of the idolatrous, devil-worshipping "Indians." "We were lax" or "negligent" is a vague and limited acceptance of responsibility on the part of the Mexica, who do not admit sin or guilt in the Christian moral sense. Their age, the fifth cosmic age, "was a time of relative chaos," and they knew well that disorderly periods were inevitable. The conquest therefore need not imply sinful conduct, as the Spaniards insisted. Indigenous morality here survives in Christian attire and Christianity is situated within the boundaries of Nahua culture.[224]

The invocation of Ipalnemoani in "Huexotzincayotl" naturally brings to mind Tezcatlipoca or Huitzilopochtli, both embodying the supreme deity in the eyes of the Mexica, although the latter, as we have seen, "was identified with both the sun and the ancient and powerful Tezcatlipoca."[225] According to León-Portilla, the song to Huitzilopochtli was one of the most important hymns in the Mexica rite. In *Cantares mexicanos*, Huitzilopochtli may appear openly or

221 J. Lee, *The Allure of Nezahualcoyotl: Pre-Hispanic History, Religion, and Nahua Poetics* (Albuquerque, NM, 2008), 201.

222 In J. Lockhart, ed. and trans., *We People Here: Nahuatl Accounts of the Conquest of Mexico* (Berkeley, CA, 1993), 257, 269, 271.

223 Burkhart, *Slippery Earth*, 28, 39, 57. See also, Burkhart, *Holy Wednesday*, 95.

224 Burkhart, *Slippery Earth*, 57, 193. For similarities and differences between Christian and Nahua notions of sin, damage, penance, and merit, see ibid., 28–34, 141–50.

225 Ibid., 189.

hide behind such a name as Ipalnemoani. "Identified with the sun and divine warrior par excellence," León-Portilla notes, Huitzilopochtli "had become the supreme god" of the Tenochca and, as already mentioned, featured prominently in foundational lore and omens about the fall of the city.[226] Bierhorst explains that "one of the avowed purposes of Aztec warfare was to provide human blood for the nourishment of the gods, especially the sun," which, in the morning, "needed food for its journey to the zenith."[227] Sacrificial rituals (see fig. 16) to Huitzilopochtli were framed as acts of reciprocity, offering human blood to the life-giving sun to keep its course uninterrupted. Among sacrificial victims we encounter war captives. Bioarchaeologist Ximena Chávez Balderas reports that during the ceremony at the Templo Mayor, Tenochtitlan's main temple, the priest would extract the heart by making an incision in the abdomen before sliding the hand inside the thorax in order to cut the heart with a stone instrument.[228]

The notion of slippage from victor to victim and sacrificing to being sacrificed, discussed earlier, was not alien to the Mexica, whose one-on-one combat style in the so-called flower wars, or "guerras floridas," against the Huexotzinca and Tlaxcalteca underscored the ephemerality of life as well as the shifting fortunes of victory and defeat.[229] We know that in the Mexica imagination the Mimixcoa were the "main food of the gods." They represented the archetypal sacrificial warriors,[230] only outshined by Mixcoatl, the god of hunting and exemplary warrior and "conquistador," who was deemed to be "the prototype of all victims."[231] According to *Customs of New Spain* (*Costumbres de Nueva España*) (ca. 1553), during Quecholli, the twenty-day Nahua month dedicated to Mixcoatl, sacrificial victims would dress like him and so would the supreme ruler of the Mexica. In fact, when the latter died, he would be

226 León-Portilla, *Pre-Columbian Literatures*, 64, and León-Portilla, *Cantares*, 1:197.

227 Bierhorst, *Cantares*, 30.

228 Chávez Balderas, "Bioarqueología," 59–60. Bioarchaeological evidence suggests that sacrificial victims were obtained from a range of sources, including war, slave purchase, and tributes.

229 Aguilar-Moreno, *Handbook*, 123. "Aztec warfare," says Hajovsky (*On the Lips of Others*, 31), "was highly individualistic, especially because battle was hand to hand and was intended to capture an enemy and bring him back to the main temple for sacrifice."

230 G. Olivier, "El simbolismo sacrificial de los Mimixcoa: Cacería, guerra, sacrificio e identidad entre los mexicas," in *El sacrificio humano en la tradición religiosa mesoamericana*, ed. L. López Luján and G. Olivier (Mexico City, 2010), 453–82, at 461.

231 M. Graulich, *Fiestas de los pueblos indígenas: Ritos aztecas. Las fiestas de las veintenas* (Mexico City, 1999), 175, 176.

buried with that attire.[232] The Mexica sovereign, Michel Graulich informs us, would lead the ritual hunting during Quecholli disguised as Mixcoatl, while his hunters were dressed as Mimixcoa (fig. 18).[233] (Interestingly, Durán recounts that Mixcoatl was the patron god of the Huexotzinca, and his importance was matched only by that of Huitzilopochtli to the Mexica.[234]) Hajovsky similarly notes that when the captive's skin was peeled off in ceremonial sacrifices during Tlacaxipehualiztli, the Mexica captor would wear it for twenty days "until it shriveled away." Throughout this period, he adds, "the captor (whether warrior or priest) and enemy captive were physically merged."[235]

Resignified from within, "Huexotzincayotl" allows for a shift from ritual victory to ritual lament—"Tears [choquiztli] are pouring, teardrops [yxayotl] are raining there in Tlatelolco" (5)—which takes on a more narrative character in the second half of the song. "True it is [ynic neltic].[236] They forsake [oyacahua] the city of Mexico. The smoke is rising, the haze is spreading.[237] This is your doing, O Life Giver," we hear in stanza 6, which announces the dramatic reconstruction of the closing moments of the siege. After an unsuccessful attempt to capture Tenochtitlan in 1520, Cortés returned in May 1521 and camped at Coyoacan south of the island cities. In the final stage of the conquest, writes Ross Hassig, Spaniards formed less than one percent of Cortés's army, the rest being composed of indigenous groups, mainly from Huexotzinco, Tlaxcala, and Chalco, but also from other areas.[238] From Coyoacan Cortés's troops progressed along the causeway into Acachinanco. Thirteen portable brigantines built in Tlaxcala using native labor were carried "piece by piece" all the way

232 F. Gómez de Orozco, ed., "Costumbres, fiestas, enterramientos y diversas formas de proceder de los indios de Nueva España," *Tlalocan: A Journal of Source Materials on the Native Cultures of Mexico* 2.1 (1945): 37–63, at 50, 52: "y yua moteçuma vestido de la vestidura que el mismo covail [que] sacrificauan ... quando este moria enterrauan con el la Ropa."

233 Graulich, *Fiestas de los pueblos indígenas*, 182.

234 Ibid., 173. Mixcoatl was mainly venerated in Huexotzinco, Tlaxcala, and Coatepec. I am grateful to Ximena Chávez Balderas for pointing me to Quecholli. For more on Quecholli, Mixcoatl, and the Mimixcoa, see Graulich, *Fiestas de los pueblos indígenas*, 171–90 and Olivier, "El simbolismo sacrificial."

235 Hajovsky, *On the Lips of Others*, 32.

236 Instead of "true it is," León-Portilla translates "ynic neltic" as "this is what happened" ("así ocurrió"), thus highlighting the narrative character of the second part of the song.

237 This final clause is an example of parallelism and asyndeton, two rhetorical devices amply used in *Cantares mexicanos*. For asyndeton, see also "tears are pouring, teardrops are raining" (5). Asyndeton, or unmarked conjunction, is very common in Nahuatl (J. R. Andrews, *Introduction to Classical Nahuatl* [Norman, OK, 2003], 54).

238 R. Hassig, *Mexico and the Spanish Conquest* (Norman, OK, 2006), 148–49.

Fig. 18. The Mexica sovereign dressed as Mixcoatl and hunters adorned as Mimixcoa during Quecholli. In B. de Sahagún, *Primeros memoriales (Códice Matritense)*, sixteenth century, Madrid, Biblioteca del Palacio Real, MS 3280, fol. 252. Courtesy of the Palacio Real. © Patrimonio Nacional.

through the mountains to Texcoco, where they were assembled.[239] When Cortés stormed the main square of Tenochtitlan through the Eagle Gate on its southern side, Emperor Cuauhtemoc fled together with other Mexica leaders, among them Tlacotzin, Motelchiuh, and Oquiztzin, to Tlatelolco, where they resisted the siege until Tuesday, 13 August. Their last stand, says Bierhorst, was in Coyonacazco at the northern end of the island (fig. 19). Eventually, Cuauhtemoc and his men were captured and taken to Coyoacan, where, according to information from the anonymous author of the *Annals of Tlatelolco* and the Texcoca

239 Bierhorst, *Cantares*, 472–73, and B. E. Mundy, *The Death of Aztec Tenochtitlan, the Life of Mexico City* (Austin, TX, 2015), 75. Similarly, Mehmed II had his ships dragged overland to outflank the chain that the Byzantines had placed across the Golden Horn (J. Harris, *The Lost World of Byzantium* [New Haven, CT, 2015], 238).

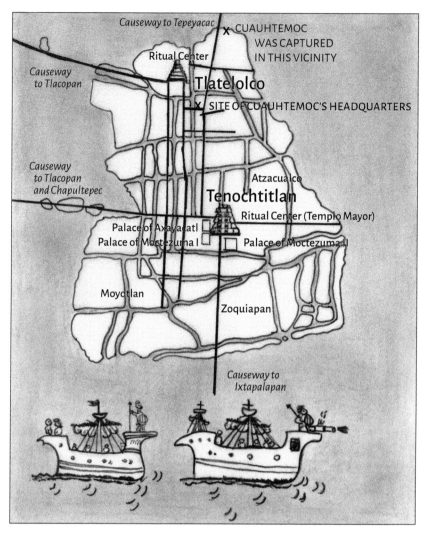

Fig. 19. Tenochtitlan-Tlatelolco, 1521. Map by Anthi Andronikou, after R. F. Townsend, *The Aztecs* (London, 2000), 29, and C. McEwan and L. López Luján, eds., *Moctezuma: Aztec Ruler* (London, 2009), 61.

historian Fernando de Alva Ixtlilxochitl (d. 1648), "the Spaniards tortured them by fire in the hope of learning the whereabouts of hidden gold."[240]

We are told that Cortés beat the Mexica with his surviving army of nine hundred Spaniards, thirteen brigantines, sixteen pieces of artillery, and eighty

240 Bierhorst, *Cantares*, 434, 473.

horses. Yet the most crucial roles were performed by his indigenous allies, some two hundred thousand men. The end of the Mexica Empire, concludes Hassig, was "more a coup or at most a rebellion than a conquest."[241] After an almost three-month-long siege, Tenochtitlan-Tlatelolco fell on 13 August 1521, although the looting and massacre continued for four days, after which the city was filled with thousands of corpses. Some people had died in battle but most passed away from starvation.[242] Over the following days, the survivors walked out of the city, throwing themselves into Lake Texcoco to avoid capture.[243] As they "went into the water," the *Florentine Codex* reports, "on some the water reached to the stomach; some, to the chest; and on some it reached to the neck. And some were all submerged, there in the deeps. Little children were carried on the backs [of the elders]; cries of weeping arose."[244]

In the song, the dramatic exodus from the ravaged city is acted out to the beats of huehuetl or teponaztli or both, and to the litany, or meaningless vocable, "ohuaya" at the end of stanza 5:[245] "The Mexica have gone into the water; along with the women they go. There we go, our friends, [*ohuaya*]." The first person plural enables the identification of the audience with the victims and secures their participation in the ritual of commemoration,[246] perhaps as a chorus, which "comes in on the litany."[247] Similarly, through the use of the imperative, a stock element in *Cantares mexicanos*, in stanzas 7 and 9 the singer

---

241 Hassig, *Mexico and the Spanish Conquest*, 175, 183.

242 Ibid., 174–75.

243 J. Gurría Lacroix, *Itinerario de Hernán Cortés / Itinerary of Hernan Cortes* (Mexico City, 1973), 175.

244 Sahagún, *Florentine Codex*, book 12, ch. 40, 118.

245 See n. 160, above. These vocables are not included in the translation. Scholars have long speculated on their function, which must have been related to rhythm and humming. They probably introduced music and signaled the passage from one stanza to the next, and they may have been performed by the singer as well as the actor(s). Their use generated "different effects of rhythm and assonance" (Garibay, *Poesía náhuatl*, xxxiii, and Karttunen and Lockhart, "La estructura de la poesía náhuatl," 23). Bierhorst confirms that the "heterometric" and "heterorythmic" songs of *Cantares mexicanos* relied heavily on them (Bierhorst, *Cantares*, 80). See also Lockhart, *Nahuas and Spaniards*, 146.

246 This is an English rendition of León-Portilla's translation: "Se han ido por el agua los mexicas; / mezclados con mujeres ya se van; allá vamos, amigos nuestros" (León-Portilla, *Cantares*, 2.1:85). Bierhorst translates: "The Mexican women have gone into the lagoon. It's truly thus. So all are going. And where to, comrades?" (Bierhorst, *Cantares*, 153). In Bierhorst's translation, the audience's identification with the victims and participation in the commemorative ritual is achieved through the vocative at the end of the stanza.

247 Bierhorst, *Cantares*, 100.

invites the audience first to "remember" (*xiquilnamiquican*) Coyonacazco,[248] the Mexica's last bastion of resistance in northeastern Tlatelolco and the place where their leaders (Tlacotzin, Motelchiuh, and Oquiztzin in stanza 8) eventually surrendered.[249] Listeners are then exhorted to "weep" (*xachocacan*), as in an icnocuicatl, and "acknowledge" (*xoconmaticā*) the fact that they have "abandoned" (*ticcauhque*) Tenochtitlan and, by extension, Mexicaness (*Mexicayotl*) during the exodus.[250] Because the abandonment of Tenochtitlan is linked to divine sanctions ("This is the doing of Life Giver [Ipalnemoani] in Tlatelolco"), the icnocuicatl is resonant with universal themes about the abandonment of the city by its gods found in early city laments from the ancient Near East.

In theory, sorrow and weeping in the song, literally a case of what Connerton has referred to as performative memory, or bodily social memory, should ensure the endurance of collective trauma, presented as a sore on the social body. More than a rhetorical trope of "misery" and destitution, the reference in stanza 9 to "bitter" water and food (*atl chichix . . . tlaqualli chichix*)—note the repetition of "chichix"[251] at the end of each phrase, a device known as epiphora—matches historical reality. Tenochtitlan-Tlatelolco depended on aqueducts supplying freshwater from Chapultepec, located on the shores of the lake, west of the island. By mid-May the aqueducts had been cut by the Spaniards and the Mexica were relying entirely on springs across the city; but these were soon drained and people were only left with salty groundwater.[252] The allusion to salty water is mirrored in the *Annals of Tlatelolco*: "What we suffered is cause for tears and sorrow. The water we drank was salt. . . . We ate . . . grass from the salt flats."[253] If "Anakalema" echoes Kritoboulos's account of the sack of Constantinople, "Huexotzincayotl" redrafts with considerable accuracy details of the siege of Mexico found in book 12 of the *Florentine Codex*, the *Annals of Tlatelolco*, and other native sources. Similarities between the song and the *Florentine Codex* in particular are coming from the same scholarly context in Tlatelolco, where

---

248 *Ilnamiqui* = to remember (Bierhorst, *Nahuatl-English Dictionary*, 166). Bierhorst (*Cantares*, 46) refers to the use of the imperative as "ejaculation."

249 Bierhorst, *Cantares*, 434, 473. See Sahagún, *Florentine Codex*, book 12, ch. 39, 115.

250 *Choca* = to weep; *mati* = to know, to realize; *cahua* = to leave or abandon—the latter verb is repeated throughout the song (6, 8, and 9) (Bierhorst, *Nahuatl-English Dictionary*, 56, 85, 205).

251 *Chichiya* = to be bitter, to turn bitter (ibid., 78).

252 Mundy, *Death of Aztec Tenochtitlan*, 75.

253 In Lockhart, *We People Here*, 267. Lockhart speculates that the anonymous author of the *Annals of Tlatelolco*, originally written in alphabetized Nahuatl, was "trained by Spanish ecclesiastics, though probably of the generation of fray Pedro de Gante [ca. 1480–1572] rather than the generation of Sahagún [1500–1590] and Motolinia [1482–1568]" (ibid., 42).

eyewitness accounts were edited by Nahua intellectuals. As indicated earlier, these scholars also wrote the *Colloquios* and possibly the song.

The trauma process culminates in the final stanza, where the author commemorates the "exemplary behavior" of the Mexica leaders Motelchiuh (the captain of the army of Mexico) and Tlacotzin (a Mexica noble) as they are taken to the fire at Cortés's camp.[254] Prospecting for gold, the Spaniards, we read in the *Annals of Tlatelolco*, "turned to the Tenochtitlan rulers and interrogated them. At this time they burned Quauhtemoctzin on the feet."[255] I have argued that in "Huexotzincayotl" the Mexica celebrate not a triumphant victory over the Huexotzinca, but their own tragic destruction. The Huexotzinca, in fact, are not mentioned anywhere save for the title, nor are any other native groups. As the Mexica come to occupy the space formerly reserved for their opponents (see fig. 16), the agents become victims sacrificed *to* and *by* Life Giver (see fig. 17). The abandonment of Mexicayotl is ritualized here with no reference to the Spanish or indigenous culprits, among them thousands of Huexotzinca. The Mexica's native rivals are nonetheless present in their absence, making the sorrow all the more profound and spectacular as the interpretive void they leave behind is filled with the trauma claim of the defeated. Somewhere subtextually and through a spell of reflexivity, the Mexica are told to bear the invasive trauma "with song" (10), as did their leaders when taken, like sacrificial victims, to the fire.

While divinity takes up the space of the perpetrator in "Huexotzincayotl," "Tlaxcaltecayotl" attributes responsibility to the indigenous factions of the Spanish-native alliance. The latter song, which appears in two variants, imaginatively reconstructs the events of the siege just as "Huexotzincayotl," albeit in less detail.[256] A Mexica composition, the song comprises five cantos of nine, three, six, four, and eight stanzas that focus on the indigenous warriors, mainly

---

254 Bierhorst, *Cantares*, 434, and idem, *A Nahuatl-English Dictionary*, 218, 328.

255 In Lockhart, *We People Here*, 271. Cuauhtemoc and other nobles did not actually die in Coyoacan. The last Mexica emperor, along with Tetlepanquetzal of Tacuba, was hanged from a tree in Itzamkanac or Acalan (in the present-day state of Campeche) during Cortés's march to Honduras in 1525. Cortés allegedly suspected them of plotting a revolt (Bierhorst, *Cantares*, 463, 476; Restall, *Seven Myths*, 147, 150). The *Annals of Tlatelolco* confirm that Cortés did not execute the Tenochtitlan rulers in 1521 (in Lockhart, *We People Here*, 273). On Cuauhtemoc's death, see Restall, *Seven Myths*, 147–57.

256 All references here are to the first version of "Tlaxcaltecayotl" that appears on fols. 54r–55v. Bierhorst reports that the second version on fols. 83r–85r only differs in the following stanzas: 1, 3, 10, 12, 13, 16, 17, 23, and 28. Stanza 30 is also absent in the variant (Bierhorst, *Cantares*, 514). The original Nahuatl text and its English translation can be found in ibid., 318–23 (for the variant, see 418–25). For Spanish translations, see León-Portilla, *Cantares*, 2.2:792–813 (for the variant, see 1168–89), and Garibay, *Poesía indígena*, 57–62.

the Tlaxcalteca and Huexotzinca, within a context that is highly subversive.[257] Referring to the use of Mexica sarcasm in this song, Bierhorst writes that "with a smirk," the singer "is inviting the enemy to destroy him." The scholar borrows from Franciscan friar Juan de Torquemada's account, according to which "when the Mexicans saw their buildings burned, they taunted their Indian foes, saying, 'burn and destroy the houses! We'll make you come back and build better ones if we win. If the Castilians win, you'll build for them too.'"[258] Sarcasm, mimicry, and tragic spoof all contribute to the disruptive effect of the utterance. The fusion of the tragic and the comic in the song—like a Euripidean tragedy—"intensif[ies]" the affliction that has befallen Mexicayotl, "toughening it with parody."[259] From the lips of the Mexica singer, "Tlaxcaltecayotl" no longer makes honorable mention of the feats of the enemy, as Hernández reported, but instead denigrates those whose deeds have turned the Tenochca and Tlatelolca into trophies. The song can thus be read as a parody of the subgenre (if the latter, as discussed before, is taken as praise or covert self-praise), a satire of the foe (already present in the subgenre as a travesty), and a poignant trauma claim that hinges on an ironic twist of fate (the new element stemming from the semantic slippage). During the four-day pillage of Tenochtitlan-Tlatelolco, the Mexica became the enemy's booty, literally assuming the role of the Mimixcoa (see fig. 18).

The unusual syntax, lack of punctuation, and obscure vocabulary of the *Cantares mexicanos* have given rise to a wealth of approaches and, not unexpectedly, to conflicting translations. "Translation of any of the more complex passages," admits Lockhart, "is something of a guess in the best of cases." In addition to these difficulties, "the texts are shot through with vocables or nonsense syllables," both within and between words, meaning that translators are left to decide what constitutes a vocable and what does not. Lockhart adds that even though Nahuatl generally distinguishes between third person and direct address, such distinctions in the *Cantares mexicanos* "seem to be widely ignored."[260] As a result, it is often difficult to tell who the speaker is, and this is precisely what happens in "Tlaxcaltecayotl." Bierhorst, for instance, translates the opening stanza as "*You*'ve arrived here in Tenochtitlan!

257 For the use of the term "canto," see n. 160, above.

258 Bierhorst, *Cantares*, 473.

259 For the fusion of the comic and the tragic in Euripides, see W. Arrowsmith, "A Greek Theater of Ideas," *Arion: A Journal of Humanities and the Classics* 2.3 (1963): 32–56, at 42.

260 Lockhart, *Nahuas and Spaniards*, 146.

'Be strong, Tlaxcalans! Huexotzincans!,'" whereas León-Portilla and I opt for "*We*'ve arrived here in Tenochtitlan!"[261]

Despite the enunciative ambiguity here and elsewhere in the song, it is obvious that the more the indigenous warriors are openly praised, the more they are degraded connotatively. Their most important feat is their greatest defeat. "Those with metal weapons are wrecking [*quixixinia*] the city, they're wrecking [*quixixinia*] Mexicaness [Mexicayotl]!," we hear in stanza 4 with reference to the Spaniards.[262] Through the use of anaphora, the destruction of Mexico is emotively staged and the roles of victims and victimizers are clearly assigned in a way similar to that of "Anakalema," where the symbol creator, through the emperor's dramatic monologue, affectively reenacts the final attack of the Turks as they enter Constantinople, "destroying" him and his subjects (lines 28–29; see fig. 11).

The enemy's triumph is contrasted with the Mexica trauma in the moving antithesis of dancing and hair-cutting: "See [*xiquimottacan*] them dancing with their shields! We've cut off our hair [*otonnexineque*], O Tehuetzquiti, O Tecoatzin! What else would you do? Onward! Let there be dancing! Sing [*xicuica*], brothers!" (10).[263] We know from the *Annals of Tlatelolco* that the "Tenochca who were war captains cut off their hair [to avoid recognition], and all the subordinate leaders cut their hair."[264] The reference to the cutting of hair is also echoed elsewhere in the *Annals*, and so is the "wrecking" of the city: "And on the roads lay shattered bones and scattered hair; the houses were unroofed, red [with blood]; worms crawled on the roads; and the walls of the houses are slippery with brains. And the water seemed red, as though it were dyed, and thus we drank it."[265] The twice repeated "What . . . brothers!" in stanza 10 further accentuates the affliction, which deepens and widens with the rhetorical

---

261 "Hemos llegado aquí, a Tenochtitlan, / esforzaos / vosotros tlaxcaltecas, huexotzincas." Another example is found in stanza 11. Compare Bierhorst's translation, "This we've abandoned . . . this Tenochtitlan. . . . *They* move toward Tlatelolco," to León-Portilla's: "We've abandoned . . . Tenochtitlan. . . . *We*'re arriving . . . in Tlatelolco" ("Hemos abandonado . . . Tenochtitlan. . . . Ya llegaremos . . . a Tlatelolco") (my emphasis).

262 *Xixinia* = to destroy, wreck (Bierhorst, *Nahuatl-English Dictionary*, 392).

263 The *xicuica* in this stanza should be read as *xicuicacan*. *Xiquimonittacan* > *itta* = to see something, to look at something; *nexintli* = haircut; *cuica* = to sing (ibid., 171–72, 238, 107). León-Portilla translates *otonnexineque* as "those who look like the Otomi" ("los que tienen aspecto de otomíes"), while, according to Bierhorst, the literal meaning is "we've become haircut owners" (ibid., 238).

264 In Lockhart, *We People Here*, 263.

265 Ibid., 313. For León-Portilla's translation, see M. León-Portilla, ed., *The Broken Spears: The Aztec Account of the Conquest of Mexico*, trans. L. Kemp (Boston, MA, 2006), 137–38. Although not a poem, León-Portilla renders the passage in verse.

question addressing the Mexica lords: "What else would you do?" Whether dancing and singing are intratextually linked to the triumph of the Tlaxcalteca and the Huexotzinca or to the Mexica's tragic sarcasm in acknowledging their defeat or both, extratextually they both ritualize the cultural trauma quite literally, as the singer calls on the audience to participate in the performative act by dancing and singing to the beats of huehuetl: "Let there be dancing!" (10) and "Sing, brothers!" (10–12). León-Portilla's previous distinction between "Huexotzincayotl"/icnocuicatl and "Tlaxcaltecayotl"/yaocuicatl is now blurred and blunted. The victors' celebration of triumphant war (yaocuicatl) is coopted by the defeated, who turn it into ritual lament (icnocuicatl). It is in this ambivalent, double-coded space that the composer inscribes and performs his trauma claim, intensifying and toughening the tragedy with parody.

The theme of the abandonment of the city found in "Huexotzincayotl" is rehearsed here in stanza 11. In a typically reflexive fashion, the singer invites the audience to "hear" his song-cum-trauma claim ("Truly we've abandoned— hear [xicaqui][266] my songs [nocuic]![267]—this, our city, this Tenochtitlan, here in Mexico. Oh I sing them in earnest, I utter them, ah!"), while stanzas 14–18 elicit a kind of self-praise—"the actual (though limited) military successes enjoyed by the Mexicans during the siege."[268] As in "Anakalema," particularly the commemorative rituals of makarismos and goos, the claim process here is foregrounded by aural and visual imagery. A performative genre, the cantar involves the physical participation ("hear," "sing," "see") of the audience in the reenactment of the siege by means of Connerton's bodily social memory, or mnemonics of the body.[269]

The events culminate in canto D (19–22), where we learn of Cuauhtemoc's capture and the grand exodus: "They've even seized [conanque][270] Cuauhtemoc. All the Mexica lords go off through the water" (22). Like the Byzantine emperor, who metonymically stands for Romania, the last Mexica ruler is a synecdoche for the Mexica Empire; his capture heralds the fall of Mexicayotl. Repeated at the end of all four stanzas, the refrain, "Tenochcans are surrounded [yaoyahualolo], Tlatelolcans are surrounded [yaoyahualolo]," reconstructs,

---

266 Caqui = to hear something (Bierhorst, Nahuatl-English Dictionary, 62).

267 Nocuic = my song (cuicatl with the first person singular possessive prefix) (T. D. Sullivan, Compendio de la gramática náhuatl [Mexico City, 2014], 45, 47).

268 Bierhorst, Cantares, 474.

269 Connerton, How Societies Remember, 71–72, 74.

270 Ana = to take, seize (Bierhorst, Nahuatl-English Dictionary, 39).

through emotive parallelism and anaphora,[271] and accompanied by the sound of drum beats, the final dramatic moments of the siege, when the Tlaxcalteca, Huexotzinca, Chimpaneca, and Acolhua, together with the Castilians, seize Mexico (19–22) (fig. 15). From the perspective of the Mexica, the numerical superiority of the enemy, emphasized by the repetition of the verb *yaoyahualoa* (to surround something in battle)[272] seven times in four consecutive stanzas, is obviously due to the involvement of their indigenous rivals. Cortés's indigenous allies are blamed for the fall of the empire, already dramatized in the refrain of canto C, which is repeated six times: "Tlaxcalans, hey! Huexotzincans, hey!" (13–18).[273] The cultural trauma is attributed to the usual suspects, a claim that is consistent with the native view of the conquest as an anti-imperial revolt.

Responsibility shifts from divine abandonment in "Huexotzincayotl" to historical circumstances and traditional antagonisms in "Tlaxcaltecayotl." In the final canto (23–30), the Mexica lords surrender in Coyonacazco, and the women are raped or coerced into marriage with the Spaniards. As in "Anakalema," this involuntary union is painted against the trauma of the conquest: "My dear Tlaxcalan nephews, now remember [*xiquilnamiquican*] how we did it in Coyonacazco: the Mexica women [*Mexica ye cihua*][274] muddied their faces [*Neiçoquihuiloc*],[275] and all the masters [*tlacahuaque*][276] made their choices" (23).[277] The *Florentine Codex* reports this incident: "And [the Spaniards] seized and set apart the pretty women—those of light bodies, the fair[-skinned] ones. And some women, when they were [to be] assaulted, covered their faces with mud and put on old, mended skirts and rags for their shifts. They put all rags on themselves."[278] The reference to the women "mudd[ying] their faces" to make themselves unattractive evidently points to the forced marriages, both literal and figurative, that ensued from the conquest.

---

271 The refrain appears with slight variations as follows: "yaoyahualolo in tenochcatlaya yaoyahualolo in tlatelolcatl" (19); "yaoyahualolo in Tenochcatla yaoyahualolo in Tlatelolcatla" (20–21); "yaoyahualolo in Tenochcatl in Tlatelolcatla" (22).

272 Bierhorst, *Nahuatl-English Dictionary*, 405.

273 "tlaxcalteca ỹ meetlo ye huexotzinca y meetla."

274 *Cihuatl* = woman, wife (Bierhorst, *Nahuatl-English Dictionary*, 87).

275 *Izoquihuia* = to cover one's face with mud (ibid., 181).

276 *Tlacahuah* = master of slaves (ibid., 323).

277 León-Portilla's translation of this stanza is almost identical to that of Bierhorst except for the final clause: "they are chosen by those who will become their masters" ("son escogidas por quienes serán sus dueños").

278 Sahagún, *Florentine Codex*, book 12, ch. 40, 118.

Enunciated in the following stanza in the form of a refrain—"This is how we did it in Coyonacazco: the Mexica women muddied their faces, and all the masters made their choices" (24)—the Mexica tragedy is embodied by Doña Isabel or Tecuichpotzin, the daughter of Emperor Moctezuma Xocoyotzin and wife of Cuauhtemoc. Stanza 29 describes what the songwriter sees, through the eyes of the last Mexica emperor, as the forced union between the Mexica and the Spaniards in the figures of Isabel and Cortés: "The ruler Cuauhtemoc says, 'O my little niece! You're seized, you're taken![279] Who are you sitting beside [ac ynahuac]?[280] The Captain General [Genelal Capitan]. Truly it's Doña Isabel [yxapeltzina]!' 'O my little niece!' Aya! It's true. And lords [teteuctin][281] are seized [necuilolo]" (29).[282] The capture of the Mexica nobility (teteuctin) and the withering of Mexicayotl is rehearsed in the refrain of the final stanza through the affective language of repetition—"'O my little niece! You're seized, you're taken! Who are you sitting beside? The Captain General. Truly it's Doña Isabel!' And lords are seized [ye necuilolo ya teteucti aayo]. Yes, lords are seized [ye necuilolo ya teteuctin ayyo]" (30). Together with the refrain of stanzas 27 and 28—"Yes, all you lords are seized [necuilolo]!"—the final stanza brings the commemorative reenactment of the fall of the empire to a close.

The traumatic events of the conquest are the focal point of the song. As the Mexica women (Mexica ye cihua) become the trophies of the Spanish "masters" (tlacahuaque), Mexicayotl falls into the hands of Cortés and its traditional foes. As in "Huexotzincayotl" (7), the audience here is invited to "remember" (xiquilnamiquican) (23) Coyonacazco as the last stronghold of the Mexica and the place where Cuauhtemoc and his men were forced to surrender. Despite commemorating the same events and being shaped through a kindred semantic

---

279 León-Portilla attributes the invocation not to Cuauhtemoc (who was a cousin of Moctezuma) but to an unknown speaker addressing Cuauhtemoc: "They tell lord Cuauhtemoc: my nephew, have you been seized, taken?" ("Le dicen al señor Cuauhtémoc: sobrino mío, has sido capturado, apresado?"). For this reason, León-Portilla translates "my nephew" instead of "my little niece" both here and in the final stanza.

280 Ac inahuac = beside whom (Bierhorst, Nahuatl-English Dictionary, 222).

281 Plural of teuctli = nobleman (ibid., 317).

282 Bierhorst understands necuiloa (passive, necuilolo) as ihcuiloa, meaning "to paint, to immortalize" (ibid., 154), and therefore translates "delineated." Frances Karttunen, however, reports that necuiloa means "to bend or twist something" (F. Karttunen, An Analytical Dictionary of Nahuatl [Norman, OK, 1992], 161). See also R. Siméon, Diccionario de la lengua náhuatl o mexicana (Mexico City, 1981], 313. By translating necuilolo as "seized" ("apresados"), León-Portilla seems to adopt the latter sense of the word and so do I. Since necuiloa also means "to engage in commerce," the passive necuilolo could suggest that the captive lords have been reduced to merchandise (Karttunen, Analytical Dictionary, 161).

slippage, the two texts nevertheless differ substantially in their trauma claim. On the one hand, "Huexotzincayotl" reads the cultural trauma as divine intervention and makes no explicit reference to the native groups who, as active agents in the alliance, played a key part in the fall of Tenochtitlan-Tlatelolco, although the latter are connotatively present thanks to the subgenre's interpretive grid. "Tlaxcaltecayotl," on the other, shows no sign of divine involvement and places the indigenous enemies at the core of its meaning-making process. Contrary to "Huexotzincayotl," where we find no mention of Cortés and his men, this song makes numerous comments on the Spaniards but shifts the focus of responsibility from them to the native players. This is evident in both the selection of the subgenre (Tlaxcaltecayotl) and the articulation of the trauma claim. Stanza 12 eloquently conveys this turn at the level of meaning-making. Even though both Castilians and Nahuas pursued Lord Anahuacatl, only the Tlaxcalteca make it into the emphatically sarcastic refrain: "with shields and swords they were chasing him, they the Tlaxcalans, aya! and they the Castilians. . . . *May it not be in vain that it has happened, Tlaxcalans! Sing, brothers!*"[283]

That Catholic missionaries salvaged *Cantares mexicanos* in alphabetized form is a truism. What is less clear is the extent to which the process of collecting and recording may have altered the songs' content. When teaching at the Colegio de Santa Cruz, the Franciscan friar Andrés de Olmos (d. 1571) gathered indigenous ethnographic data through questionnaires that he sent to surviving native nobles, specifically his students' parents. This methodology, writes Lee, which was coopted by Sahagún, the man likely behind the *Cantares mexicanos* project, surely influenced the content and topics of the assembled information, and may have led indigenous informants to "tailo[r] their responses to the expectations of the missionaries," thus modifying the requested material.[284] I have suggested, however, that at least one of our songs, if not both, was probably composed by Nahua intellectuals at the Colegio de Santa Cruz. Whether true or not, the absence of a potent anti-Spanish rhetoric in these texts may have to do less with Spanish censorship and expectations, or the position of the composers, informants, and collectors in early colonial society, and more with the Nahua belief system (e.g., rotational ordering scheme, disorderly periods, and breach of sacred rituals), as well as with the native view of the conquest as an act of defiance against a powerful empire.

Both texts are the end products of trauma processes that, in Smelser's terms, associate the traumatic experience of the siege and fall of Mexico with

283 The refrain is indicated in italics.
284 Lee, "*Mestizaje*," 902–3.

"a strong negative affect."[285] At the same time, the fact that one of them has survived in two variants implies a degree of diffusion and possibly of popularity. Among the ninety-one compositions of the *Cantares mexicanos* only two are repeated in their entirety—"Tlaxcaltecayotl" and a "plain song" that does not deal with the events of the conquest.[286] This may be telling of the relative dissemination of this particular trauma claim in the second half of the sixteenth century, despite the somewhat unwelcoming backdrop of early colonial Mexico for this type of narrative. As the events of the conquest are dramatized, "Tlaxcaltecayotl" and "Huexotzincayotl" become commemorative rituals in a recognizable language that, potentially, could gestate or perpetuate, if we agree that the songwriters did not have firsthand experience of the events, the postmemory of the cultural trauma.

285 Smelser, "Psychological Trauma," 36.
286 The two versions of the "plain song" appear on fol. 3v and fols. 25r–25v.

FIVE

TEXTS AND THEIR AFTERLIFE

O N THE CUSP OF MODERNITY, THE EASTERN ROMAN AND MEXICA EMPIRES FELL into the hands of two rising Old World powers. The doomsday of the Byzantines turned out to signal a global cognitive remapping. Sixty-eight years and several thousand miles apart, Romania and Mexicayotl were faced with the aftermath of their conquest. "Traumatic status," Alexander reminds us, "is attributed to real or imagined phenomena, not because of their actual harmfulness or their objective abruptness, but because these phenomena are believed to have abruptly, and harmfully, affected collective identity.... Only if the patterned meanings of the collectivity are abruptly dislodged," he insists, is an event ascribed with traumatic status. Simply put, "it is the meanings that provide the sense of shock and fear, not the events in themselves."[1] "Anakalema," "Huexotzincayotl," and "Tlaxcaltecayotl" are solid examples of such meanings. Through the vocabulary of negative affect, they relate the trauma of the fall of an empire as a fissure in the social fabric and an open wound on the body politic. They are the workings of creators who use symbolic resources and historical particulars to articulate, in a familiar language, the trauma of the conquered.

We have seen that "Anakalema" calls on the long tradition of threnoi, folk songs, and monodies about the fall of cities, as well as on ancient tragedy, ritual lamentation, funerary practices, and lore. "Huexotzincayotl" and "Tlaxcaltecayotl" are similarly fixed in the context of pre-Hispanic cantares

---

1   Alexander, "Toward a Theory," 9–10.

and sacrificial practices. Remodeled from within, the songs enable a dramatic slippage from ritualized victory to ritual lamentation, and a semantic shift from triumph to defeat. In "Anakalema" and "Huexotzincayotl," the trauma claim is uttered in an accessible language that could reach broader intergenerational audiences. Negative affect is conveyed through identifiable forms of lament: threnoi and ritual lamentation in the case of "Anakalema," icnocuicatl in "Huexotzincayotl" and "Tlaxcaltecayotl" (in the latter, lamentation is hardened by sarcasm and parody). At the same time, the trauma claim is rhetorically constructed through, among others, anaphora, parallelism, and repetition. The authors address the four critical questions on the nature of the pain, the nature of the victim, the relation of the victim to the wider community, and the attribution of responsibility. "Anakalema" clearly blames the enemy, who is denigrated through the metaphor of the "dog." The poem may cut loose from the idea of theodicy, which pervades other learned laments of the time, but it does not depart from the notion of divine involvement. "Huexotzincayotl" puts divine intervention at the center of its trauma claim while making no explicit mention of the foe. The latter is invoked in "Tlaxcaltecayotl," where the weight of responsibility slides from the Spaniards to the Mexica's historical antagonists, particularly the Tlaxcalteca and Huexotzinca, who are degraded through parody. In the same song, we come across references to the rape of women by the conquerors, an act of violence that is also developed in graphic detail in "Anakalema."

All three texts bear signs of reflexivity, implying a conscious effort on the part of the composers to create widely available accounts of collective grief.[2] "Huexotzincayotl" and "Tlaxcaltecayotl" are performative subgenres and as such belong to the public realm, whereas a learned poem like "Anakalema" is theoretically associated with the private sphere. I say "theoretically" because the poem may have been transmitted orally, and possibly publicly, before it was written down. A literal case of performative memory or mnemonics of the body, the Nahuatl songs were accompanied by music and, probably, acting. Though not a folk song, "Anakalema" is nevertheless inflected with the sounds and rhythms of popular songs and folk laments for the dead (moirologia). The figurative reconstruction of ritual lament and popular funerary practices, and the use of literary devices such as dialogue, dramatic monologue, and tragic irony, all lend the poem a strong sense of immediacy and performativity. Through an imaginative reenactment of the disruptive events mirrored in contemporary sources, the threnos and the cantares seek to impart their trauma claims to the broader

2   Ibid., 26.

community. The three texts are imbued with pessimism—Constantinople is now a "city of Turks" (*Tourkopole*) (line 60) and Tenochtitlan has been abandoned ("Huexotzincayotl": 8–9; "Tlaxcaltecayotl": 11). In principle, all three accounts could empower postmemory, serving as vehicles for the transgenerational transmission of trauma. For that to happen, they would need to enter the "public 'theatre' of history," where "dramas concerning 'our' history" are enacted.[3] In reality, different historical contexts gave rise to different historical routes.

The conquest of Constantinople may have brought the end of the empire, but it did not put an end to the Byzantine tradition, nor did it prevent Greeks from finding ways to adapt to the Ottoman era. Historical and political specificities aside, the surviving religious and secular aristocracy (*archontes*) of Byzantium as well as various intellectuals, like the colonial Nahuas, hammered out a place for themselves in Ottoman society, and so did an emerging Greek economic elite that took advantage of the fact that the Genoese and Venetians lost the commercial privileges they had enjoyed before the conquest. Kritoboulos, we have seen, became Mehmed II's biographer. In his *History*, he focuses on the transfer to Ottoman rule and makes several references to his personal role in this transition. Gennadios Scholarios, who had opposed the union of the Greek and Latin churches, served as the first Greek Orthodox patriarch under the Ottomans, albeit reluctantly and intermittently, from 1454 to 1465. The Greek church would strengthen its power gradually over the next three hundred years, profiting from many concessions and Ottoman expansion in the Mediterranean. "Catholic bishops," says Molly Greene, "will fall to the wayside and Orthodox metropolitans will hurry to take their place."[4]

The scions of the greatest noble families of the Byzantine Empire, such as the Palaiologoi and Kantakouzenoi, gained important official posts in the first few decades of Ottoman rule and, similar to the Nahua ruling class, were involved in tax collection. Like other Palaiologoi, the last despot of the Morea in the Peloponnese, Demetrios Palaiologos, became "a tax farmer of Ottoman state monopolies" in Constantinople.[5] Often sons of Byzantine nobles who had

3 Popular Memory Group, "Popular Memory: Theory, Politics, Method," in *Making Histories: Studies in History-Writing and Politics*, ed. R. Johnson et al. (Abingdon, 2007), 205–52, at 207.

4 M. Greene, *The Edinburgh History of the Greeks, 1453 to 1768: The Ottoman Empire* (Edinburgh, 2015), 30, 36; Stathakopoulos, Μικρή ιστορία, 325, 327; Neville, *Guide to Byzantine Historical Writing*, 308. See also P. Bádenas, "Τα συμφιλιωτικά ρεύματα Ελλήνων λογίων στην αυλή του Μεγάλου Τούρκου," in *Ο ελληνικός κόσμος ανάμεσα στην Ανατολή και τη Δύση 1453–1981*, 2 vols., ed. A. Argyriou, K. A. Dimadis, and A. D. Lazaridou (Athens, 1999), 2:409–19.

5 Greene, *Edinburgh History*, 24; Stathakopoulos, Μικρή ιστορία, 326.

been taken to the sultan's palace and converted later held high offices in the government. Among them we find the last Byzantine emperor's own nephew and nominal heir to the Byzantine throne (Konstantinos Palaiologos was childless), the grand vizier Mesih Pasha. The example of Mahmud Pasha Angelović, another grand vizier and a former member of the Byzantine nobility who had entered Mehmed II's palace at a young age only to lead the conquest of Serbia against his own brother years later, may recall the numerous Nahua and Maya conquerors in colonial Mexico, even if the historical terms and conditions in each case are hardly comparable.[6]

Constantinople, now the capital city of Mehmed II's empire, was repopulated partly with Christian Greeks, who in 1477 made up over twenty-five percent of its population. Mehmed, Kritoboulos tells us, actively sought to revive the glorious capital city and for this reason granted significant power to Orthodox Greeks, whose presence in trade, tax farming, and the guilds came to be very strong, despite the fact that throughout the Ottoman period non-Muslims were treated as inferior.[7] Greene observes that early postconquest Constantinople was "a remarkably Greek and even Byzantine city," considering that just a few years earlier the Byzantines had been defeated and the city suffered damage during the siege and subsequent plundering. But the prominent role of the Greeks in early Ottoman Constantinople, a consequence of Mehmed's readiness "to come to terms with his Christian subjects," was nevertheless temporary. The children of those who had converted to Islam were rooted firmly in Islamic society and the Byzantine aristocracy became extinct, while the conquest of Egypt and Syria in the early sixteenth century placed the Ottoman Empire in an orbit that was more decidedly Islamic.[8]

The diffusion of prophecies about liberating Constantinople in the two centuries after the conquest may be suggestive of their relevance to different generations, and so might the survival of folk poetry about the sack of the city (halosis) in the rural areas of the Greek-speaking world at least up to the nineteenth century, when most of the songs were recorded. But it is not easy to gauge this relevance, particularly from the early sixteenth to the late seventeenth century, nor is it clear whether the epithet Romaios or Romios (Roman)— "Rum" in Turkish—was consistently used from the fall of Constantinople to the

---

6 Greene, *Edinburgh History*, 24, 27; Stathakopoulos, Μικρή ιστορία, 325–26.

7 Greene, *Edinburgh History*, 24–25, 27; Reinsch, "Εισαγωγή," 10–13. See also H. Inalcik, "The Policy of Mehmed II toward the Greek Population of Istanbul and the Byzantine Buildings of the City," *Dumbarton Oaks Papers* 23–24 (1969–1970): 229–49.

8 Greene, *Edinburgh History*, 28, 54.

dissolution of the Ottoman Empire in the early twentieth century. Following the conquest, Orthodox Greeks, notes Greene, gradually came to think of themselves principally as Christians, while the Ottomans began to call them "Rum" only in the late seventeenth century. This shift in terminology implies that at some point after the fall, the use of the word "Roman" to mean the Greek Orthodox living in Ottoman territories either faded away entirely or shrank in comparison to the epithet "Christian." She speculates that this was the result of the waning of the Byzantine ruling class, which in the past had referred to itself as "Roman," and links the comeback of the term in the late seventeenth century to the emergence of the Phanariots, the Greek Orthodox Constantinopolitan aristocracy with "strong Hellenizing tendencies."[9] These were members of powerful Greek families in Phanar, the northern neighborhood of Constantinople by the Golden Horn, where the patriarchate had moved in 1601.[10]

During the Ottoman period, the history of the patriarchate and Hellenism were inextricably connected. It is doubtful, says Greene, that the Greek elites within and close to the patriarchate "ever abandoned their Hellenic biases," adding that "even if these sentiments were somewhat attenuated in the sixteenth and seventeenth centuries, they came roaring back in the eighteenth with the rise of the Phanariots."[11] This is not the place to ascertain the shape and form of Hellenic sentiments in Ottoman Constantinople or other imperial territories, but we may safely assume that up until the early sixteenth century, the dream of liberating Byzantium was alive, nursed by Greek scholars who had fled Constantinople before or after 1453, by their descendants, and by their students. Collective petitions or poems in both Latin and Greek would be sent to Western monarchs encouraging them to take action against the Ottoman conquerors.[12]

Although absent in "Anakalema," the idea of recapturing Constantinople from the Turks with the help of the Christian world is present in folk poetry and in threnoi like the "Sack of Constantinople" by Limenitis.[13] Similarly, Stephen Reinert writes that prophetic narratives regarding the retaking of the city, especially the so-called *Oracula Leonis*, were in circulation until the seventeenth

---

9   Ibid., 50–52. Greene points out that in the thirteenth century the term "Rum" began to be used with reference to the Muslims who lived in the Byzantine Empire, or Romania.

10   E. Thomopoulos, *The History of Greece* (Santa Barbara, CA, 2012), 47.

11   Greene, *Edinburgh History*, 52.

12   Stathakopoulos, Μικρή ιστορία, 336.

13   For Limenitis's threnos, see Zoras, Βυζαντινή ποίησις, 183–197.288–1045.

century.[14] A relevant illustration of *Oracula Leonis* with the title "Blood" ("Haima/Sanguis") (fig. 20) by Cretan painter Georgios Klontzas in Codex Bute (ca. 1575–1577) shows a Christian coalition reconquering Constantinople. The infantry floods the city, while in the middle of the Christian fleet, on the water, we read: "The Power of Alliance" ("Dunamis sunodike / Potentia Conspirata").[15] Well known by the 1150s, the Leonine oracles apparently grew very popular in the two hundred years following the fall, when they were seen to forecast the liberation of the Queen City from the Turks.[16] The extraordinary number of manuscript copies produced in the sixteenth and seventeenth centuries attests to the popularity of these oracles.

In the eighteenth century, Orthodox Greeks managed to gain greater social cohesiveness by carving out a niche in the Ottoman order that was "more institutionally distinct, and more distinctly Christian" than before.[17] Members of the Greek elite, both Orthodox and converts, studied at the University of Padua, the official university of the Republic of Venice and birthplace of the Greek Enlightenment. As the century progressed, there was an increasing focus on publications by Greek presses outside the Ottoman Empire and on the foundation of Greek Orthodox schools within the empire, often funded by wealthy merchants.[18] Greene argues that these merchants, along with the Phanariots and the church, constituted "the backbone of the Greek Enlightenment"; by the last quarter of the century, self-determination had become an "explicit programme" not only for the Enlightenment intellectuals of the Greek diaspora, but also for some of these Ottoman Greeks.[19] The long investment in education had surely paid off, but the desire for independence was equally nurtured through historical circumstances. In the late eighteenth century the Ottoman Empire was in

---

14 Reinert, "Fragmentation," 280. Melissenos identifies Emperor Leo VI (r. 886–912) as Leo the Wise. Falsely associated with Leo VI, the Leonine oracles should probably be attributed to Leo the Mathematician or the Philosopher (ninth century). See P. Lurati, "*Oracula Leonis* (Leonine Oracles)," in *Byzantium: Faith and Power, 1261–1557*, ed. H. C. Evans (New York, 2004), 408–9, at 409, and P. Stephenson, *The Legend of Basil the Bulgar-Slayer* (Cambridge, 2003), 99.

15 The phrase is visible in red letters in the original fig. 20. Reinert makes reference to a variation of this illustration in MS Barocci 170, fol. 11v (1577) held in the Bodleian Library (Reinert, "Fragmentation," 280, ill. 281). For a color illustration, see A. Rigo, *Oracula Leonis: Tre manoscritti greco-veneziani degli oracoli attribuiti all'imperatore bizantino Leone il Saggio (Bodl. Baroc. 170, Marc. gr. VII.22, Marc. gr. VII.3)* (Padua, 1988), 30.

16 Stephenson, *Legend of Basil*, 99.

17 Greene, *Edinburgh History*, 213.

18 Ibid., 192, 208–9.

19 Ibid., 209, 212–13.

Fig. 20. Prophecies about recapturing Constantinople by Georgios Klontzas. "Haima/ Sanguis," in *Oracula Leonis*, Greek with Latin translation by Francesco Barozzi, ca. 1575– 1577, *Codex Bute*, fol. 10v, private collection. In J. Vereecken and L. Hadermann-Misguich, eds., *Les oracles de León le Sage illustrés par Georges Klontzas: La version Barozzi dans le Codex Bute* (Venice, 2000), 295. Courtesy of the Vikelaia Library of Heraklion and the Hellenic Institute of Venice.

turmoil and Christians were targeted, with prominent Greeks losing long-held privileges.[20] The way for the Greek Revolution of 1821 was already being paved.

In independent Greece, threnoi and folk songs about the sack of Constantinople would find their place in school curricula, the "institutional arenas" that had disseminated them up to this point[21] not as historical vestiges of Hellenism or Romiosune (Romanness) but as living evidence of a deep-seated trauma. The collection of these orally transmitted songs in the nineteenth and early twentieth centuries overlapped as much with the nascent Hellenic state and the processes of nation building as it did with Greek irredentism, and was often informed by Greek politics. Inaugurated with Ioannis Kolettis's speech to the National Assembly on 14 January 1844, the irredentist "great idea" or *megali idea* was the ideological core of the Greek nation-state for about a century, and was essentially the outcome of "the Greek encounter with modernity." It stemmed from the obvious difference between statehood and ethnicity—"the plain fact that the Greeks as a people did not all reside within the Greek state."[22] For grand visionaries (*megaloïdeates*) like Kolettis, Constantinople, not Athens, should become the capital of a fully fledged Hellas.[23]

Similar to Enlightenment scholars and political thinkers like Rigas Velestinlis and Adamantios Korais, who laid the groundwork for the War of Independence from the barracks of the Greek diaspora,[24] the link between classical past and modern present and the notion of national rebirth, or *palingenesia*, were crucial to the postrevolution intellectual and political elites. Korais's project of cultural regeneration, for instance, entailed a linguistic reform, which, although moderate, led to the development of *katharevousa*, a purified language meant to revive classical Greek through lexical and grammatical correction.[25] Meanwhile, philhellenism played a critical part in the struggle for independence, with Romantic poets such as Percy Bysshe Shelley claiming that the world had a moral obligation

---

20 Ibid., 212–13.

21 Alexander, "Toward a Theory," 15.

22 G. Jusdanis, *Belated Modernity and Aesthetic Culture: Inventing National Literature* (Minneapolis, MN, 1991), 115–16.

23 L. J. Frary, *Russia and the Making of Modern Greek Identity, 1821–1844* (New York, 2015), 78, and M. Herzfeld, *Ours Once More: Folklore, Ideology, and the Making of Modern Greece* (Austin, TX, 1982), 123.

24 On Greek Enlightenment, see P. M. Kitromilides, ed., *Adamantios Korais and the European Enlightenment* (Oxford, 2010), and P. M. Kitromilides, *Enlightenment and Revolution: The Making of Modern Greece* (Cambridge, MA, 2013).

25 For Korais's linguistic views, see P. Mackridge, "Korais and the Greek Language Question," in Kitromilides, *Adamantios Korais*, 127–49.

to help the Greeks, the scions of "those glorious beings" to whom Westerners "owe their civilization."[26] The rhetoric of national rebirth, writes Roderick Beaton, crystallized the idea that it was the children of the ancient Greeks that now lived in the lands of old Hellas, and, being their legitimate descendants, they deserved to be free.[27] The word "Hellenes" is used in the first Greek constitution of 1822 in relation to the citizens of the emerging state who, until then, had called themselves Romaioi or Graikoi. By the early nineteenth century this revivalist narrative was so widespread within Greek and philhellenic circles that it drew the criticism of historians like Jakob Philipp Fallmerayer, who in his *Geschichte* (1830) argued that the cultural and racial ties with ancient Hellas had been ruptured by Slav and Albanian invasions during the Byzantine period.[28] Among the intellectuals who staunchly refuted his theory was Konstantinos Paparrigopoulos, a professor of history at the National and Kapodistrian University of Athens. In Paparrigopoulos's multivolume *History of the Greek Nation* (*Historia tou hellenikou ethnous*) published from 1860 to 1877, and in the work of the Heptanesian scholar Spyridon Zambelios, we see a shift from the rhetoric of cultural rebirth to that of continuity, one that is still current today.[29]

Popular tradition was key to establishing this continuity between antiquity and modern times, with Byzantium acting as the connecting link. Thanks to Fallmerayer's controversial views, the study of folklore, or *laographia*, a term coined by professor of Greek mythology Nikolaos Politis in 1884, would soon take center stage, eventually becoming a national discipline.[30] In the preface to his anthology of Greek folk songs three decades later, Politis posited that in folk poetry one could find the "national character . . . imprinted, pure and

26 R. Beaton, "Introduction," in *The Making of Modern Greece: Nationalism, Romanticism, and the Uses of the Past (1797–1896)*, ed. R. Beaton and D. Ricks (Farnham, 2009), 1–18, at 3, and Percy Bysshe Shelley, *Hellas: A Lyrical Drama* (London, 1822), 8–10. On Shelley's *Hellas*, see R. Beaton, "Re-Imagining Greek Antiquity in 1821: Shelley's *Hellas* in Its Literary and Political Context," in *Re-Imagining the Past: Antiquity and Modern Greek Culture*, ed. D. Tziovas (New York, 2014), 47–58.

27 Beaton, "Introduction," 3.

28 Ibid., 4–5. On the use of the terms Hellenes, Romaioi, and Graikoi, see T. A. Kaplanis, "Antique Names and Self-Identification: *Hellenes, Graikoi,* and *Romaioi* from Late Byzantium to the Greek Nation-State," in Tziovas, *Re-Imagining the Past*, 81–97.

29 Beaton, "Introduction," 5.

30 Herzfeld, *Ours Once More*, 79–80, and D. Tziovas, *The Other Self: Selfhood and Society in Modern Greek Fiction* (Lanham, MD, 2003), 36.

genuine."[31] Folk songs on the fall of Constantinople in particular were granted special status within the relevant literature of lamentation because "with profound simplicity, they express a feeling of perseverance throughout the great national travails and the enslaved people's certain hope of being restored to its freedom and to its rightful position."[32] Politis's comment was meant as a prelude to a famous folk song in which the Virgin and the icons weep at the news of the fall: "Hush, Our Lady, don't weep, don't cry; / with the years, with time, all will be yours again."[33] Variously titled "The Capture of the City" ("To parsimo tes Poles"), "Hagia Sophia," or "The Sack of Constantinople" ("He halosis tes Konstantinoupoleos"), the song has survived in several variants that bear witness to its significance and dissemination,[34] while the closing line, slightly altered, turned into the mantra of Greek nationalism, both elite and popular. Whenever "all will be yours again" appeared isolated from the rest of the song, notes Michael Herzfeld, the "yours" of the Virgin was replaced with the first person plural possessive pronoun, a small but consequential modification reflecting the workings of a far-reaching national narrative: "all will be ours again."[35]

Folk poetry has played an important role in Greek education, despite the language question that persisted during the nineteenth century and a good part of the twentieth century, splitting politicians and literati into two camps: those who insisted that the vernacular, or *dimotiki*, should be the official language of the state, and those who promoted the purist *katharevousa*. One hundred eight out of a total of one hundred twenty-nine secondary school manuals of modern Greek from the years 1884–1977 gathered by Chrysanthi Koumbarou-Chanioti contain about two hundred fifty different folk songs or their variants, often repeated in multiple books. The prevalence of folk poetry in these manuals is only rivaled by the works of the Greek national bard Kostis Palamas, who nevertheless features in less than half as many entries and fewer books.[36]

---

31 N. Politis, *Εκλογαί από τα τραγούδια του ελληνικού λαού* (Athens, 1914), vi: Εις τα τραγούδια . . . ο εθνικός χαρακτήρ αποτυπώνεται ακραιφνής και ακίβδηλος.

32 Ibid., 4 (translated by Herzfeld, *Ours Once More*, 131): Τα δημοτικά άσματα . . . εκφράζουν με βαθείαν απλότητα συναίσθημα εγκαρτερήσεως προς τα μεγάλα εθνικά δεινά και βεβαίαν την ελπίδα του δουλωθέντος γένους περί ελευθερίας και ανορθώσεως.

33 Kehayoglou, "Συνοδευτικά έμμετρα κείμενα," 125.12–13: Σώπα, Κυρία Δέσποινα, μην κλαίεις, μη δακρύζεις· / πάλε με χρόνους, με καιρούς, πάλε δικά σου είναι.

34 See M. Philippides, "Tears of the Great Church: The Lamentation of Santa Sophia," *Greek, Roman, and Byzantine Studies* 52 (2012): 714–37.

35 Herzfeld, *Ours Once More*, 130, 132.

36 C. Koumbarou-Chanioti, *Τα νεοελληνικά αναγνώσματα στη μέση εκπαίδευση: Συγγραφείς και ανθολογημένα κείμενα (1884–1977)* (Athens, 2003), 191, 193.

Among the folk songs on the fall of Constantinople, the one with the highest frequency by far is "The Capture of the City," which crops up, many times along with "Anakalema," in variants, always preserving the final two lines. From 1917 to 1975 the song was included in twenty-one secondary school textbooks and numerous readers for primary education,[37] such as Galateia Kazantzaki's *The Soldier* (*Ho stratiotes*) (1914) and Kostas Pasayanis's *The Little Greek* (*To helle-nopoulo*) (1931), in which the "all will be ours again" variation is favored.[38] In primary school manuals, the song makes its appearance as early as 1899 in Michael Sakellaropoulos's *Reader* (*Anagnosmatarion*), while "Anakalema" emerges in high school textbooks three decades later, in Alexandros Saris's *Modern Greek Readings* (*Neoellenika anagnosmata*) (1930).[39] In the period 1930–1979 alone, the poem was incorporated in six out of fourteen manuals for the tenth grade, and it continues to figure in contemporary textbooks, with no other relevant threnos having the same rate of occurrence.[40]

It is a truism that the exigencies of nation building and the rhetoric of cultural continuity informed the collection, dating, and interpretation of Greek folk poetry. So too is the fact that folk laments and threnoi have been projected as signs of an open wound that has profoundly shaped the identity of Greeks from the Ottoman occupation (*tourkokratia*) to the nineteenth century and the inception of the "great idea," which came to an end with the equally "great" Asia Minor Disaster (*mikrasiatiki katastrophi*) in 1922. Memory is "social" and "deeply connected to the contemporary sense of the self," writes Alexander. Likewise, Smelser reminds us that "once a historical memory is established as a national trauma," it has to be "continuously and actively sustained and reproduced in order to continue in that status."[41] Through successive "re-territorializations"[42] and resignifications, the trauma of the fall of Constantinople has become an archsignifier of all the traumas of the nation, including the Turkish invasion of Cyprus (the *tourkiki eisvoli*) in 1974. A kind of urtrauma, *halosis* is understood as

---

37 Ibid., 173.

38 G. Kazantzaki, *Ο στρατιώτης: Ελληνικόν αναγνωσματάριον προς χρήσιν των μαθητών της πέμπτης τάξεως του δημοτικού σχολείου* (Athens, 1914), 184, and K. Pasayanis, *Το ελληνόπουλο: Αναγνωστικό για την δ' του δημοτικού* (Athens, 1931), 171.

39 M. K. Sakellaropoulos, *Αναγνωσματάριον προς χρήσιν των μαθητών της δ' τάξεως των δημοτικών σχολείων* (Athens, 1899), 62, and A. Saris, *Νεοελληνικά αναγνώσματα διά τους μαθητάς της ε' τάξεως των γυμνασίων και λυκείων* (Athens, 1930), 266–68.

40 Koumbarou-Chanioti, *Τα νεοελληνικά αναγνώσματα*, 38.

41 Alexander, "Toward a Theory," 22, and Smelser, "Psychological Trauma," 38.

42 I. Spasić, "The Trauma of Kosovo in Serbian National Narratives," in Eyerman, Alexander, and Breese, *Narrating Trauma*, 81–105, at 83.

foundational of modern Greek identity, but also as a "traumatizing interpretive framework" and an "entrenched story" for the Greeks.[43]

Mexico's case is different, and so is the fate of the *Cantares mexicanos,* whose manuscript was apparently forgotten until it was rediscovered in the second half of the nineteenth century.[44] For one thing, colonial censorship surely played a part in this, as we can gather from Sahagún's references to the "pagan" areítos. The hermetic language of *Cantares mexicanos* as a whole may have been another reason for its withering by the end of the sixteenth century, by which date the songwriters must have all passed away. In Bierhorst's view, "it is hardly surprising that the intricately cerebral song recitals died out."[45] But there is one more reason, a crucial one, for the phasing out of the trauma claim of "Huexotzincayotl" and "Tlaxcaltecayotl" in particular.

One strategy against trauma, argues Smelser, is to turn a negative occurrence into a positive event. Similarly, Eyerman notes that founding narratives often speak of a traumatic incident from which the collectivity has allegedly emerged. This "primal scene," he explains, "is usually given positive connotation, but it can also be negative."[46] So was this the case with early colonial Nahuas? The answer is no. Colonial Nahua society, as we have seen, was not especially inclined to such trauma claims, therefore laments like "Huexotzincayotl" and "Tlaxcaltecayotl" were exceptions rather than the rule. The siege and fall of Tenochtitlan-Tlatelolco did not acquire the status of collective trauma among Nahuas, not even among the Mexica elite. This was partly because of the Nahua sociopolitical system that saw periodic rotations of power rather than ruptures and watershed events, partly because of the continuity narrative as a survival strategy, and partly because of the conquest as a massive indigenous enterprise against a much hated empire. This, of course, does not mean that the conquest could not have been retrospectively read and projected as cultural trauma in later centuries.[47] But it never quite happened.

---

43 Ibid., 83, 93. Ivana Spasić speaks of the Serbian cultural trauma originating in the Battle of Kosovo in 1389, which led to the Ottoman occupation of Serbia that lasted, as with Greece, until the early nineteenth century.

44 For the history of the manuscript, see Bierhorst, *Cantares,* 14–15.

45 Ibid., 69.

46 Smelser, "Psychological Trauma," 54; Eyerman, "Past in the Present," 163.

47 On retrospective trauma, see R. Eyerman, *Cultural Trauma: Slavery and the Formation of African American Identity* (Cambridge, 2001), 1–5, and E. Zhukova, "From Ontological Security to Cultural Trauma: The Case of Chernobyl in Belarus and Ukraine," *Acta Sociologica* 59.4 (2016): 332–46.

During the seventeenth and eighteenth centuries, the works of such intellectuals as Carlos de Sigüenza y Góngora and Francisco Xavier Clavijero inspired a criollo patriotism that contested the colonial order by forging an identity distinct from Spain. Patriotic criollos (those of European descent who were born and raised in Spanish America) revalidated Mexico's preconquest past and thought up "symbolic genealogies" to assert a figurative Nahua ancestry.[48] Yet idealizing the native past had little to do with the indigenous present, while reading the Spanish invasion and conquest as a collective trauma would put criollo-ness (or *criollismo*) into an impossible position. The metaphorical affiliation of criollo patriotism with precontact civilizations was rarely accompanied by a genuine interest in the peoples that were now lumped under the undifferentiated heading of "Indian" (*indio*).

Those involved in the War of Independence in the nineteenth century (Mexico declared independence in 1821, a few months after the Greek War of Independence broke out) exploited similar strategies to justify their emancipation struggle. Historians like Carlos María Bustamante portrayed "Aztec emperors as patriotic forefathers of the new nation," but by the end of the century these began to give way to the heroes of independence.[49] Meanwhile, the preconquest past, says Kathleen Ann Myers, continued to be cut off from the indigenous present in nationalist rhetoric. For all that Mexican secretary of public education José Vasconcelos's (1921–1924) notional championing of *mestizaje* (the term *mestizo* originally referred to people of mixed indigenous and European origins) and the indigenism (*indigenismo*) movement of the early twentieth century tried to resolve this contradiction, in reality they cemented the hegemonic position of the ruling class and had a hand in "the further erasure of living indigenous cultures."[50]

With his influential 1925 concept of "the cosmic race" (*la raza cósmica*), which crucially did not overlap with the existing "brown race" (*raza de bronce*), Vasconcelos envisaged the subsumption of the indigenous cultures (essentially considered obsolete) under the category of a superior, "synthetic race." The latter, even though not "white" but a compound of the best qualities of all the living "races," was nevertheless imagined as the "new race to which the White

48   K. A. Myers, *In the Shadow of Cortés: Conversations along the Route of Conquest* (Tucson, AZ, 2015), 7. On criollo patriotism and nationalism, see D. A. Brading, *The First America: The Spanish Monarchy, Creole Patriots, and the Liberal State, 1492–1867* (Cambridge, 1991), and R. Earle, *The Return of the Native: Indians and Myth-Making in Spanish America, 1810–1930* (Durham, NC, 2007).

49   Myers, *In the Shadow of Cortés*, 8.

50   Ibid.; Earle, *Return of the Native*, 211.

himself will have to aspire with the object of conquering the synthesis."[51] Within a decade the mestizo had been established "as the cultural icon of the Mexican Revolution."[52] The birth of the mestizo narrative is commonly traced in the Porfirio Díaz regime, which preceded the Revolution (1910–1920), specifically in the writings of such intellectuals as Justo Sierra, who had also served as secretary of public education in the years 1905 to 1911. For Sierra, the "mestizo family" was "the dynamic factor" in Mexican history.[53] "When Tlatelolco . . . had been bled and razed," he claimed, "the end had come. . . . We Mexicans are the sons of two countries and two races."[54]

With the mestizo ideological construct at the core of postrevolution rhetoric, modern Mexico was literally thought to have been born with the conquest. In the meantime, indigenous difference was obliterated from the nation's narrative.[55] Thus unlike the modern Greek reading of *halosis* as a rupture, an open wound, and a deep-rooted cultural trauma, and in contrast to the Nahua counternarrative of continuity in early colonial Mexico, twentieth-century Mexican nationalism put a positive spin on the conquest through the discourse of *mestizaje*. The fall of Tenochtitlan-Tlatelolco was retrospectively seen by the urban elites as a new start, the dawn of the mestizo nation, while *mestizaje* became the foundational myth of the Mexican nation-state.

During this time, the image of Malintzin, Malinche, or Doña Marina, who appears in stanza 2 of "Tlaxcaltecayotl" as Cortés's interpreter, was cast and recast in positive and negative terms alike. Negative because, in her role as translator, strategist, and companion of Cortés, the native woman from Veracruz performed a key role in the conquest of Mexico; positive because she is considered the mother of the modern nation and the single figure who, in her capacity as translator, "appears to understand the two cultures."[56] Even though

51 J. Vasconcelos, *The Cosmic Race / La raza cósmica*, trans. D. T. Jaén (Baltimore, MD, 1997), 18, 32; Earle, *Return of the Native*, 207. For differences between Vasconcelos's notion of *mestizaje* and that of Manuel Gamio, see Lee, "Mestizaje," 892–94.

52 Earle, *Return of the Native*, 204–5.

53 J. Sierra, "México social y político: Apuntes para un libro," *Revista nacional de letras y ciencias* 1 (1889): 13–19, at 19; Earle, *Return of the Native*, 205.

54 J. Sierra, *The Political Evolution of the Mexican People*, trans. C. Ramsdell (Austin, TX, 2011), 62.

55 S. D. Morris, "Between Neo-Liberalism and Neo-Indigenismo: Reconstructing National Identity in Mexico," *National Identities* 3.3 (2001): 239–55, at 240.

56 S. Greenblatt, *Marvelous Possessions* (Chicago, IL, 1991), 143. For Malintzin as a strategist, see C. Townsend, *Malintzin's Choices: An Indian Woman in the Conquest of Mexico* (Albuquerque, NM, 2006). For Malintzin's role as an interpreter, see M. L. Spoturno, "Revisiting Malinche: A Study of Her Role as an Interpreter," in *Translators, Interpreters, and Cultural Negotiators:*

the heated debate on the rhetorical imaginings of Malintzin is out of the scope of this discussion, we may add that in the early twentieth century the idea of Malintzin and Cortés as the nation's progenitors gained currency.[57] Perceived as the Mexican Adam and Eve, the couple exemplified the union of the two worlds that gave birth to modern Mexico, a mestizo nation symbolically embodied by their son, Martín Cortés el Mestizo (born ca. 1523).[58] Following the Mexican Revolution, notes Ann McBride-Limaye, Malintzin is identified as "the mother of the *mestizo* race, the Mexican Eve" but is also connected to *malinchismo*, which implies love and admiration of the foreign at the expense of the local.[59]

Despite the fact that it is still regarded as a violent and in many ways problematic historical juncture, the fall of the Mexica Empire has never achieved the status of cultural trauma. In the twentieth century the rhetoric of *mestizaje*, a backdated reading of the conquest, excluded the possibility of retrospectively associating the events with a strongly negative affect. For traumas to become collective, argue Alexander and Breese, they must be "conceived as wounds to social identity."[60] But if the conquest should signal the birth of a nation, it could not at the same time be taken as a "national threat" arousing negative affect.[61] Whether linked with native or nonnative agency, the traumatic events commemorated in "Huexotzincayotl" and "Tlaxcaltecayotl" could not be held as

---

Mediating and Communicating Power from the Middle Ages to the Modern Era, ed. F. M. Federici and D. Tessicini (London, 2014), 121–35.

57 For the construction of the image of Malintzin, see S. M. Cypess, *La Malinche in Mexican Literature: From History to Myth* (Austin, TX, 1991). For Malintzin as a "treacherous translator," see N. Alarcón, "Traddutora, Traditora: A Paradigmatic Figure of Chicana Feminism," in *Scattered Hegemonies: Postmodernity and Transnational Feminist Practices*, ed. I. Grewal and C. Kaplan (Minneapolis, MN, 1994), 110–33, and P. Godayol, "Malintzin/La Malinche/Doña Marina: Re-Reading the Myth of the Treacherous Translator," *Journal of Iberian and Latin American Studies* 18 (2012): 61–76. Pilar Godayol ("Malintzin," 63) reports that the earliest references to Malintzin are found in the works of Spanish chroniclers, namely, in *True History of the Conquest of New Spain* by Díaz del Castillo, *Account of the Affairs of Yucatán (Relación de las cosas de Yucatán)* (1566) by the Franciscan friar Diego de Landa, *History of the Conquest of Mexico (Historia de la conquista de México)* (1552) by Francisco López de Gómara, and in Cortés's letters to Emperor Charles V, published as *Cartas de relación (Letters from Mexico)*.

58 S. M. Cypess, "'Mother' Malinche and Allegories of Gender, Ethnicity, and National Identity," in *Feminism, Nation, and Myth: La Malinche*, ed. R. Romero and A. N. Harris (Houston, TX, 2005), 14–27, at 15, and Godayol, "Malintzin," 66.

59 A. McBride-Limaye, "Metamorphoses of La Malinche and Mexican Cultural Identity," *Comparative Civilizations Review* 19 (1988): 1–28, at 11.

60 Alexander and Breese, "Introduction," xii.

61 Smelser, "Psychological Trauma," 36, 40.

traumatizing because the conquest was seen as constitutive, not disruptive, of modern Mexicanness.[62]

In theory, of course, carrier groups among the indigenous peoples in postindependence Mexico could have completed the trauma process in retrospect as a response to the mestizo narrative, but these did not usually have access to the institutional power, "resources," or "authority" with which to compellingly disseminate a trauma claim.[63] Not all individuals, groups, classes, or nations have the same power "to claim the territory of memory," says Michael Schudson.[64] Indigenous peoples in modern Mexico have been largely unable to access that territory and, along with it, the intricate mechanisms of cultural memory construction. At the turn of the twenty-first century, millions of indigenous Mexicans from nearly sixty ethnic groups found themselves at the bottom of all socioeconomic indicators. Although indigenous movements like the Zapatista Army of National Liberation have questioned the role of the indigenous in the nation's self-imagining,[65] the official discourse continues to be couched in the traditional rhetoric of *mestizaje*, reflected in the celebration of the Día de la Raza, or Race Day. October 12, which is Spain's national day, variously called Columbus Day, Race Day, and Hispanic Day (Día or Fiesta de la Hispanidad), is now celebrated across the Americas.

While the trauma of the Ottoman conquest is firmly fixed in the modern Greek imagination, the historical contours of colonial and postindependence Mexico did not allow for the same to happen. "The status of trauma as trauma," Smelser tells us, "is dependent on the sociocultural context of the affected society."[66] Today "Huexotzincayotl" and "Tlaxcaltecayotl" entertain a close circle of Pre-Columbianists and early modernists and may be found in specialized university courses. Renditions of the two songs by Garibay, partially presented and camouflaged under the ad hoc titles "The Fall of Tenochtitlan" and "Flowers and Songs of Sorrow," and "The Imprisonment of Cuauhtemoc,"[67] feature as "elegies" in León-Portilla's collection of native accounts of the conquest,

---

62 On trauma and national identity, see also A. G. Neal, *National Trauma and Collective Memory: Major Events in the American Century* (Armonk, NY, 1998).

63 Alexander, "Toward a Theory," 27.

64 M. Schudson, "The Past in the Present versus the Present in the Past," in *The Collective Memory Reader*, ed. J. K. Olick, V. Vinitzky-Seroussi, and D. Levy (New York, 2011), 287–90, at 290.

65 Morris, "Between Neo-Liberalism and Neo-Indigenismo," 239, 241.

66 Smelser, "Psychological Trauma," 36.

67 "Huexotzincayotl," stanzas 5–6, 8–9, and 1–4, and "Tlaxcaltecayotl," stanzas 22, 27–30, and refrain of stanzas 19–22, respectively.

The Broken Spears (*Visión de los vencidos*), first published in 1959.[68] Despite the author's monumental contribution to Nahuatl literary studies (it is thanks to his and Garibay's work that the discipline came to prominence in the second half of the twentieth century), the relaxed scholarly approach, which dismisses the original titles, makes only a curt mention of the manuscript,[69] provides no folio numbers, and clamps together distinct parts of the compositions rather freely, uproots the songs from their *Cantares mexicanos* context and offers only a taste of disembodied "elegiac" responses to the conquest. León-Portilla's collection appeared as suggested reading in the curriculum of "Mexican and Latin American Literature" of the National Preparatory High School. Redesigned in 1996 by the National Autonomous University of Mexico and only updated recently, this final-year course comprised eight units, of which the first two were dedicated to pre-Hispanic and sixteenth-century colonial literature. In the first unit, there were texts from the Maya and Nahuatl traditions, including some songs that Garibay and León-Portilla have ascribed to King Nezahualcoyotl (1402–1472), report-edly chosen for their treatment of "philosophical and existential themes."[70] It was within the latter unit that we could find a recommendation of León-Portilla's book, although here the emphasis was clearly on Spanish chronicles.[71]

Contrary to "Anakalema," "Huexotzincayotl" and "Tlaxcaltecayotl" are not standard inclusions in high school manuals, not even in the veiled form in

---

68 León-Portilla, *Broken Spears*, 146, 148–49. The 1969 Spanish version of the book offers slightly different titles: "The Mexica Nation Has Been Lost" ("Se ha perdido el pueblo mexícatl") for "Huexotzincayotl," and "The Wrecking of the Tenochca and Tlatelolca" ("La ruina de tenoch-cas y tlatelolcas") and "The Imprisonment of Cuauhtemoc" ("La prisión de Cuauhtémoc") for "Tlaxcaltecayotl" (M. León-Portilla, ed., *Visión de los vencidos: Relaciones indígenas de la conquista* [Mexico City, 1969], 165–69).

69 León-Portilla, *Broken Spears*, 145, and idem, *Visión de los vencidos*, 164. That León-Portilla's book "is not a critical edition of the native texts," but is aimed at "the general reader," does not justify the arbitrary treatment of the texts (León-Portilla, *Broken Spears*, xlviii).

70 A. de Teresa Ochoa and E. Achugar Díaz, *Literatura mexicana e iberoamericana* (Naucalpan de Juárez, 2014), 22: "temas filosóficos y existenciales."

71 See UNAM, Escuela Nacional Preparatoria, "Programa de estudios de la asignatura de Literatura Mexicana e Iberoamericana. Clave: 1602" (Mexico City, 1996): 1–37, at 33, accessed 7 July 2020, http://www.dgire.unam.mx/contenido/normatividad/enp/prog _indicativos/60/IV/1602.pdf. Updated in 2016, the revised curriculum comprises six units, which are organized around themes as opposed to historical periods. Here there is still no mention of *Cantares mexicanos* beyond León-Portilla's collection, which appears twice, in units two and four (UNAM, Escuela Nacional Preparatoria, "Programa Literatura Mexicana e Iberoamericana. Clave: 1602" [Mexico City, 2016]: 1–24, at 6, 9, accessed 7 July 2020, http://dgenp.unam.mx/planesdeestudio/actualizados/sexto-2018/1602_literatura _mxna_e_iberoamericana.pdf).

which they figure in *The Broken Spears*. Recent textbooks by Josefina Chorén, Guadalupe Goicoechea, and María de los Ángeles Rull or Adriana de Teresa Ochoa and Eleonora Achugar Díaz do not anthologize any song dealing with the conquest, in spite of the fact that since 2011 the entire corpus of *Cantares mexicanos* has been available in Spanish.[72] The attention that the 1996 curriculum of the National Preparatory High School paid to *mestizaje* was evident in the course description, which specified that students were expected to "consolidate a true nationalism based on the richness of our indigenous and colonial past" and "better understand our identity," while unit two in particular foregrounded "the *mestizaje* and *criollismo* of our culture."[73] The erosion of indigenous difference in *The Broken Spears* and school manuals alike is not unrelated to *mestizaje*, nor is Garibay's and León-Portilla's application of Western literary categories (e.g., epic, lyric, and dramatic poetry) to preconquest traditions, a domesticating strategy coopted in the textbooks and prefigured in the work of sixteenth-century missionaries like Olmos, Sahagún, Durán, and Motolinía.[74]

Garibay, a Catholic priest and a contemporary of Vasconcelos and Manuel Gamio, saw the conquest as the birth of modern Mexico, and so did León-Portilla. Lee goes as far as to suggest that Garibay's Nahuatl project is a paradigm of "nationalist cultural *mestizaje* in contemporary Mexican history."[75] Meanwhile, present-day indigenous authors continue to have no place in the curriculum and, more generally, in histories of Spanish American literature, where native traditions are almost always crammed under the rubric "Pre-Columbian."[76] Severed from the here and now, they are thought of as museum pieces or *antiguallas* (old things, relics), as if moored to a "mythical past."[77] At the other end, "Anakalema" enjoys a privileged position in today's textbooks, as a

---

72 J. Chorén, G. Goicoechea, and M. de los Ángeles Rull, *Literatura mexicana e hispanoamericana* (Mexico City, 2014), and De Teresa Ochoa and Achugar Díaz, *Literatura mexicana*.

73 UNAM, "Programa de estudios," 3, 9: "El estudio de lo mexicano será excelente para afianzar un verdadero nacionalismo sustentado en la riqueza de nuestro pasado indígena y colonial ... a fin de poder comprender mejor nuestra identidad" and "el mestizaje y el criollismo de nuestra cultura." These comments were removed from the revised curriculum, which is substantially shorter in length.

74 See Lee, "*Mestizaje*," 899–904.

75 Ibid., 890–92. For León-Portilla's and Garibay's views on *mestizaje*, and for the differences between the latter's and Vasconcelos's understanding of the notion, see ibid., 892, 894, 898.

76 See M. del R. Castañeda Reyes, "La enseñanza de la literatura en el bachillerato: Comparación México-Francia," *Tiempo de educar: Revista interinstitucional de investigación educativa* 8.15 (2007): 69–112, at 102–3.

77 J. A. Barisone, "Problemas en el estudio de las literaturas indígenas," *Zama* 5 (2013): 153–67, at 159. For exceptions, see ibid., 163.

Fig. 21. View of the archaeological site of the Templo Mayor, Tenochtitlan, facing Calle Donceles, Mexico City. Photograph by the author.

composition that "describes with realism, sensitivity, and restrained emotion some of the episodes of the siege, as well as the suffering that followed for the now enslaved Christians of the Greek East, victims of the cruelty of the conquerors, the looting and plundering."[78] Far from being treated as an *antigualla*, the poem is glossed as a lament for the loss of Constantinople, which in turn is projected as a watershed event that "resonated deeply and painfully with the soul of the people and was considered a tragic sign for the fate of the Nation as a whole."[79] In the assigned function and standing of these texts of the past there are mirrored the complexities of two pervading narratives of the present.

During a 2016 trip to Mexico I asked for León-Portilla's 2011 Spanish translation of *Cantares mexicanos* at one of the biggest and oldest bookshops in the country, situated on Calle Donceles opposite the Templo Mayor, at the heart

78 Ministry of Education and Culture, Pedagogical Institute, *Κείμενα κυπριακής λογοτεχνίας* (Nicosia, 2017), 94: περιγράφονται με ρεαλισμό, ευαισθησία και συγκρατημένη συγκίνηση τόσο κάποια από τα επεισόδια της πολιορκίας, όσο και τα δεινά που ακολούθησαν για τους υπόδουλους πλέον χριστιανούς της ελληνικής Ανατολής, θύματα της αγριότητας των κατακτητών, της λεηλασίας και των διαρπαγών.

79 Ministry of Education, Research, and Religious Affairs, Institute of Educational Policy, *Κείμενα νεοελληνικής λογοτεχνίας*, vol. 1, Α' Γενικού Λυκείου (Athens and Patras, 2017), 68: Το πάρσιμο της Πόλης . . . είχε βαθιά και οδυνηρή απήχηση στην ψυχή του λαού και θεωρήθηκε ως τραγικό σημάδι για τη μοίρα ολόκληρου του Έθνους.

of ancient Tenochtitlan (fig. 21). Two members of staff who were keen to help but had not heard of the work searched through the bookshop's database only to find out that the multivolume translation was available in just one of their thirty branches in Mexico City, about four miles away. Other attempts in nearby *librerías* were also unsuccessful. In the meantime, "Anakalema" has crept into anthologies of folk songs, including one sanctioned by the Academy of Athens, and features in schoolbooks in both Greece and Cyprus. If the fall of Constantinople has generated a "hypertrophy of memory" among modern Greeks,[80] the trauma of the siege and fall of Tenochtitlan-Tlatelolco in many respects has largely been relegated to the realm of hypotrophic memory. Like Lake Texcoco, the tears once pouring in Tlatelolco have dried up in collective memory, but in the passage from Romiosune to Hellenism, the trauma of the siege and fall of Constantinople keeps playing in the background.

---

80   A. Huyssen, *Present Pasts: Urban Palimpsests and the Politics of Memory* (Stanford, CA, 2003), 3, and V. Roudometof and M. Christou, "1974 and Greek Cypriot Identity: The Division of Cyprus as Cultural Trauma," in Eyerman, Alexander, and Breese, *Narrating Trauma*, 163–87, at 163.

REFERENCES

Academy of Athens. *Ελληνικά δημοτικά τραγούδια*. 2 vols. Athens, 1962–68.

———. *Ιστορικόν λεξικόν της νέας ελληνικής*. 4 vols. Athens, 1933–53.

Adorno, R. *Polemics of Possession in Spanish American Narrative*. New Haven, CT, 2007.

Afentoulidou-Leitgeb, E. "The *Dioptra* of Philippos Monotropos: Didactic Verses or Poetry?" In *Poetry and Its Contexts in Eleventh-Century Byzantium*, ed. F. Bernard and K. Demoen, 181–91. London and New York, 2012.

Agapitos, P. A. "Public and Private Death in Psellos: Maria Skleraina and Styliane Psellaina." *Byzantinische Zeitschrift* 101.2 (2008): 555–607.

Aguilar-Moreno, M. *Handbook to Life in the Aztec World*. New York, 2007.

Alarcón, N. "Traddutora, Traditora: A Paradigmatic Figure of Chicana Feminism." In *Scattered Hegemonies: Postmodernity and Transnational Feminist Practices*, ed. I. Grewal and C. Kaplan, 110–33. Minneapolis, MN, 1994.

Alexander, J. C. "Toward a Theory of Cultural Trauma." In *Cultural Trauma and Collective Identity*, ed. J. C. Alexander, R. Eyerman, B. Giesen, N. J. Smelser, and P. Sztompka, 1–30. Berkeley, CA, 2004.

Alexander, J. C., and E. B. Breese. "Introduction: On Social Suffering and Its Cultural Construction." In Eyerman, Alexander, and Breese, *Narrating Trauma*, xi–xxxv.

Alexiou, M. *The Ritual Lament in Greek Tradition*, rev. D. Yatromanolakis and P. Roilos. Lanham, MD, 2002.

Allen, J. S. "Constantine Dragaš." In Kazhdan et al., *The Oxford Dictionary of Byzantium*, 1:505–6.

Andrews, J. R. *Introduction to Classical Nahuatl*. Norman, OK, 2003.

Angelov, D. G. "Byzantinism: The Imaginary and Real Heritage of Byzantium in Southeastern Europe." In *New Approaches to Balkan Studies*, ed. D. Keridis, E. Elias-Bursać, and N. Yatromanolakis, 3–23. Dulles, VA, 2003.

Arrowsmith, W. "A Greek Theater of Ideas." *Arion: A Journal of Humanities and the Classics* 2.3 (1963): 32–56.

Asselbergs, F. "Stories of Tlaxcalteca and Quauhquecholteca Conquistadors." In *Indian Conquistadors: Indigenous Allies in the Conquest of Mesoamerica*, ed. L. E. Matthew and M. R. Oudijk, 65–101. Norman, OK, 2007.

Bádenas, P. "Τα συμφιλιωτικά ρεύματα Ελλήνων λογίων στην αυλή του Μεγάλου Τούρκου." In *Ο ελληνικός κόσμος ανάμεσα στην Ανατολή και τη Δύση 1453–1981*, 2 vols., ed. A. Argyriou, K. A. Dimadis, and A. D. Lazaridou, 2:409–19. Athens, 1999.

Barbaro, N. *Diary of the Siege of Constantinople*, trans. J. R. Jones. New York, 1969.

———. *Giornale dell'assedio di Costantinopoli 1453*, ed. E. Cornet. Vienna, 1856.

Barisone, J. A. "Problemas en el estudio de las literaturas indígenas." *Zama* 5 (2013): 153–67.

Beaton, R. *Folk Poetry of Modern Greece.* Cambridge, 1980.

———. "Introduction." In *The Making of Modern Greece: Nationalism, Romanticism, and the Uses of the Past (1797–1896)*, ed. R. Beaton and D. Ricks, 1–18. Farnham, 2009.

———. *The Medieval Greek Romance.* London, 1996.

———. "Re-Imagining Greek Antiquity in 1821: Shelley's *Hellas* in Its Literary and Political Context." In *Re-Imagining the Past: Antiquity and Modern Greek Culture*, ed. D. Tziovas, 47–58. New York, 2014.

Bierhorst, J., ed. and trans. *Ballads of the Lords of New Spain: The Codex* Romances de los Señores de la Nueva España. Austin, TX, 2009.

———, ed. and trans. *Cantares mexicanos: Songs of the Aztecs.* Stanford, CA, 1985.

———. *A Nahuatl-English Dictionary and Concordance to the* Cantares Mexicanos*: With an Analytic Transcription and Grammatical Notes.* Stanford, CA, 1985.

———. "Translating an Esoteric Idiom: The Case of Aztec Poetry." In *Born in the Blood: On Native American Translation*, ed. B. Swann, 370–97. Lincoln, NE, 2001.

Boone, E. H. "Aztec Pictorial Histories: Records without Words." In *Writing without Words: Alternative Literacies in Mesoamerica and the Andes*, ed. E. H. Boone and W. D. Mignolo, 50–76. Durham, NC, 1994.

Bouboulidis, F. Κρητική λογοτεχνία. Athens, 1955.

Boucher, P. P. *Cannibal Encounters: Europeans and Island Caribs, 1492–1763.* Baltimore, MD, 1992.

Brading, D. A. *The First America: The Spanish Monarchy, Creole Patriots, and the Liberal State, 1492–1867.* Cambridge, 1991.

Braude, B. "The Success of Religion as a Source for Compromise in Divided Empires: Ottoman and Safavid, Past and Present." In *Power Sharing in Deeply Divided Places*, ed. J. McEvoy and B. O'Lear, 176–97. Philadelphia, PA, 2013.

Brinton, D. G. *Ancient Nahuatl Poetry, Containing the Nahuatl Text of XXVII Ancient Mexican Poems—with a Translation, Introduction, Notes, and Vocabulary.* Philadelphia, PA, 1890.

Browning, R. "A Note on the Capture of Constantinople in 1453." *Byzantion* 22 (1952): 379–87.

Bryennios, I. Ἰωσὴφ μοναχοῦ τοῦ Βρυεννίου τὰ εὑρεθέντα, ed. E. Voulgaris. 2 vols. Leipzig, 1768.

Buffon, G.-L. Leclerc, Comte de. *Histoire naturelle générale et particulière, avec la description du Cabinet du Roy*, Suppl. 5. Paris, 1778.

Burke, P. *A Social History of Knowledge: From Gutenberg to Diderot.* Malden, MA, 2000.

———. *Varieties of Cultural History.* Ithaca, NY, 1997.

Burkhart, L. M. "Doctrinal Aspects of Sahagún's *Colloquios*." In *The Work of Bernardino de Sahagún: Pioneer Ethnographer of Sixteenth-Century Aztec Mexico*, ed. J. Klor de Alva, H. B. Nicholson, and E. Quiñones Keber, 65–82. Albany, NY, 1988.

———. *Holy Wednesday: A Nahua Drama from Early Colonial Mexico.* Philadelphia, PA, 1996.

———. "Introduction." In *Aztecs on Stage: Religious Theater in Colonial Mexico*, ed. L. M. Burkhart, trans. L. M. Burkhart, B. D. Sell, and S. Poole, 3–29. Norman, OK, 2011.

———. "Introduction." In *Words and Worlds Turned Around: Indigenous Christianities in Colonial Latin America*, ed. D. Tavárez, 4–26. Boulder, CO, 2017.

———. *The Slippery Earth: Nahua-Christian Moral Dialogue in Sixteenth-Century Mexico.* Tucson, AZ, 1989.

Cabranes-Grant, L. *From Scenarios to Networks: Performing the Intercultural in Colonial Mexico.* Evanston, IL, 2016.

Cameron, A. "The History of the Image of Edessa: The Telling of a Story." In *Okeanos: Essays Presented to Ihor Ševčenko on His Sixtieth Birthday by His Colleagues and Students* (*Harvard Ukrainian Studies* 7 [1983]): 80–94.

Caplow, D. *Leopoldo Méndez: Revolutionary Art and the Mexican Print.* Austin, TX, 2007.

Carder, J. N. "The Architectural History of Dumbarton Oaks and the Contribution of Armand Albert Rateau." In Carder, *A Home of the Humanities*, 93–115.

———, ed. *A Home of the Humanities: The Collecting and Patronage of Mildred and Robert Woods Bliss.* Washington, DC, 2010.

———. "Mildred and Robert Woods Bliss: A Brief Biography." In Carder, *A Home of the Humanities*, 1–25.

Carrasco, D. *City of Sacrifice: The Aztec Empire and the Role of Violence in Civilization.* Boston, MA, 1999.

Castañeda Reyes, M. del R. "La enseñanza de la literatura en el bachillerato: Comparación México-Francia." *Tiempo de educar: Revista interinstitucional de investigación educativa* 8.15 (2007): 69–112.

Chávez Balderas, X. "Bioarqueología del sacrificio humano: La ofrenda de vida." *Arqueología mexicana* 24.143 (2017): 56–61.

Choniates, N. *O City of Byzantium, Annals of Niketas Choniates*, trans. H. J. Magoulias. Detroit, MI, 1984.

Chorén, J., G. Goicoechea, and M. de los Ángeles Rull. *Literatura mexicana e hispanoamericana.* Mexico City, 2014.

Christensen, M. Z. *Translated Christianities: Nahuatl and Maya Religious Texts.* University Park, PA, 2014.

Clendinnen, I. *Aztecs: An Interpretation.* New York, 1993.

Columbus, C. *The Four Voyages*, ed. and trans. J. M. Cohen. London, 1969.

Congourdeau, M.-H. "Byzance et la fin du monde." In *Les traditions apocalyptiques au tournant de la chute de Constantinople*, ed. B. Lellouch and S. Yerasimos, 55–97. Paris, 1999.

———. "Les Byzantins face aux catastrophes naturelles sous les Paléologues." *Revue des études byzantines* 67.1 (2009): 151–63.

Connerton, P. *How Societies Remember.* Cambridge, 1996.

Correa, P. *La cultura literaria de los aztecas.* Madrid, 1994.

Cortés, H. *Letters from Mexico*, ed. and trans. A. Pagden. New Haven, CT, 1986.

Cummins, T. "Competing and Commensurate Values in Colonial Conditions: How They Are Expressed and Registered in the Sixteenth-Century Andes." In *The Construction of Value in the Ancient World*, ed. J. K. Papadopoulos and G. Urton, 358–75. Los Angeles, CA, 2012.

Cypess, S. M. *La Malinche in Mexican Literature: From History to Myth*. Austin, TX, 1991.

———. "'Mother' Malinche and Allegories of Gender, Ethnicity, and National Identity." In *Feminism, Nation, and Myth: La Malinche*, ed. R. Romero and A. N. Harris, 14–27. Houston, TX, 2005.

Darrouzès, J. "Bulletin critique." *Revue des études byzantines* 25 (1967): 259–60.

Davis, J., trans. "Lament on the Fall of Constantinople." In *The Greek Poets: Homer to the Present*, ed. P. Constantine, R. Hadas, E. Keeley, and K. Van Dyck, 348–50. New York, 2010.

Del Mar, A. *The Worship of Augustus Caesar*. New York, 1900.

De Teresa Ochoa, A., and E. Achugar Díaz. *Literatura mexicana e iberoamericana*. Naucalpan de Juárez, 2014.

Díaz del Castillo, B. *The Memoirs of the Conquistador Bernal Díaz del Castillo*, trans. J. I. Lockhart. 2 vols. London, 1844.

Doukas, M. *Decline and Fall of Byzantium to the Ottoman Turks*, trans. H. J. Magoulias. Detroit, MI, 1975.

———. *Michaelis Ducae Nepotis Historia byzantina*, ed. I. Bekker. New York, 2012.

Dussel, E. *The Invention of the Americas: Eclipse of "the Other" and the Myth of Modernity*, trans. M. D. Barber. New York, 1995.

———. *The Underside of Modernity: Apel, Ricœur, Rorty, Taylor, and the Philosophy of Liberation*, trans. E. Mendieta. New York, 1996.

Earle, R. *The Return of the Native: Indians and Myth-Making in Spanish America, 1810–1930*. Durham, NC, 2007.

Escobar, A. "'Mundos y conocimientos de otro modo': El programa de investigación de modernidad/colonialidad latinoamericano." *Tabula rasa* 1 (2003): 51–86.

Eyerman, R. *Cultural Trauma: Slavery and the Formation of African American Identity*. Cambridge, 2001.

———. "The Past in the Present: Culture and the Transmission of Memory." *Acta Sociologica* 47.2 (2004): 159–69.

Eyerman, R., J. C. Alexander, and E. B. Breese, eds. *Narrating Trauma: On the Impact of Collective Suffering*. Boulder, CO, 2011.

Fleming, K. E. "Constantinople: From Christianity to Islam." *The Classical World* 97.1 (2003): 69–78.

Frary, L. J. *Russia and the Making of Modern Greek Identity, 1821–1844*. New York, 2015.

García Ortega, R., and A. I. Fernández Galvín. *Trenos por Constantinopla: Estudio preliminar, traducción y comentarios*. Granada, 2003.

Garibay K., A. M. *Llave del náhuatl*. Mexico City, 1961.

———, ed. and trans. *Poesía indígena de la altiplanicie: Divulgación literaria*. Mexico City, 1940.

———, ed. and trans. *Poesía náhuatl II: Cantares mexicanos, manuscrito de la Biblioteca Nacional de México*. Mexico City, 1965.

Geanakoplos, D. J. *Byzantium: Church, Society, and Civilization Seen through Contemporary Eyes*. Chicago, IL, 1984.

Gibbon, E. *The History of the Decline and Fall of the Roman Empire*. 6 vols. London, 1997.

Godayol, P. "Malintzin/La Malinche/Doña Marina: Re-Reading the Myth of the Treacherous Translator." *Journal of Iberian and Latin American Studies* 18 (2012): 61–76.

Goldwyn, A. "'I come from a cursed land and from the depths of darkness': Life after Death in Greek Laments about the Fall of Constantinople." In *Wanted: Byzantium. The Desire for a Lost Empire*, ed. I. Nilsson and P. Stephenson, 93–108. Uppsala, 2014.

Gómez de Orozco, F., ed. "Costumbres, fiestas, enterramientos y diversas formas de proceder de los indios de Nueva España." *Tlalocan: A Journal of Source Materials on the Native Cultures of Mexico* 2.1 (1945): 37–63.

Gouma-Peterson, T. "Manuel and John Phokas and Artistic Personality in Late Byzantine Painting." *Gesta* 22.2 (1983): 159–70.

Graulich, M. *Fiestas de los pueblos indígenas: Ritos aztecas. Las fiestas de las veintenas.* Mexico City, 1999.

Greenblatt, S. *Marvelous Possessions*. Chicago, IL, 1991.

Greene, M. *The Edinburgh History of the Greeks, 1453 to 1768: The Ottoman Empire.* Edinburgh, 2015.

Grivaud, G. "Ο πνευματικός βίος και η γραμματολογία κατά την περίοδο της Φραγκοκρατίας." In *Ιστορία της Κύπρου*, ed. T. Papadopoullos, vol. 5, *Μεσαιωνικόν βασίλειον: Ενετοκρατία*, part 2, *Πνευματικός βίος, παιδεία, γραμματολογία, βυζαντινή τέχνη, γοτθική τέχνη, νομισματοκοπία, βιβλιογραφία*, 863–1207. Nicosia, 1996.

Guran, P. "Eschatology and Political Theology in the Last Centuries of Byzantium." *Revue des études sud-est européennes* 45 (2007): 73–85.

Gurría Lacroix, J. *Itinerario de Hernán Cortés / Itinerary of Hernan Cortes*. Mexico City, 1973.

Gutiérrez, G. "Mexico-Tenochtitlan: Origin and Transformation of the Last Mesoamerican Imperial City." In *The Cambridge World History*, vol. 3, *Early Cities in Comparative Perspective, 4000 BCE–1200 CE*, ed. N. Yoffee, 491–512. Cambridge, 2015.

Haarer, F. "Writing Histories of Byzantium: The Historiography of Byzantine History." In *A Companion to Byzantium*, ed. L. James, 9–21. Oxford, 2010.

Hajovsky, P. T. *On the Lips of Others: Moteuczoma's Fame in Aztec Monuments and Rituals.* Austin, TX, 2015.

Hanks, W. F. "Birth of a Language: The Formation and Spread of Colonial Yucatec Maya." *Journal of Anthropological Research* 68.4 (2012): 449–71.

Harris, J. *The End of Byzantium*. New Haven, CT, 2010.

———. *The Lost World of Byzantium*. New Haven, CT, 2015.

Hassig, R. *Mexico and the Spanish Conquest*. Norman, OK, 2006.

Heinrich, G. S. "Ποιος έγραψε το ποίημα Άλωσις της Κωνσταντινουπόλεως (ΒΒ 1, 177–197)." In *Constantinopla: 550 años de su caída / Κωνσταντινούπολη: 550 χρόνια από την άλωση*, 3 vols., ed. E. Motos Guirao and M. Morfakidis Filactos, 2:405–14. Granada, 2006.

Hernández, F. *Obras completas*, vol. 6, *Escritos varios*, ed. E. C. del Pozo et al. Mexico City, 1984.

Herzfeld, M. *Ours Once More: Folklore, Ideology, and the Making of Modern Greece*. Austin, TX, 1982.

Hill, G. *A History of Cyprus*, vol. 3, *The Frankish Period, 1432–1571*. Cambridge, 1948.

Hirsch, M. "Connective Histories in Vulnerable Times." *PMLA* 129.3 (2014): 330–48.

———. *The Generation of Postmemory: Writing and Visual Culture after the Holocaust*. New York, 2012.

Holton, D. "The Cretan Renaissance." In *Literature and Society in Renaissance Crete*, ed. D. Holton, 1–16. New York, 1991.

Horn, R. "Indigenous Identities in Mesoamerica after the Spanish Conquest." In *Native Diasporas: Indigenous Identities and Settler Colonialism in the Americas*, ed. G. D. Smithers and B. N. Newman, 31–78. Lincoln, NE, 2014.

———. *Postconquest Coyoacan: Nahua-Spanish Relations in Central Mexico, 1519–1650*. Stanford, CA, 1997.

Huyssen, A. *Present Pasts: Urban Palimpsests and the Politics of Memory*. Stanford, CA, 2003.

Inalcik, H. "The Policy of Mehmed II toward the Greek Population of Istanbul and the Byzantine Buildings of the City." *Dumbarton Oaks Papers* 23–24 (1969–1970): 229–49.

Ioannou, G. *Τα δημοτικά μας τραγούδια*. Athens, 1996.

Jacobs, J. "The City Lament Genre in the Ancient Near East." In *The Fall of Cities in the Mediterranean: Commemoration in Literature, Folk-Song, and Liturgy*, ed. M. R. Bachvarova, D. Dutsch, and A. Suter, 13–35. New York, 2016.

Jaenen, C. J. "'Les Sauvages Ameriquains': Persistence into the 18th Century of Traditional French Concepts and Constructs for Comprehending Amerindians." *Ethnohistory* 29.1 (1982): 43–56.

Jauss, H. R. "Modernity and Literary Tradition," trans. C. Thorne. *Critical Inquiry* 31.2 (2005): 329–64.

Jeffreys, E. "Poetry." In Kazhdan et al., *The Oxford Dictionary of Byzantium*, 3:1688–89.

Jusdanis, G. *Belated Modernity and Aesthetic Culture: Inventing National Literature*. Minneapolis, MN, 1991.

Kaldellis, A. *Hellenism in Byzantium: The Transformations of Greek Identity and the Reception of the Classical Tradition*. Cambridge, 2007.

———. *A New Herodotos: Laonikos Chalkokondyles on the Ottoman Empire, the Fall of Byzantium, and the Emergence of the West*, Dumbarton Oaks Medieval Library Suppl. Washington, DC, 2014.

Kaoulla, C. "Queen Helena Palaiologina of Cyprus (1442–1458): Myth and History." *Επετηρίς του Κέντρου Επιστημονικών Ερευνών* 32 (2006): 109–50.

Kaplanis, T. A. "Antique Names and Self-Identification: *Hellenes, Graikoi*, and *Romaioi* from Late Byzantium to the Greek Nation-State." In *Re-Imagining the Past: Antiquity and Modern Greek Culture*, ed. D. Tziovas, 81–97. Oxford, 2014.

Karanika, A. "Messengers, Angels, and Laments for the Fall of Constantinople." In *The Fall of Cities in the Mediterranean: Commemoration in Literature, Folk-Song, and Liturgy*, ed. M. R. Bachvarova, D. Dutsch, and A. Suter, 226–51. New York, 2016.

Karttunen, F. *An Analytical Dictionary of Nahuatl*. Norman, OK, 1992.

Karttunen, F., and J. Lockhart. "La estructura de la poesía náhuatl vista por sus variantes." *Estudios de cultura náhuatl* 14 (1980): 15–64.

Kazantzaki, G. *Ο στρατιώτης: Ελληνικόν αναγνωσματάριον προς χρήσιν των μαθητών της πέμπτης τάξεως του δημοτικού σχολείου*. Athens, 1914.

Kazhdan, A. P. "Theater." In Kazhdan et al., *The Oxford Dictionary of Byzantium*, 3:2031.

Kazhdan, A. P., et al. *The Oxford Dictionary of Byzantium*. 3 vols. New York, 1991.

Kefala, E., ed. *Negotiating Difference in the Hispanic World: From Conquest to Globalisation*. Oxford, 2011.

Kehayoglou, G. *Από τον ύστερο Μεσαίωνα ως τον 18ο αιώνα: Εισαγωγή στα παλαιότερα κείμενα της νεοελληνικής λογοτεχνίας*. Thessaloniki, 2009.

———. "Επίμετρο." In Kriaras, *Ανακάλημα της Κωνσταντινόπολης*, 35–100.

———. "Συνοδευτικά έμμετρα κείμενα." In Kriaras, *Ανακάλημα της Κωνσταντινόπολης*, 102–45.

———. "Το γραμματειακό 'πολυσύστημα' του ύστερου Μεσαίωνα και η ποικιλία της ελληνόγλωσσης λόγιας, ημιλόγιας, δημώδους και ιδιωματικής λογοτεχνίας ως το τέλος της φραγκοκρατίας (12ος αι.–1489)." In *Ιστορία της νεότερης κυπριακής λογοτεχνίας*, ed. G. Kehayoglou and L. Papaleontiou, 19–90. Nicosia, 2010.

Kitromilides, P. M., ed. *Adamantios Korais and the European Enlightenment*. Oxford, 2010.

———. *Enlightenment and Revolution: The Making of Modern Greece*. Cambridge, MA, 2013.

Klor de Alva, J. "The Aztec-Spanish Dialogues of 1524." *Alcheringa: Ethnopoetics* 4.2 (1980): 52–55.

———. "Nahua Colonial Discourse and the Appropriation of the (European) Other." *Archives de sciences sociales des religions* 77 (1992): 15–35.

Kontoglou, F. "Θρηνητικὸν συναξάριν Κωνσταντίνου τοῦ Παλαιολόγου." *Κιβωτός* 17–18 (1953): 193.

Koumbarou-Chanioti, C. *Τα νεοελληνικά αναγνώσματα στη μέση εκπαίδευση: Συγγραφείς και ανθολογημένα κείμενα (1884–1977)*. Athens, 2003.

Kriaras, E. "Ανακάλημα της Κωνσταντινόπολης." In Kriaras, *Ανακάλημα της Κωνσταντινόπολης*, 21–27.

———, ed. *Ανακάλημα της Κωνσταντινόπολης*. Thessaloniki, 2012.

———. "Εισαγωγή." In Kriaras, *Ανακάλημα της Κωνσταντινόπολης*, 9–17.

———. *Λεξικό της μεσαιωνικής ελληνικής δημώδους γραμματείας, 1100–1669*. 21 vols. Thessaloniki, 1968–.

———, ed. *Το Ανακάλημα της Κωνσταντινόπολης: Κριτική έκδοση με εισαγωγή, σχόλια και γλωσσάριο*. Thessaloniki, 1956.

Kritoboulos, Michael. *Critobuli Imbriotae Historiae*, ed. D. R. Reinsch. Berlin, 1983.

———. *History of Mehmed the Conqueror by Kritovoulos*, trans. C. T. Riggs. Princeton, NJ, 1954.

———. Ἱστορία, ed. and trans. D. R. Reinsch and F. Kolovou. Athens, 2005.

Lambros, S. P. Νέος Ἑλληνομνήμων, vol. 5. Athens, 1908.

L'Écuy, J.-B., ed. *De capta a Mehemethe II Constantinopoli, Leonardi Chiensis et Godefridi Langi narrationes, sibi invicem collatae*. Paris, 1823.

Lee, J. *The Allure of Nezahualcoyotl: Pre-Hispanic History, Religion, and Nahua Poetics*. Albuquerque, NM, 2008.

———. "*Mestizaje* and the Creation of Mexican National Literature: Ángel María Garibay Kintana's Nahuatl Project." *Bulletin of Spanish Studies* 91.6 (2014): 889–912.

Legrand, É. *Collection de monuments pour servir à l'étude de la langue néo-hellénique*. 26 vols. Athens, 1869–75.

León-Portilla, M. *Aztec Thought and Culture: A Study of the Ancient Nahuatl Mind*, trans. J. E. Davis. Norman, OK, 1963.

———, ed. *The Broken Spears: The Aztec Account of the Conquest of Mexico*, trans. L. Kemp. Boston, MA, 2006.

———, ed. and trans. *Cantares mexicanos*. 3 vols. Mexico City, 2011.

———. *Pre-Columbian Literatures of Mexico*, trans. G. Lobanov and M. León-Portilla. Norman, OK, 1969.

———, ed. *Visión de los vencidos: Relaciones indígenas de la conquista*. Mexico City, 1969.

Lietaert Peerbolte, L. J. "Antichrist." In *Dictionary of Deities and Demons in the Bible*, 2nd ed., ed. K. van der Toorn, B. Becking, and P. W. van der Horst, 62–64. Leiden and Grand Rapids, MI, 1999.

Lockhart, J. *The Nahuas after the Conquest: A Social and Cultural History of the Indians of Central Mexico, Sixteenth through Eighteenth Centuries*. Stanford, CA, 1992.

———. *Nahuas and Spaniards: Postconquest Central Mexican History and Philology*. Stanford, CA, 1991.

———. *Of Things of the Indies: Essays Old and New in Early Latin American History*. Stanford, CA, 1999.

———, ed. and trans. *We People Here: Nahuatl Accounts of the Conquest of Mexico*. Berkeley, CA, 1993.

Lurati, P. "*Oracula Leonis* (Leonine Oracles)." In *Byzantium: Faith and Power, 1261–1557*, ed. H. C. Evans, 408–9. New York, 2004.

Lusignan, S. *Description de toute l'isle de Cypre*. Paris, 1580.

Machairas, L. Χρονικόν Κύπρου / *Chronique de Chypre*, ed. E. Miller and C. Sathas. Paris, 1882.

Mackridge, P. "Korais and the Greek Language Question." In Kitromilides, *Adamantios Korais*, 127–49.

Magaloni Kerpel, D. *The Colors of the New World: Artists, Materials, and the Creation of the Florentine Codex*. Los Angeles, CA, 2014.

Magdalino, P. "The Year 1000 in Byzantium." In *Byzantium in the Year 1000*, ed. P. Magdalino, 233–70. Leiden, 2003.

Mango, C. "Byzantinism and Romantic Hellenism." *Journal of the Warburg and Courtauld Institutes* 28 (1965): 29–43.

———. "Constantinople." In Kazhdan et al., *The Oxford Dictionary of Byzantium*, 1:508–12.

Matthew, L. E., and M. R. Oudijk, eds. *Indian Conquistadors: Indigenous Allies in the Conquest of Mesoamerica*. Norman, OK, 2007.

McBride-Limaye, A. "Metamorphoses of La Malinche and Mexican Cultural Identity." *Comparative Civilizations Review* 19 (1988): 1–28.

McEwan, C., and L. López Luján, eds. *Moctezuma: Aztec Ruler*. London, 2009.

Mignolo, W. D. *The Idea of Latin America*. Oxford, 2005.

Miklas, H., and J. Fuchsbauer, eds. *Die kirchenslavische Übersetzung der Dioptra des Philippos Monotropos*. Vienna, 2013.

Ministry of Education and Culture, Pedagogical Institute. *Κείμενα κυπριακής λογοτεχνίας*. Nicosia, 2017.

Ministry of Education, Research, and Religious Affairs, Institute of Educational Policy. *Κείμενα νεοελληνικής λογοτεχνίας*, vol. 1, *Α' Γενικού Λυκείου*. Athens and Patras, 2017.

Montesquieu, C.-L. de Secondat, Baron de. *Considerations of the Causes of the Grandeur and Decadence of the Romans*, trans. J. Baker. New York, 1882.

Morgan, G. "Cretan Poetry: Sources and Inspiration." *Κρητικά χρονικά* 14 (1960): 7–68, 203–70, 379–434.

Morris, S. D. "Between Neo-Liberalism and Neo-Indigenismo: Reconstructing National Identity in Mexico." *National Identities* 3.3 (2001): 239–55.

Mourtzopoulos, A. T. "Διορθωτικό στο Ἀνακάλημα της Κωνσταντινόπολης." *Ἑλληνικά* 23.2 (1970): 337–46.

Mullett, M. "Do Brothers Weep? Male Grief, Mourning, Lament, and Tears in Eleventh- and Twelfth-Century Byzantium." In *Greek Laughter and Tears: Antiquity and After*, ed. M. Alexiou and D. Cairns, 312–37. Edinburgh, 2017.

———. "Rhetoric, Theory, and the Imperative of Performance: Byzantium and Now." In *Rhetoric in Byzantium*, ed. E. Jeffreys, 151–70. Aldershot, 2003.

———. *Theophylact of Ochrid: Reading the Letters of a Byzantine Archbishop*. Aldershot, 1997.

Mundy, B. E. *The Death of Aztec Tenochtitlan, the Life of Mexico City*. Austin, TX, 2015.

Myers, K. A. *In the Shadow of Cortés: Conversations along the Route of Conquest*. Tucson, AZ, 2015.

Neal, A. G. *National Trauma and Collective Memory: Major Events in the American Century*. Armonk, NY, 1998.

Nelson, R. S. "Byzantium and the Rebirth of Art and Learning in Italy and France." In *Byzantium: Faith and Power, 1261–1557*, ed. H. C. Evans, 515–23. New York, 2004.

Nestor-Iskander. *The Tale of Constantinople (of Its Origin and Capture by the Turks in the Year 1453)*, trans. W. K. Hanak and M. Philippides. New Rochelle, NY, 1998.

Neville, L. *Guide to Byzantine Historical Writing*. Cambridge, 2018.

Nicol, D. M. *The Immortal Emperor*. Cambridge, 1992.

Nicolle, D. "Constantinople 1453." In *The Fall of Constantinople: The Ottoman Conquest of Byzantium*, ed. D. Nicolle, J. Haldon, and S. Turnbull, 174–243. Oxford, 2007.

Olivier, G. "El simbolismo sacrificial de los Mimixcoa: Cacería, guerra, sacrificio e identidad entre los mexicas." In *El sacrificio humano en la tradición religiosa mesoamericana*, ed. L. López Luján and G. Olivier, 453–82. Mexico City, 2010.

Ortiz de Montellano, B. "Ghosts of the Imagination: John Bierhorst's Translation of *Cantares mexicanos.*" *Tlalocan: A Journal of Source Materials on the Native Cultures of Mexico* 11 (1989): 469–79.

Papadopoullos, T., ed. "Ο θρήνος της Κύπρου." *Κυπριακαί σπουδαί* 44 (1980): 1–78.

Papayianni, A. "*He Polis healo*: The Fall of Constantinople in 1453 in Post-Byzantine Popular Literature." *Al-Masāq* 22.1 (2010): 27–44.

Pasayanis, K. *Το ελληνόπουλο: Αναγνωστικό για την δ' του δημοτικού.* Athens, 1931.

Passow, A. *Popularia carmina Graeciae recentioris.* Leipzig, 1860.

Pertusi, A., ed. *La caduta di Costantinopoli,* vol. 2, *L'eco nel mondo.* Verona, 1999.

Petropoulos, D. *Ελληνικά δημοτικά τραγούδια.* 2 vols. Athens, 1958–59.

Philippides, M. "Tears of the Great Church: The Lamentation of Santa Sophia." *Greek, Roman, and Byzantine Studies* 52 (2012): 714–37.

Philippides, M., and W. K. Hanak. *The Siege of Constantinople in 1453: Historiography, Topography, and Military Studies.* Farnham, 2011.

Politis, N. *Εκλογαί από τα τραγούδια του ελληνικού λαού.* Athens, 1914.

Polylas, I. *Η φιλολογική μας γλώσσα.* Athens, 1892.

Popular Memory Group. "Popular Memory: Theory, Politics, Method." In *Making Histories: Studies in History-Writing and Politics,* ed. R. Johnson, G. McLennan, B. Schwarz, and D. Sutton, 205–52. Abingdon, 2007.

Preger, T., ed. *Scriptores originum Constantinopolitanarum.* 2 vols. Leipzig, 1901–7.

Puchner, W. *Greek Theatre between Antiquity and Independence: A History of Reinvention from the Third Century BC to 1830.* Cambridge, 2017.

Quijano, A. "Colonialidad del poder, eurocentrismo y América Latina." In *La colonialidad del saber: Eurocentrismo y ciencias sociales. Perspectivas latinoamericanas,* ed. E. Lander, 201–45. Caracas, 2000.

———. "Colonialidad del poder y clasificación social." *Journal of World-System Research* 6.2 (2000): 342–86.

Reinert, S. "Fragmentation (1204–1453)." In *The Oxford History of Byzantium,* ed. C. Mango, 248–83. Oxford, 2002.

Reinsch, D. R. "Εισαγωγή." In Kritoboulos, *Ιστορία,* 7–19.

Restall, M. *Seven Myths of the Spanish Conquest.* New York, 2003.

———. *When Montezuma Met Cortés: The True Story of the Meeting That Changed History.* New York, 2018.

Restall, M., and F. Asselbergs. *Invading Guatemala: Spanish, Nahua, and Maya Accounts of the Conquest Wars.* University Park, PA, 2007.

Rigo, A. *Oracula Leonis: Tre manoscritti greco-veneziani degli oracoli attribuiti all'imperatore bizantino Leone il Saggio (Bodl. Baroc. 170, Marc. gr. VII.22, Marc. gr. VII.3).* Padua, 1988.

Roudometof, V., and M. Christou. "1974 and Greek Cypriot Identity: The Division of Cyprus as Cultural Trauma." In Eyerman, Alexander, and Breese, *Narrating Trauma,* 163–87.

Runciman, S. *The Fall of Constantinople 1453.* London, 1965.

Sahagún, B. de. *Colloquios y doctrina christiana,* ed. and trans. J. Klor de Alva. *Alcheringa: Ethnopoetics* 4.2 (1980): 56–193.

———. *Florentine Codex: General History of the Things of New Spain*, ed. and trans. A. J. O. Anderson and C. E. Dibble. 12 vols. in 13. Santa Fe, NM, 1950–1982.

Sakellarios, A. *Τα κυπριακά: Ἤτοι γεωγραφία, ιστορία και γλώσσα της Κύπρου από των αρχαιοτάτων χρόνων μέχρι σήμερον.* 2 vols. Athens, 1890–91.

Sakellaropoulos, M. K. *Αναγνωσματάριον προς χρήσιν των μαθητών της δ΄ τάξεως των δημοτικών σχολείων.* Athens, 1899.

Saris, A. *Νεοελληνικά αναγνώσματα διά τους μαθητάς της ε΄ τάξεως των γυμνασίων και λυκείων.* Athens, 1930.

Saunier, G. "Οι αρχές του ιστορικού τραγουδιού και η εθνική συνείδηση." In *Ελληνικά δημοτικά τραγούδια: Συναγωγή μελετών (1968–2000),* ed. G. Andriomenos, trans. I. Botouropoulou, 249–64. Athens, 2001.

———. "Πικρότητα και θάνατος, πικρός και φαρμάκι στα ελληνικά δημοτικά τραγούδια." In *Ελληνικά δημοτικά τραγούδια: Συναγωγή μελετών (1968–2000),* ed. G. Andriomenos, trans. I. Botouropoulou, 361–85. Athens, 2001.

Schudson, M. "The Past in the Present versus the Present in the Past." In *The Collective Memory Reader,* ed. J. K. Olick, V. Vinitzky-Seroussi, and D. Levy, 287–90. New York, 2011.

Scodel, R. *An Introduction to Greek Tragedy.* New York, 2010.

Segala, A. *Literatura náhuatl: Fuentes, identidades, representaciones,* trans. M. Mansour. Mexico City, 1990.

Shelley, Percy Bysshe. *Hellas: A Lyrical Drama.* London, 1822.

Sierra, J. "México social y político: Apuntes para un libro." *Revista nacional de letras y ciencias* 1 (1889): 13–19.

———. *The Political Evolution of the Mexican People,* trans. C. Ramsdell. Austin, TX, 2011.

Sievernich, G., ed. *America de Bry, 1590–1634,* trans. A. Kovacsics. Madrid, 2003.

Siméon, R. *Diccionario de la lengua náhuatl o mexicana.* Mexico City, 1981.

Smelser, N. J. "Psychological Trauma and Cultural Trauma." In *Cultural Trauma and Collective Identity,* ed. J. C. Alexander, R. Eyerman, B. Giesen, N. J. Smelser, and P. Sztompka, 31–59. Berkeley, CA, 2004.

Spasić, I. "The Trauma of Kosovo in Serbian National Narratives." In Eyerman, Alexander, and Breese, *Narrating Trauma,* 81–105.

Spatharakis, I. *Dated Byzantine Wall Paintings of Crete.* Leiden, 2001.

Spoturno, M. L. "Revisiting Malinche: A Study of Her Role as an Interpreter." In *Translators, Interpreters, and Cultural Negotiators: Mediating and Communicating Power from the Middle Ages to the Modern Era,* ed. F. M. Federici and D. Tessicini, 121–35. London, 2014.

Stathakopoulos, D. *Μικρή ιστορία της Βυζαντινής Αυτοκρατορίας.* Athens, 2017.

Stephenson, P. *The Legend of Basil the Bulgar-Slayer.* Cambridge, 2003.

Sullivan, T. D. *Compendio de la gramática náhuatl.* Mexico City, 2014.

Suter, A. "Introduction." In *The Fall of Cities in the Mediterranean: Commemoration in Literature, Folk-Song, and Liturgy,* ed. M. R. Bachvarova, D. Dutsch, and A. Suter, 1–12. New York, 2016.

Thomopoulos, E. *The History of Greece.* Santa Barbara, CA, 2012.

Tomlinson, G. *The Singing of the New World: Indigenous Voice in the Era of European Contact.* Cambridge, 2007.

Townsend, C. *Malintzin's Choices: An Indian Woman in the Conquest of Mexico.* Albuquerque, NM, 2006.

Townsend, R. F. *The Aztecs.* London, 2000.

Tziovas, D. *The Other Self: Selfhood and Society in Modern Greek Fiction.* Lanham, MD, 2003.

UNAM, Escuela Nacional Preparatoria. "Programa de estudios de la asignatura de Literatura Mexicana e Iberoamericana. Clave: 1602," http://www.dgire.unam.mx /contenido/normatividad/enp/prog_indicativos/60/IV/1602.pdf, 1–37. Mexico City, 1996.

———. "Programa Literatura Mexicana e Iberoamericana. Clave: 1602," http://dgenp .unam.mx/planesdeestudio/actualizados/sexto-2018/1602_literatura_mxna_e _iberoamericana.pdf, 1–24. Mexico City, 2016.

Vasconcelos, J. *The Cosmic Race / La raza cósmica,* trans. D. T. Jaén. Baltimore, MD, 1997.

Vasiliev, A. A. *History of the Byzantine Empire, 324–1453.* Madison, WI, 1952.

Vereecken, J., and L. Hadermann-Misguich, eds. *Les oracles de León le Sage illustrés par Georges Klontzas: La version Barozzi dans le Codex Bute.* Venice, 2000.

Voltaire. *Les œuvres complètes,* vol. 26A, *Essai sur les mœurs et l'esprit des nations,* ed. B. Bernard, J. Renwick, N. Cronk, and J. Godden. Oxford, 2013.

———. *Les œuvres complètes,* vol. 67, *Œuvres de 1768,* ed. S. Davies, J. Renwick, B. Guy, and C. Todd. Oxford, 2007.

Wittkower, R. "Eagle and Serpent: A Study in the Migration of Symbols." *Journal of the Warburg Institute* 2.4 (1939): 293–325.

Wood, S. *Transcending Conquest: Nahua Views of Spanish Colonial Mexico.* Norman, OK, 2003.

Xirouchakis, A. *Ο κρητικός πόλεμος (1645–1669): Ἡ συλλογή των ελληνικών ποιημάτων Ανθίμου Διακρούση, Μαρίνου Ζάνε.* Trieste, 1908.

Yangoullis, K. *Θησαυρός κυπριακής διαλέκτου.* Nicosia, 2009.

Zachariadou, E. "Η επέκταση των Οθωμανών στην Ευρώπη ως την άλωση της Κωνσταντινουπόλεως (1354–1453)." In *Ιστορία του ελληνικού έθνους: Βυζαντινός ελληνισμός, μεσοβυζαντινοί χρόνοι (1071–1204), υστεροβυζαντινοί χρόνοι (1204–1453),* vol. 9, 184–213. Athens, 1979.

Zhukova, E. "From Ontological Security to Cultural Trauma: The Case of Chernobyl in Belarus and Ukraine." *Acta Sociologica* 59.4 (2016): 332–46.

Ziolkowski, J. M. "Foreword." In Carder, *A Home of the Humanities,* xiii–xiv.

Zoras, G. T. *Βυζαντινή ποίησις.* Athens, 1956.

———. *Περί την άλωσιν της Κωνσταντινουπόλεως.* Athens, 1959.

INDEX

Page numbers in *italics* indicate illustrations and inset translations.

Acachinanco, 75, 77, 104

Acamapichtli, 1

Achugar Díaz, Eleonora, 134

Aeschylean tragedy, 39, 93n182

Agapitos, Panagiotis, xi

Alexander, Jeffrey, 24, 25, 40, 47, 50, 52, 53, 62, 67–68, 117, 127, 131

Alexiou, Margaret, 15, 37, 39, 41, 44, 52, 63

allegory in "Anakalema," 29, 35–37, 56, 64–65

alphabetized Nahuatl, 4, 71, 89, 108n253, 115

altepetl, 85

Alva Ixtlilxochitl, Fernando de, 106

America. *See* Mexica world

Anagnosmatarion (*Reader*; Sakellaropoulos), 127

Anahuacatl, 77, 115

"Anakalema tes Konstantinopoles" ("Lament for Constantinople"), x, 15–20, 27–70; allegory in, 29, 35–37, 56, 64–65; angel guarding city, departure of, 37, 66–67, 69; Antichrist or *anomos* in, 37, 61n101, 64, 67; as city lament, 64–66, 65; cultural trauma/collective memory theories and, 24–26, 38, 39–41, 47, 50–54, 62–65, 67, 70, 117–19; death, fall of Constantinople as form of, 45; on departure of angel guarding city, 37, 66–67, 69; divine abandonment instead of theodicy in, 67–69, 70, 118; dog metaphors, 31–37, 48, 50, 56, 60, 62, 67, 69, 118; dramatic narration of pillage, rape, and enslavement, 33–35, 56–63; emperor's head, iconization of, 53–54; emperor's lament and death in, 31–33, 46–54, 111; eschatological expectations in, 63–64, 67; folk poetry and, 15–16, 27, 29, 40, 41, 44, 45, 46, 50, 56, 63, 69, 118, 127; on Hagia Sophia, 37, 64–66, 65; Kontoglou's "Ho threnos Konstantinou tou Palaiologou" and, 54–56, 55; language, authorship, dating, and origins of, 16–18, 17, 26, 29, 56n87, 61–62, 69; male versus female lamentation, 52–53; manuscript and publication history, 27–29, 28; modern use of, 127, 134–36; as performative work, 18–19, 47–48; political verse (*politikos stichos*), use of, 15; rhyme, lack of, 29; ships' dialogue in, 29, 31–33, 40–46, 43; structure of, 29; sun and moon, apotropaic invocations of, 62–64; text and translation, 30–37; as *threnos* or poetic lament, x, 15–16, 18–19, 29, 38–39, 45, 117; "Tlaxcaltecayotl"/"Huexotzincayotl" compared, 71, 86, 88n165, 95, 98, 99, 108, 111, 112, 113, 117–19, 133–36; transmission of, 20

anaphora, 48, 50, 70, 100, 111, 113, 118

angel guarding city, departure of, in "Anakalema," 37, 66–67, 69

Angelović, Mahmud Pasha, 120

Annals of Tlatelolco (*Anales de Tlatelolco*), 71, 88, 102, 105, 108, 109, 111

Antichrist or *anomos* in "Anakalema," 37, 61n101, 64, 67

Antiquities of New Spain (*Antigüedades de la Nueva España*; Hernández), 91–96, 98, 99, 101, 110 antithesis, as rhetorical device, 46, 66–67, 111

antiunionist sentiment, 68–69, 119

Apano Symi, Crete, church of Saint George, dedicatory inscription, 45

apotropaic invocations of sun and moon, in "Anakalema," 62–64

Asia Minor Disaster (1922), 127

Assizes (Cypriot legal corpus), 18

asyndeton, 46, 50, 104n237

Ayocuan of Tecamachalco, 90

Azcapotzalco, 71, 88, 90

Aztecs or Aztecah. See Mexica world

Aztlan, x

Barbaro, Nicolò, 41, 42, 49n59

Beaton, Roderick, 15–16n3, 125

Benavente, Toribio (Motolinía), 22, 108n253, 134

Benvenuto of Ancona, 49, 50, 57, 70

Bessarion, Cardinal, 57n91

Bierhorst, John: Cantares mexicanos, translation of, 21–23, 71, 128; on "Huexotzincayotl," 80–81, 87–88, 90–93, 95, 96n192, 97n194, 98–99, 101, 103, 105, 107n246; on "Tlaxcaltecayotl," 110, 111n265, 113n277, 114n282

Bion, 63n106

birds as messengers, in Greek laments, 44–45

bitter/salty water, in "Huexotzincayotl," 75, 108

Bliss, Mildred Barnes, and Robert Woods, ix–x

Boone, Elizabeth, 84

Borges, Jorge Luis, ix

Boustronios, Georgios, chronicle of, 18, 56n87

Breese, Elizabeth, 25, 40, 47, 53, 131

Brinton, Daniel, 91

The Broken Spears (Visión de los vencidos; León-Portilla), 133–34

Browning, Robert, 42–43

Buffon, comte de, 12

Burke, Peter, 53

Burkhart, Louise, 7, 71, 84, 101, 102

Bustamante, Carlos María, 129

Codex Bute, 122, 123

Buzantinotourkike historia (Turco-Byzantine History; Doukas), 49, 60–61, 70

Byzantine world: aftermath of Ottoman conquest in, 119–28, 123; antiunionist sentiment in, 68–69, 119; archsignifier or urtrauma of Greek nation, fall of Constantinople as, 127–28, 130, 132, 134–35; Avar siege of Constantinople (626), 46n47; eagle and snake, trope of struggle between, 7–8, 8; endogenous inferiorization of European past, modernity requiring, 13–14; eschatological expectations, 1–4, 2, 63; first siege of Constantinople by Ottomans (1422), 66; Latin sack of Constantinople (1204), 61; liberation of Constantinople, 120–26, 123; map of Constantinople, 43; megali idea, 56n85, 124–27; modern Greek nationalism and, 124–26, 127–28, 130, 132; Orthodox Church in, 38, 50, 54, 55, 68–69, 81, 119–22; rhetoric in, 19; Romaioi, Rum, and Byzantines, as terms, x–xi, 38, 120–21; second siege and fall of Constantinople to Ottomans (1453), 3, 5, 5–6, 27, 46–47, 47, 56–59, 105n239, 127–28, 130 (See also "Anakalema tes Konstantinopoles"); Trebizond, Pontic songs about fall of, 69. See also modernity, Byzantium, and Mexica world

calmecac, 23, 88–89

Cantares mexicanos (Mexica Songs), x, 21–23, 72–73; "Huexotzincayotl" in, 71–81, 72–73, 87, 88, 90, 91, 93, 95, 98–99, 102–3, 107; in modern Mexico, 128, 133, 134, 135–36; "Tlaxcaltecayotl" in, 71–81, 110, 115–16

"The Capture of the City" ("To parsimo tes Poles")/"The Sack of Constantinople" ("He halosis tes Konstantinoupoleos"), 50, 56n86, 126–27

"The Capture of the City" ("To Parsimotes Poles") (Pontic song), 44

Carrasco, David, 94

Catholicism and antiunionist sentiment, 68–69, 119

Chalkokondyles, Laonikos, 61n100

Charles V (Holy Roman emperor and king of Spain), 71

Chávez Balderas, Ximena, 103

Choniates, Niketas, 61n101

Chorén, Josefina, 134

Christianity: Antichrist or *anomos* in "Anakalema," 37, 61n101, 64, 67; antiunionist sentiment, 68–69, 119; Mexica world, Christianity and indigenous belief in, 81, 84, 85–86, 102; Orthodox church, 38, 41n24, 50, 54, 55, 68–69, 68n128, 81, 119–22

Christonymos, Manuel, 56n86, 61nn99–100

Chronicon Maius (Melissenos/Pseudo-Sphrantzes), 48–49

churches, "Anakalema" on looting of, 56, 59–60

cihuacuicatl ("female song"), 95

city lament, "Anakalema" as, 64–66, 65

Clavijero, Francisco Xavier, 129

Coaihuitl, 77

Codex Bute, 122, 123

Codex Magliabechiano, 96

Codex Matritense, 105

Codex Mendoza, 84

Codex Parisinus Graecus, 27–29, 28

Colbert, Jean-Baptiste, 27

Colegio de San José de los Naturales, 88

Colegio de Santa Cruz de Tlatelolco, 4, 87, 88, 89, 100, 101, 115

collective memory/trauma. *See* cultural trauma and collective memory

Colloquios (*Debates*), 100–101, 109

colonialism: modern Mexican understanding of Spanish conquest, 129–36; modernity and, 11–14

Columbus, Christopher, 2–3, 3, 12

commemorative practices, cultural trauma, and collective memory, 53–54

Connerton, Paul, 53, 108, 112

Constantine the Great (Roman emperor), xi, 7–8, 64, 66

Constantinople. *See* Byzantine world; *specific sites, e.g.,* Hagia Sophia

Correa, Pedro, 97

Cortés, Hernán: conquest of Tenochtitlan and Tlatelolco by, 4, 104–6, 109, 113–15; exogenous inferiorization by, 12; and Doña Isabel/Tecuichpotzin, 79, 114; Nahua counternarrative of continuity to conquest as rupture and, 82–85, 89; letters to Charles V, 71; Malintzin/Malinche/Doña Marina and, 130–31; on marketplace at Tlatelolco, 4–5; as Mexican national progenitor, 131

Cortés el Mestizo, Martin, 131

"cosmic race," 129–30

Council of Ferrara-Florence (1438–1439), 68

Coyonacazco, 75, 79, 105, 108, 113, 114

criollismo and *mestizaje* concepts in modern Mexico, 129–32, 134

Cuauhtemoc, 79, 105, 109n255, 112, 114

Cuauhtencoztli, 77, 81

Cuextecayotl, 91–92

cultural trauma and collective memory: "Anakalema" and, 24–26, 38, 39–41, 47, 50–54, 62–65, 67, 70, 117–19; archsignifier or urtrauma of Greek nation, fall of Constantinople as, 127–28, 130, 132, 134–35; commemorative practices and, 53–54; eschatological narratives and, 63–64, 67; imagination, role of, in construction of trauma, 52; Nahua counternarrative of continuity versus conquest as rupture interfering with, 81–87, 83, 128; modern Mexican understanding of Spanish colonialism not encompassing, 129–36; negative affect, use of vocabulary of, 38, 50, 98, 116–18, 131; postmemory, 51–52, 116, 119; theodicy and, 67–68; theories of, x, 14, 24–26, 117–19, 131; "Tlaxcaltecayotl"/"Huexotzincayotl" and, 24–26, 86, 95, 98, 99, 108–9, 112, 114–19, 131–32

Cummins, Tom, xii, 4

Customs of New Spain (*Costumbres de Nueva España*), 103

Cyprus, Turkish invasion of (1974), 127

Darrouzès, Jean, 16–17, 29

Davanzo, Piero, 41

de los Ángeles Rull, María, 134

de Teresa Ochoa, Adriana, 134

del Mar, Alexander, 2, 9, 11

Demetrios Palaiologos (despot of the Morea), 119

Description de toute l'isle de Cypre (Lusignan), 20

Día de la Raza (Race Day) in Americas, 132

Díaz, Porfirio, 130

Díaz del Castillo, Bernal, 4, 71, 131n57

Dioptra (*Mirror*; *Monotropos*), 38–39, 63

divine involvement: "Anakalema," divine abandonment instead of theodicy in, 67–69, 70, 118; in "Huexotzincayotl," 101–3, 108, 109, 115, 118

dog metaphors in "Anakalema," 31–37, 48, 50, 56, 60, 62, 67, 69, 118

Doña Isabel (Tecuichpotzin), 79, 114

double mistaken identity, 85

Doukas, Michael, 49, 60–61, 70

Dragaš, Helena and Konstantinos, 46n45

Durán, Diego, 22, 94, 104, 134

Durán Codex, 9

Dussel, Enrique, 12

eagle and snake, trope of struggle between, 7–9, *8*, *9*

emperor's lament and death in "Anakalema," 31–33, 46–54, 111

endogenous inferiorization, 13–14

enjambment, 15n2

Enlightenment, 11–12, 14, 122, 124

epiphora, 108

Epitaphios of Adonis (attrib. Bion), 63

eschatological expectations: in Byzantine world, 1–4, *2*, 63–64, 67; cultural trauma/collective memory and, 63–64, 67

Euripides, 110n259

exogenous inferiorization, 12–13

Eyerman, Ron, 25, 128

Fallmerayer, Jakob Philipp, 125

Fernández Galvín, Ana Isabel, 44, 63, 68n122

Ferrara-Florence, Council of (1438–1439), 68

Flaying of Men Ceremony (Tlacaxipehualiztli), 94, 101, 104

Florentine Codex, 4–5, 6, 7, 23, 71, 87, 88, 93, 97, 101, 107, 108, 113

flower wars, 103–4

flower-song metaphor in "Huexotzincayotl," 98–99

folk poetry, Greek: "Anakalema" and, 15–16, 27, 29, 40, 41, 44, 45, 46, 50, 56, 63, 69, 118, 127; modern Greek nationalism and, 120, 124–27; moirologia (folk laments), 14, 16, 44, 48, 69, 118

Franciscans, 4, 71, 88, 89, 100, 110, 115

French Revolution, 12

Gamio, Manuel, 130n51, 134

Gante, Pedro de, 108n253

García Ortega, Rosario, 44, 63, 68n122

Garibay, Fray Ángel María, 21, 90, 96, 98, 132–34

Gelasius (pope), 11

gender: "Anakalema" on rape and enslavement of Constantinopolitan women and boys, 35, 56–63; *cihuacuicatl* ("female song"), 95; Greek lamentation, male versus female, 52–53; Spanish conquistadors, forced union between Mexica women and, 79, 93, 113–14

Gennadios Scholarios, 1, 119

Geschichte (Fallmerayer), 125

"ghost-song" theory, 80–81n137, 98n197

Giustiniani, Guglielmo Longo, 46–47
Giustiniani, Leonardo, 42, 49n59, 57
Goicoechea, Guadalupe, 134
Golden Horn, Constantinople, 42–43, 43, 46, 121
Goldwyn, Adam, 45, 68
goos, 52–54, 112
Goudeles, Nikolaos, 57n91
Grado, Diego de, 88
Graulich, Michael, 104
Great Palace, Istanbul, eagle and snake mosaic, *8*, 9n19
Greek nationalism, modern, 124–26, 127–28, 130, 132
Greek Orthodox church, 38, 41n24, 50, 54, 55, 68–69, 68n128, 81, 119–22
Greek War of Independence (1821), 124–25, 129
Greene, Molly, 119, 120, 121, 122
Guatemala, conquest of, 82

Hagia Sophia, Constantinople, 5, 5–6, 7, 37, 56n86, 64–66, *65*, 69
Hajovsky, Patrick, 93, 103n229, 104
"Halosis Konstantinoupoleos" ("Sack of Constantinople"), 50, 63n108, 68, 121
"He halosis tes Konstantinoupoleos" ("The Sack of Constantinople")/"To parsimo tes Poles" ("The Capture of the City"), 50, 56n86, 126–27
Hanak, Walter, 6n11, 43, 46–47, 48, 49, 56, 57n91, 66
Hanks, William, 89
Hassig, Ross, 104, 107
Heinrich, Günther Steffen, 68
Helena Palaiologina (queen of Cyprus), 51
To hellenopoulo (*The Little Greek*; Pasayanis), 127
Hernández, Francisco, 91–96, 98, 99, 101, 110
Herzfeld, Michael, 126
Hill, George, 20
Hirsch, Marianne, 51–52
Historia verdadera de la conquista de la Nueva España (*True History of*

the Conquest of New Spain; Díaz del Castillo), 4, 71, 131n57
Histories (Chalkokondyles), 61n100
History of Mehmed the Conqueror (Kritoboulos), 6, 42, 57–62, 70, 108, 119, 120
History of the Greek Nation (Paparrigopoulos), 125
History of Tlaxcala (*Lienzo de Tlaxcala*), 82, *83*
Holton, David, xiii
huehuetl, 22, 107, 112
huehue cuicatl ("old man song"), 95
"Huexotzincayotl." *See* "Tlaxcaltecayotl" ("Tlaxcala Piece") and "Huexotzincayotl" ("Huexotzinca Piece")
Huitzilopochtli (deity): as Blue Tezcatlipoca, 101; burning of Temple of, 6–7, *7*; at Coateocalli, 94; as preeminent deity, 101–4; sacrifices to, 102–3
human sacrifice, in "Tlaxcaltecayotl"/ "Huexotzincayotl," 92n182, 94, 98–99, 101, 103–4, 118
Hyalinas (ship's captain), 42–43

icnocuicatl or songs of sorrow, "Tlaxcaltecayotl"/"Huexotzincayotl" as, x, 21, 96–98, 118
iconization of emperor's head, in "Anakalema," 53–54
imagination, role of, in construction of trauma, 52
Industrial Revolution, 12
Ipalnemoani/Ipalnemohuani (deity), 101–3
Isidore, Cardinal, 49, 50, 57n91, 62, 64, 67, 70
Istanbul, Topkapi Palace, Kritoboulos MS, 61

Jacobita, Martín, 88, 100
Justinian I (Byzantine emperor), 7, 8, 64

Kallistos, Andronikos, 56n86
Kantakouzenoi, 119

Karanika, Andromache, 37, 38, 43, 46, 52, 53, 63n105, 66

Karttunen, Frances, 114n282

Kazantzaki, Galateia, 127

Kehayoglou, Giorgos, 18, 29, 36, 38, 41, 44, 51, 56n87

Klontzas, Giorgos, 122, 123

Klor de Alva, Jorge, 84–85

koine Greek, 16, 18, 69

Kolettis, Ioannis, 124

Kolovou, Fotini, 59n95

Konstantinos XI Palaiologos (Byzantine emperor), 42, 46–54, 55, 120

Kontoglou, Fotis, 54–56, 55

Korais, Adamantios, 124

Kosovo, Battle of (1389), 128n43

Koumbarou-Chanioti, Chrysanthi, 126

Kriaras, Emmanuel, 16–18, 29, 36

Kritoboulos, Michael, 6, 42, 57–62, 70, 108, 119, 120

"Lament and Weeping for Constantinople" ("Threnos kai klauthmos peri tes Konstantinoupoleos"; Matthaios of Myra), 68

"Lament for Constantinople." See "Anakalema tes Konstantinopoles"

"Lament for Constantinople" ("Threnos Konstantinoupoleos"), 68

"Lament for Constantinople" ("Threnos tes Konstantinoupoleos"), 41n24, 50, 68n128

"Lament for Cyprus" ("Threnos tes Kuprou"; Rodinos), 18, 19–20

"Lament for Konstantinos Palaiologos" ("Ho threnos Konstantinou tou Palaiologou"; Kontoglou), 54–56, 55

"Lament of the Four Patriarchates" ("Threnos ton tessaron patriarcheion"), 41n24, 68n128

Lee, Jongsoo, 101–2, 115, 134

Legrand, Émile, 27, 37

Leo VI the Wise (emperor), 122n14

Leo the Mathematician/Philosopher, 122n14

Leonardo, Andrés, 88, 100

Leonine oracles, 121–22

León-Portilla, Miguel: The Broken Spears (Visión de los vencidos), 133–34; Cantares mexicanos, translation of, 21, 80–81, 135–36; on "Huexotzincayotl," 87–88, 90–91, 93, 96, 98n197, 101–3, 104n236, 107n246; on "Tlaxcaltecayotl," 90–91, 111, 112, 113n277, 114n279, 114n282

Lienzo de Tlaxcala (History of Tlaxcala), 82, 83

Limenitis, Emmanuel Georgilas, threnoi composed by, 68, 121

The Little Greek (To hellenopoulo; Pasayanis), 127

Lockhart, James, 21, 83, 85, 90, 98, 108n253, 110

Lomellino, Angelo Giovanni, 57

London, British Museum Add. MS 34060, 42

Louis XIV (king of France), 27

Lusignan, Stefano, 20

Machairas, Leontios, chronicle of, 18, 38

Codex Magliabechiano, 96

makarismos, 52–54, 112

Malintzin/Malinche/Doña Marina, 77, 81, 130–31

Malta, Ottoman siege of (1565), 20

Mandylion of Edessa, 53, 54

Manuel I (Byzantine emperor), 53

Manuel II Palaiologos (Byzantine emperor), 1

manuscripts. See specific name or location

Codex Matritense, 105

Matthaios of Myra, 68

Maximiliano, Bonifacio, 88

McBride-Limaye, Ann, 131

megali idea, 56n85, 124–27

Mehmed II (sultan), 3, 6, 29, 42, 46, 48, 49, 50, 57, 62, 66, 67, 105n239, 119, 120

Melissenos, Makarios (Pseudo-Sphrantzes), 48–49

memory/trauma. See cultural trauma and collective memory

Codex Mendoza, 84

Mesarites, Nikolaos, 61–62n101

Mesih Pasha, 120

mestizaje and *criollismo* concepts in modern Mexico, 129–32, 134

Mexica world: aftermath of Spanish conquest in, 128–36, *135*; Christianity and indigenous belief in, 81, 84, 85–86, 102; Columbus's "discovery" of America (1492), 2–3, *3*; *criollismo* and *mestizaje* concepts in modern Mexico and, 129–32; eagle and snake, trope of struggle between, 8–9, *9*; European conquest of New World inaugurating modernity, 11–14; Nahua counternarrative of continuity versus conquest as rupture, 81–87, *83*, 128; Nahua, Mexica, and Aztecs or *Aztecah* as terms, x–xi, 23n43; omens and portents before Spanish conquest, 6–7; siege and fall of Tenochtitlan and Tlatelolco to Spanish (1521), 4, 71 (*See also* "Tlaxcaltecayotl" ["Tlaxcala Piece"] and "Huexotzincayotl" ["Huexotzinca Piece"]); Temple of Huitzilopochtli, burning of, 6–7, *7*; uneasy first encounters between Europe and, 4–5. *See also* modernity, Byzantium, and Mexica world

Mexican Revolution (1910–1920), 130, 131

Mexican War of Independence (1821), 129

Mexico City: Biblioteca Nacional de Antropología e Historia, *History of Tlaxcala*, *83*; Biblioteca Nacional de México, MS 1628 bis, 71–80, *72–73*; siege and fall of Tenochtitlan and Tlatelolco to Spanish (1521), 4, 71 (*See also* "Tlaxcaltecayotl" ["Tlaxcala Piece"] and "Huexotzincayotl" ["Huexotzinca Piece"])

Middle Ages, concept of, 13–14

Mimixcoa, 103–4, *105*, 110

Mirror (*Dioptra*; Monotropos), 38–39, 63

"missionary" or "reduced" Nahuatl, 87, 89

Mixcoatl (deity), 103–4, *105*

Moctezuma I, 95

Moctezuma II Xocoyotzin, 82, 87, 94, 114

Modern Greek Readings (*Neoellenika anagnosmata*; Saris), 127

modernity, Byzantium, and Mexica world, ix–xiii, 1–14; concept of modernity, 11–12; cultural trauma and collective memory, theories of, x, 14, 24–26 (*See also* cultural trauma and collective memory); Dumbarton Oaks, commingling of Byzantine and Pre-Columbian studies at, ix–xiii; eagle and snake, trope of struggle between, 7–9, *8*, *9*; eschatological expectations in Byzantine world, 1–4, *2*, 63–64; exogenous and endogenous inferiorization, modernity as process of, 11–14; Greek encounter with modernity and vision of Constantinopolitan reconquest, 124–26; lament songs compared, x, 14, 15–26, 117–19 (*See also* "Anakalema tes Konstantinopoles"; "Tlaxcaltecayotl" ["Tlaxcala Piece"] and "Huexotzincayotl" ["Huexotzinca Piece"]); Mexican *criollismo*, *mestizaje*, and understanding of Spanish colonialism, 129–32, 134; ominous signs and portents observed, 5, *5–7*, *7*; "premoderns" and "nonmoderns" as conceptual others, xi. *See also* Byzantium; Mexica world

moirologia, 14, 16, 44, 48, 69, 118

Moldovita Monastery, Romania, *Siege of Constantinople* (fresco), 46n47, *47*

monotonic orthography, 36

Monotropos, Philippos, 38–39, 63

moon and sun, apotropaic invocations of, in "Anakalema," 62–64

Morgan, Gareth, 44, 62, 64, 67

Motelchiuh, 75, 105, 108, *109*

Motolinía (Toribio Benavente), 22, 108n253, 134

Mourtzopoulos, Agamemnon, 37

Mullett, Margaret, 19, 52

Murad II (sultan), 66

Myers, Kathleen Ann, 129

Nahua. *See* Mexica world

negative affect, 38, 50, 98, 116–18, 131
Nelson, Robert, xi
Neoellenika anagnosmata (*Modern Greek Readings*; Saris), 127
Saint Neophytos Enkleistos, 18
Nestor-Iskander, 5, 5–6, 7–8, 9n19, 65, 68
Nezahualcoyotl of Texcoco, 89, 133
Nezahualpilli, 89
Nicosia, Ottoman conquest of (1570), 20
noble savage, concept of, 13
Notara family, execution of, 57

Olmos, Andrés de, 115, 134
Ometeotl (deity), 101
Oquiztzin, 75, 105, 108
Oracula Leonis, 121–22
Orthodox church, 38, 41n24, 50, 54, 55, 68–69, 68n128, 81, 119–22
Ortiz de Montellano, Bernardo, 99
Ottoman empire. *See* Byzantine world
Oxford, Bodleian Library, MS Barocci 170, 122n15

Palaiologoi, 68–69, 119–20. *See also specific Palaiologoi, e.g.,* Konstantinos XI Palaiologos
Palamas, Kostis, 126
Paparrigopoulos, Konstantinos, 125
parallelism, 64, 104n237, 113, 118
Paris, Bibliothèque nationale de France, Codex Parisinus Graecus 2873, 27–29, *28*
"To parsimo tes Poles" ("The Capture of the City")/"He halosis tes Konstantinoupoleos" ("The Sack of Constantinople"), 50, 56n86, 126–27
"To Parsimo tes Poles" ("The Capture of the City") (Pontic song), 44
Pasayanis, Kostas, 127
Patria Konstantinoupoleos (*Patria of Constantinople*), 66
Pertusi, Agostino, 41
Persians (Aeschylus), 93n182
Phanariots, 121, 122
philhellenism, 124–25

Philippides, Marios, 6n11, 43, 46–47, 48, 49, 56, 57n91, 66
Philomatis, 42, 43
Phoenician Women (Phrynichus), 93n182
Phokas, Manuel, 45
Phrynichus, 93n182
Pindar, threnoi of, 52
"The Plague of Rhodes" ("Thanatikon tes Rodou"; Limenitis), 68
Plaza Mayor, Tenochtitlan, 92, 105
Politis, Nikolaos, 125–26
Polylas, Iakovos, 29n6
polyptoton, 67, 70
postmemory, 51–52, 116, 119
Primeros memoriales (Sahagún), *105*
Pseudo-Sphrantzes (Makarios Melissenos), 48–49
Pusculo, Ubertino, 42, 49, 50, 57n91, 70

Quecholli, 103–4, *105*
Quetzalcoatl (deity), 101

race: *criollismo* and *mestizaje* concepts in modern Mexico, 129–32, 134; Día de la Raza (Race Day) in Americas, 132
rape of conquered women. *See* gender
Reader (*Anagnosmatarion*; Sakellaropoulos), 127
Real Colegio de Santa Cruz de Tlatelolco, 4, 87, 88, 89, 100, 101, 115
"reduced" or "missionary" Nahuatl, 87, 89
reflexivity, 29, 56, 65, 109, 112, 118
Reinert, Stephen, 121–22
Reinsch, Diether, 59n95
repetition, as rhetorical device, 38, 50, 67, 70, 98, 108, 113, 114, 118
Restall, Matthew, 82
rhetoric, in Byzantium, 19. *See also specific rhetorical devices, e.g.,* anaphora
Riggs, Charles, 59n95
Rodinos, Solomon, 18, 19–20
Roustika, Crete, Church of Panagia, fresco, 2

"Sack of Constantinople" ("Halosis Konstantinoupoleos"), 50, 63n108, 68, 121

"The Sack of Constantinople" ("He halosis tes Konstantinoupoleos")/ "The Capture of the City" ("To parsimo tes Poles"), 50, 56n86, 126–27

sacrifice, in "Tlaxcaltecayotl"/ "Huexotzincayotl," 92n182, 94, 98–99, 101, 103–4, 118

Sahagún, Bernardino de: *Cantares mexicanos* and, 22–23, 88, 91, 115, 128; *Colloquios* (*Debates*) and, 100; *Florentine Codex* and, 4, 88; *Primeros memoriales*, 105; on song activity, 22–23, 91, 94; as teacher, 4, 88, 100, 108n253, 115, 134

St. Elmo's fire, 6n11

Sakellaropoulos, Michael, 127

salty/bitter water, in "Huexotzincayotl," 75, 108

Saris, Alexandros, 127

Saunier, Guy, 45, 69

Schudson, Michael, 132

Segala, Amos, 71

Serbia, Ottoman occupation of, 128n43

Seven Nights (Borges), ix

Sgouros, 42, 43

Shelley, Percy Bysshe, 124–25

ships' dialogue in "Anakalema," 29, 31–33, 40–46, 43

Sierra, Justo, 130

Sigüenza y Góngora, Carlos de, 129

Simonides, threnoi of, 52

skull rack (*tzompantli*), 92

Smelser, Neil, 24–25, 38, 115–16, 128, 132

The Soldier (*Ho stratiotes*; Kazantzaki), 127

The Song of the Dead Brother, 39n14

Spain: Columbus's "discovery" of America (1492), 2–3, 3; conquest of Mexico (*See* Mexica world); fall of Granada (1492), 2

Spasić, Ivana, 128n43

Sphrantzes, 49n59

sun and moon, apotropaic invocations of, in "Anakalema," 62–64

synecdoche, 7, 40, 54, 64, 112

synteleia, 2, 3, 63–64

Tafur, Pero, 66

Tecayehuatzin of Huexotzinco, 89–90

Tecuichpotzin (Doña Isabel), 79, 114

Templo Mayor, Tenochtitlan, 92–93n182, 103, *106*, 135

teponaztli, 22, 107

Tetaldi, Jacopo, 42

Tetlepanquetzal of Tacuba, 109n255

Tezcatlipoca (deity), 101–2

"Thanatikon tes Rodou" ("The Plague of Rhodes"; Limenitis), 68

theodicy, 67–69, 118

Theophylact of Ochrid, 52–53

"Threnos kai klauthmos peri tes Konstantinoupoleos" ("Lament and Weeping for Constantinople"; Matthaios of Myra), 68

"Ho threnos Konstantinou tou Palaiologou" ("Lament for Konstantinos Palaiologos"; Kontoglou), 54–56, 55

"Threnos Konstantinoupoleos" ("Lament for Constantinople"), 68

threnos or poetic lament, "Anakalema" as, x, 15–16, 18–19, 29, 38–39, 45, 117

"Threnos tes Konstantinoupoleos" ("Lament for Constantinople"), 41n24, 50, 68n128

"Threnos ton tessaron patriarcheion" ("Lament of the Four Patriarchates"), 41n24, 68n128

Tlacaxipehualiztli ("Flaying of Men Ceremony"), 94, 101, 104

Tlacotzin, 75, 79, 105, 108, 109

"Tlaxcaltecayotl" ("Tlaxcala Piece") and "Huexotzincayotl" ("Huexotzinca Piece"), x, 21–24, 71–116; "Anakalema" compared, 71, 86, 88n165, 95, 98, 99, 108, 111, 112, 113, 117–19, 133–36; comparison of "Tlaxcaltecayotl" to

"Huexotzincayotl," 109, 115; conquest as rupture, Nahua counternarrative of continuity versus, 81–87, 83, 128; cultural trauma/collective memory theories and, 24–26, 86, 95, 98, 99, 108–9, 112, 114–19, 131–32; dancing and hair-cutting, antithesis of, 111–12; dating, authorship, and geographical origins, 21, 23–24, 24, 26, 71, 87–93, 101, 108–9, 115; divine intervention and involvement in, 101–3, 108, 109, 115, 118; flower-song metaphor, 98–99; on forced union between Mexica women and Spanish conquistadors, 79, 93, 113–14; "ghost-song" theory and, 80–81n137, 98n197; as icnocuicatl or songs of sorrow, x, 21, 96–98, 118; indigenous warriors in Spanish-native alliance, as focus of "Tlaxcaltecayotl," 109–15; language and poetic structure of, 23, 87, 89, 91, 107–8, 109–10; map of Tenochtitlan-Tlatelolco, 106; modern use of, 132–36; opponents/enemies, as songs about, 92–95, 109; performance and transmission of, 21–23, 118; reconstruction of siege of Mexico in "Huexotzincayotl," 98–109; sacrifice in, 92n182, 94, 98–99, 101, 103–4, 118; slippage between victory and lament, 95–98, 96, 97, 103–4, 109, 114–15, 118; texts and translations, 72–79; yaocuicatl or war song, drawing on traditions of, 21, 96–98

Tomlinson, Gary, 71, 98
Torquemada, Juan de, 110
trauma/memory. See cultural trauma and collective memory
Trebizond, Pontic songs about fall of, 69
True History of the Conquest of New Spain (Historia verdadera de la conquista de la Nueva España; Díaz del Castillo), 4, 71, 131n57
Turco-Byzantine History (Buzantinotourkike historia; Doukas), 49, 60–61, 70
tzompantli (skull rack), 92

Valeriano, Antonio, 88, 90, 100
Vasconcelos, José, 129–30, 134
Vegerano, Alonso, 100
Velestinlis, Rigas, 124
Villani, Filippo, 13–14
vocables, 87n160, 107, 110
Voltaire, 12, 13

Wolf, Hieronymus, xi
women. See gender
Wood, Stephanie, 84

Xipe Totec (deity), 101

Zambelios, Spyridon, 125
Zapatistas, 132
Ziolkowski, Jan, ix, xiii
Zumárraga, Juan de, 84